Praise for *The Space in Between*

"In her beautifully thoughtful and insightful book, Signe Myers Hovem guides us to reflect on what it really means to be an 'energy-aware empath' and how to understand and honor our personal sensitivities. What a valuable resource for anyone searching for truly meaningful information about the empath experience!"

—Jean Haner, author of *Clear Home, Clear Heart: Learn to Clear the Energy of People and Places*

"The line by ancient Greek poet Pindar that appears on the first and last page of *The Space in Between*—'Know who you are and be such'—captures the essence of this fearless memoir and valuable guide into what it means to be an empath. This deep dive into the places that tell you who you are promises to be an empowering read for all who seek to know and love themselves."

—Dorothy Van Soest, award-winning author of *Nuclear Option* and *Death, Unchartered*

"*The Space in Between* is an invaluable addition to the consciousness of our time. Signe Myers Hovem explores the essential questions for all who experience the 'in between' spaces and places of connection. The book is beautifully crafted, born out of deep personal experience and perception, and each page guides the reader toward rich understandings applicable to the everyday."

—Prune Harris, energy expert, educator, and author

"This field guide will help everyone who picks it up to identify and clarify their empathic nature and understand how to create boundaries as needed and tap into our gifts. If you've been labeled as an empath or a highly sensitive person, this book will help you discern, redefine where necessary, and [illegible] into who you truly are to harness your truth and [illegible]

[illegible]ell Bush, strategy consultant and wellness coach

"I believe that energy is the new language of the future and Signe Myers Hovem is a master guide for navigating a path for sensitive people through her own personal story. *The Space in Between* offers a safe space to explore our personal sensitivities and open up to our natural intuition. As an empath, I recommend this book to anyone wanting to explore their own intuition and embrace their own unique energy."

—Titanya Monique Dahlin, energy medicine practitioner and author of the Energy Medicine for Kids series

"Once I began to read *The Space in Between,* I found myself picking it up at every spare moment that I had. The content of this brilliantly written book is delivered by Signe Myers Hovem with such clarity and poise and is very relatable and easy to digest. It is very clear to me that many people in our world will benefit from reading this book—may it be read and loved widely and receive the glowing accolades that it deserves!"

—Melaney Ryan, founder and director of the Melaney Ryan Institute of Applied Consciousness

"In this book Signe Hovem expertly outlines the distinctions between being highly sensitive, having the capacity for empathy, and being an empath. We learn the value and gifts inherent in each, and their unique challenges. But maybe the strongest lesson Signe brings to us in this highly readable book is how to live within our sensitive natures with balance and functionality."

—Rosa Glenn Reilly, counselor and founder of Spectrum Center

THE SPACE IN BETWEEN

THE SPACE IN BETWEEN

An Empath's Field Guide

Signe Myers Hovem

SHE WRITES PRESS

Published 2021
Printed in the United States of America
Print ISBN: 978-1-64742-301-8
E-ISBN: 978-1-64742-302-5
Library of Congress Control Number: 2021909880

For information, address:
She Writes Press
1569 Solano Ave #546
Berkeley, CA 94707

She Writes Press is a division of SparkPoint Studio, LLC.

Interior design by Tabitha Lahr
Interior images © Shutterstock.com

Names and identifying characteristics have been changed to protect the privacy of certain individuals.

In loving memory of my father

William A. Myers

who brought me the mountains

Contents

Learn who you are and be such.

—PINDAR, ANCIENT GREEK POET

Introduction

A burning acid sensation instantly hit the back of my hand when the guard at the Luanda, Angola, airport returned my passport to me. I'd felt this particular sting before. It was a combination of malaria and strong medicines as they battled it out inside his body.

When I arrived in Angola in the spring of 2014, my first driver, Miguel, had malaria. Sitting beside him as he drove me on various errands, I became familiar with the combination of parasites and medicines that took possession of his health. I experienced a heaviness in the air around him, a stinging sensation nipping at my skin, and a fogginess coating my mind.

I looked at the airport guard kindly, smiled, and wished him a good evening in my limited Portuguese: "Boa Noite."

I took notice of the long line of passengers snaking around the security hall behind us, waiting to get through the initial passport and ticket control. The guard had a long night ahead of him. I touched the back of my hand where the acid sensation lingered and brushed my other hand over it, soothing it with an acceptance of what I felt and knew to be true—he was at work even though he wasn't well. I silently acknowledged what I sensed would bring him balance in that moment: the healing and fortification of his immune system and the rest his body craved. I thanked my hand for witnessing. My body was simply the messenger; it didn't need to hold on to the energy or the sensations once I had received the message.

This is one of the many experiences I've had over the years as an empath. This book is my account of how I traversed the arc of being an overly sensitive person at odds with my environment and culture to become an engaged and functional empath, comfortable in my own skin and all the sensations that come with that authority. My hope is that through communicating the essence of my life as an empath, you'll find a framework on these pages to better understand your own sensitivities. My goal is to help you manage these impressions and how they influence your relationship with yourself, others, and your environment.

I chose the story from Angola to illustrate what it's like to be *both* empathic and an empath, or what I call a *functional empath*. On the surface, my interaction with the guard may have seemed brief (a thirty-second encounter at most), but from my perspective, my succinct discernment and response to the acid-like sensation is the culmination of having traversed this arc.

The moment is brief and succinct precisely because both aspects of me (the empath and the empathic) were present and engaged, operating together in a balanced manner from the center of who I know I am. If we take a closer look, like a director's cut, it was my empathic sensitivities that registered the guard's compromised health through the shared space of passing my passport back and forth. Because I had past experience with that particular sensation, it was easy to discern the source. But how I processed the information—not taking it on as my own energy and staying present in the moment, while offering compassion and goodwill for him—was a pure expression of being an empath.

I haven't always been both empathic and an empath. A younger, less experienced, and less developed version of me would have wobbled or freaked out at feeling the acid sensation on the back of my hand. Long after the interaction, I would have spent time and energy worrying that something was wrong with me. I would have been quick to conclude that if I was feeling the sensation, it must have originated with me. Or if I did recognize that the sensation had something to do with the guard, I'd have had no understanding of the context. I might even have perceived it as a negative assessment of him, as in "he made me feel this way." Perhaps, regrettably, I might have even carelessly projected negative thoughts his way as a defense to distance myself from him. You see, being empathic doesn't instantly elevate you to being a spiritual, empathetic, or compassionate person.

No One Is Born an Empath

We might be born sensitive and empathic, but no one is born an empath. I evolved into one, and so can you. It's the by-product of being transformed by your empathic nature, which feels deeply and profoundly, entering spaces in an immersive manner rather than just viewing them flatly. A nature that continually promotes awareness, inclusion, and heart-centered intelligence. That recognizes fundamental truths about the world we live in: that we are sensory, energetic, creative, and multidimensional beings, and we are all connected.

Being empathic is a personal journey that challenges what you sense and feel, as well as your sense of belonging. For a large portion of my life, I have silently experienced some aspect of the life of other people—strangers and family members alike—through my body, my thoughts, and my emotions. *This is an empathic trait—to experience or mirror another person's feelings and emotions.*

Likewise, I have also entered empty spaces and been met by impressions that used my senses to determine there's more in the space than what can be physically touched or seen. *This is also an empathic trait—to have an expanded relationship to, and conversation with, the environment.*

I was slow in recognizing my empathic traits when I was younger because the culture in which I was raised didn't consider such possibilities. I struggled to feel comfortable in my own skin. I didn't trust my own experiences that were difficult to explain to others. I felt isolated and alone, and I survived by creating barriers in social settings rather than healthy boundaries.

I'm often asked when I knew I was an empath. I liken this to asking a caterpillar when it knew it was a butterfly. Truthfully, hindsight grants me a lot of insight into why I struggled in certain environments in my past and why I preferred nature over social gatherings as a child. I had the temperament of a quiet, *sensitive* child, as well as being preternaturally *empathetic*. But it wasn't until I started recognizing and accepting my *empathic* traits as a young adult that I began to understand the source of my sensitivities and my expanded relationship with my environment.

Though this acceptance was a relief initially, once the reality took hold, I was quickly overwhelmed. It was like opening a door to what you think is just another room and experiencing a deluge of formless, intangible sensations to be deciphered. This isn't a room, you discover, but another realm—a layer of energy that nevertheless correlates to the physical world.

Over time, I've learned to tune into my body and honor its service in bringing me a larger awareness of what's going on around and within me. I have spent many years establishing a baseline of my own natural rhythms—physical, emotional, and mental—based on my life experiences. An established baseline makes it easier to register when I'm personally out of balance, when I'm empathically receiving an impression from the environment, and when I'm guided by an internal wisdom toward a different path. At various points within this book, you'll read how each of these situations has helped me accept my expanded relationship with my body's sensory nature.

My empathic receptivity also expanded my reality. It conjoined the physical with the nonphysical like the wings of my cliché butterfly—each one equally important to the mechanics of flight. There are dimensions in the space around and within us, but we tend to think of the physical and nonphysical as separate from each other. We assume that our emotions and thoughts are contained within our physical body. They are . . . and they aren't. Our sensory system doesn't make this distinction. It's designed to receive impressions from the environment to aid perception whether the signal is internal or external. And this is where functional empaths balance in the space between these two realms. Hence, the title of this book: *The Space in Between.*

As empaths, we share the same intuitive mechanism for empathic reception, but how we process the information and what reaction/response we take is based on our individual life experiences. Our reception is customized to our sensibilities and our field of awareness.

As you think of your own empathic sensitivities, do you know your primary channels of receptivity? Have you considered how your life experiences fuel empathy? Do you recognize that trauma can impact your sense of safety and overall perception of your environment, creating hypersensitivity? These are questions you'll explore for yourself as you continue reading.

Function and Purpose

I have spent my life making sense of these heightened sensory experiences in pursuit of understanding their function and purpose. *What does this level of sensitivity teach me about myself and humanity? What is the difference between having empathic traits and sensitivities and having the skills and abilities of an empath?*

It became important for me to understand what purpose these sensitivities serve in my life. To feel and sense what's in a room, in the land, or emanating from a person, and to understand why those feelings are present in the first place—these are important questions we need to ask ourselves as empaths. We also need to ask ourselves what to do with the information we feel and sense.

We've been given little definition or understanding from society and external cultural authorities as to what it means to be empathic and/or an empath. This confusion is partly because there are too many unaware empathic people and partly because empathic abilities are usually labeled "paranormal," as if being an empath were a hobby or a sideshow in a traveling circus. And it certainly doesn't help that the dictionary gives it a narrow glance, placing its origin in science fiction and fantasy.

Connection

As an ordained spiritual counselor who began my practice in 2003, I've discovered that there's a spectrum of sensitivities that can impact our perception of how we fit into the world. In 1997, Dr. Elaine Aron introduced the label of Highly Sensitive Person (HSP), which researchers have gone on to identify as a genetic trait expressed in an estimated 15 to 20 percent of the population.

Sensitive people of all variations flocked to this label, finally feeling seen and given a voice of advocacy in counseling and society. But not everyone with empathic receptivity is an HSP, at least not exclusively. And the HSP brand doesn't address the non-ordinary receptivity that unaware empaths receive from their environment and accept as their own thoughts and feelings.

From my experience, there's an evolutionary arc from being an overly sensitive person who tries to survive in their environment by feeling *separate*, to that of being an engaged and functional empath who witnesses what's out of balance and honors that *connection*.

Admittedly, the awareness that we're all connected takes cultivation, and for some, it remains theoretical. For empathic people, however, its application is very much a part of our reality, which is poignantly ironic considering that many of us relish time alone. It's exactly why we sometimes struggle to feel comfortable in our own skin. The boundary between the external and internal can certainly be hard to define when you're able to feel so much. It's also why we continually question if our sensitivities are a blessing or a curse.

In 2006, I created a presentation that became the seed for this book: "Sponge or Empath: Consciously Evolving Your Sensitivity." On these pages, I want to contribute to and expand the conversation about sensitivity, empathic nature, and intuition, which is only going to continue to grow.

In the last twenty years, we've seen greater awareness and promotion of empathy as a healthy expression of mental and emotional health. The benefits of nature, sustainability, and conscious living have also been promoted in the last ten years, gaining advocacy in mainstream society. What's emerging now is how to bridge these two aspects of inside (empathy) and outside (nature). How are we connected to the environment around us, to communities, and to ourselves? Being an empath, I sense, is one of those active bridges living in the space between the two.

A Guide to Carry into the Field of Life

As you navigate the questions that come up for you, as well as examine your own evolutionary arc, I would like to be your guide to help you step into your authentic, empowered, and empathic self. While it may be complex and challenging, it will also be creative, expansive, and empowering. It's the ultimate paradox of discovering yourself inside a mystery.

This book is for anyone who has questioned their own sensitivities, particularly their empathic ones, or for anyone curious about how to manage boundaries and develop self-awareness. I hope that by sharing my awareness of energy flow, I can clarify the difference between empath and empathy, empathic and empathetic, and how it's possible to be sensitive and not be able to experience empathy. I will also explain how you can be empathic yet not fully an empath. This is more than mere semantics—it's about understanding your own unique sensory sensitivities and how you relate to, interact with, and perceive your environment.

I will share personal stories from my life as a child, adult, mother, wife, and spiritual counselor, as well as stories from the world around us. Therefore, in some parts, it will read more like a teaching memoir, reflecting the truth that our life is embedded with guidance and helps us become more centered in our own wisdom and empowerment. I speak from the authority of what I've found to be true for myself, my students, and my clients. Read with discernment, as my experiences and insights are not absolutes. What may be true for me may not be a reflection of your path and knowingness.

If you're asking why I've called the book a "field guide," it's because I'm an active outdoors person. Topography maps and field guides are part of the resources I carry with me to orient myself in a new landscape. The concept of "field" is used in many disciplines, such as the spiritual understanding that we're collectively part of a *unified field*. In psychology, there's the *field of trauma*, where different therapeutic modalities work specifically to help people heal traumatic events holistically, looking at body, mind, and spirit.

There are "fields" of study, disciplines, ecosystems, and so on. Essentially, a "field" narrows the view to a specific component that can be investigated independently or jointly in conjunction with other elements in the field. Most importantly, there are energy fields that are part of the foundation of our physical bodies, known as bioenergetics, which we'll discuss, as well as how our empathic nature emanates from these fields.

Throughout these pages, I have created field guides for five different landscapes of consciousness. These provided me with insight and movement in my own journey toward a balanced perception of the world and my place in it. They are the Field of Reflection, the Field of Definition, the Field of Sensing, the Field of Experience and Awareness, and the Field of Mystery.

Each field in the book helped me find my center and better understand energetic boundaries and relationships. Ultimately, they grounded and expanded my perception of myself as an empath. I have included an introduction to each field to present the central themes of its chapters, as well as a page of "Questions for Reflection" at the end of each chapter. These introspective tools are designed to prompt your own self-discovery. My advice is to take your time with each section. By design, this isn't a quick read.

I suggest you have a journal, your curiosity, and self-compassion at hand. Bless your journal, as a blessing lifts something into service. When I bless my meal, it's to add presence to the experience, extend gratitude for the nourishment, and affirm that it serves my body well. In the same way, when you bless your journal with the intention to create a safe space to explore in honest self-awareness, it helps you integrate wisdom and trust in your life.

I may provide my services as a guide, but your own life's tests, challenges, and joys are your most effective teachers. Let your journal be a source of connection to yourself and your environment—a place to explore, experience, and witness any truths that emerge on your journey.

I invite you to dig deep, as I have, and examine your relationship with cultural authorities (for me, it was science and religion), nature, trauma, mystery, and ultimately, your senses. I ask you to look at what makes you more fully human.

Honor your wisdom, and embrace a wholeness that only comes from being comfortable in your own skin.

With kindness and compassion,
Signe Myers Hovem

Important Guide Points

- Being empathic is not a power, so there's no reason to be afraid of it. If you do consider it a power that can be abused or that you aren't entitled to, reflect on where this belief comes from. Remember that it's just information from your environment. It may not be a power, but it *can* empower authenticity.
- You are safe. Even though your body may feel physical sensations or emotional and mental impressions, you aren't being occupied. Repeat "I am safe," and breathe deeply with a calming rhythm. Any extrasensory reception is just information, so what does it feel like? What is it communicating? What is the counter-emotion or feeling to bring balance or a neutral state? An empathic person generally experiences the information as sensations and impressions.
- Intuition is part of what I call the "Knowing Network." Empathic sensitivity is part of your intuition, but it's only one feature. Intuition provides a higher level of awareness to your own wisdom and creative intelligence.
- Contrary states create layers in an empath's emotional registry. You can experience moments of discomfort and pain and still know peace. Likewise, you can feel great joy and still know despair. An empath simultaneously samples many emotions and feelings, and this can seem manic and confusing until you develop the skills to support your nature.

Part One

The FIELD of Reflection

The FIELD of Reflection

The world is a looking-glass, and gives back to every man the reflection of his own face.

—William Makepeace Thackeray, *Vanity Fair*

I have chosen to start our journey here—in front of society and culture, in front of family and friends, and in front of the natural world. The Field of Reflection is where I want you to examine and understand what may be blocking or limiting your view of your sensitive and empathic nature. Where do you currently see yourself reflected? Which environments or groups resonate with you and support your self-image?

From the moment we're born, our eyes look outward and try to make sense of our world. We continually update our unique perception of how we fit in based on how our environment responds or reacts to us, and we do this before we ever get a look at ourselves in a mirror.

Can you remember the first time you saw your own reflection? Our parents undoubtedly introduce us to our image while we're babies. Perhaps we were mildly curious and surprised by our goofy, drooling mini-selves, but I can't imagine we were critical of what we saw.

As we develop, we begin to identify ourselves with features and traits, likes and dislikes, passions and hobbies, sensibilities and leanings. When we feel ourselves reflected in society or feel represented by authorities, we feel safe and perhaps even harmonious with our relationships and ourselves. Yet, for most of us, a distortion starts to take hold of how we see ourselves internally and in the world. It's a gradual slide, starting with the first inklings that we're different from others. We begin to compare and judge others and ourselves.

Society and culture reflect what are considered social norms or a consensus of the majority—acceptable behavior. Though this may be more about safeguards than outright intentional suppression, this standardized approach to life influences the collective perception of what's true and possible for a human experience. Society can create a box that you either feel safe within or suffocated by. Any person who envisions or experiences a contrary reality to the mainstream version will undoubtedly be pushed to question personal truths. At the very least, they will be challenged to be authentic in a world of conformity.

Each of us encounters social conditioning at some point in our childhood. I was quickly cast as the quiet bookworm kid, aloof but aware. I tepidly accepted the worldview that was taught at school, endorsed at home, or preached at church—basically, that trust was to be placed in authorities outside of ourselves. These included teachers, parents, government, doctors, and any official who presumably knew more about the world than just a mere individual, let alone a child.

This dynamic always troubled me and gave me a sense of a truncated and prescribed reality. I have never been comfortable as a conformist—I didn't even join the Brownies, the precursor to Girl Scouts, because I couldn't fathom someone telling me I had to wear a uniform to belong. Can you relate to this struggle against conformity in your own life?

I was born in the mid-1960s, the third and youngest child to parents who were striving for the American dream with the sheer determination that all they had to do was put in enough work hours. This is what was reflected to them and their generation, and it's fair to say that I'm a product of my generation. I was among the youngest viewers in front of the television to watch Apollo 11 land on the moon. Astronauts were instantly rocketed to idol status, and science was touted as the marvel that took our nation into space. Who wouldn't be star struck? My father certainly was, and I quickly declared that I would be an astronaut when I grew up. I built my childhood dream on the reflection of those inspired astronauts and my father's pride at what I could be.

My family lived in a remote, small Colorado mountain town, far away from any relatives. We didn't have strong connections to cultural traditions, but we did have a reverence and appreciation for nature. We enjoyed Sunday chicken dinners followed by family viewing of *Mutual of Omaha's Wild Kingdom*, *The Wonderful World of Disney*, and *Masterpiece Theatre*. I grew up looking for my reflection in nature and books, TV series, and later movies. This is how I tried to make sense of my experiences and my placement in the world, alternating between observing, witnessing, and waiting to see where I belonged.

Science and religion were presented to me as default authorities that presumably knew more about life than I could possibly know about my own nature. As a result, I wrestled internally with my empathic sensitivities.

The Field of Reflection section that follows will examine how science, religion, and nature simultaneously confused and comforted me as I looked for a reflection of my empathic experiences and a guide to others like myself. I suspect many of you may identify with my struggles with what I was told to believe and what I knew to be true for myself.

Let's imagine we can see behind the "looking glass," past the reflections that dim our view of our true selves. We're certainly not the first to do this. Dorothy followed the yellow brick road to Oz only to look behind the curtain and discover a wizard of ordinary origins. In the movie *The Matrix*, a curious and soul-seeking Neo chose the red pill and watched the mirror of his false world melt away and expose another reality. I may not have special transcendent props of ruby red shoes or red pills, but if a default authority like science or religion can seemingly usurp personal development and self-awareness, it's time to be brave and honest as we look within and know ourselves.

Chapter One

No Longer Science Fiction

When I was a young girl growing up in the mountain ranchlands of Colorado, one of my first Hollywood crushes was Mr. Spock, the character played by the late Leonard Nimoy in the popular TV series *Star Trek*. He was unlike anyone I'd encountered on TV or in books. His magnetism captivated my imagination—his wit and logic, his loyalty and discipline, the way he lifted his pointed eyebrows in bemusement, and his alien mystique.

Spock was confident and made no apologies for his nature. But thanks to his human half, he was still vulnerable and struggled to accept himself fully. This dilemma is perhaps what made me identify most with the character. Like him, I have spent a fair amount of my life feeling confused yet filled with wonder at the intensity and subtleties of emotions—both mine and others'.

Riveted, I watched him as he wrestled with human relationships and focused on facts to transcend ego-based dramas. Embedded in the message of his personal journey was a simple truth: emotions offer a depth that reason alone cannot. He was learning how to understand the intrinsic power of human empathy and integrate the head with the heart.

Spock was a reprieve and a treat for me as a young girl who felt alienated from others, particularly from my peers. I didn't know who to trust or what to trust—including myself. *Star Trek* opened my imagination to genres that examined the human condition outside of conventional literary forms. Sometimes, placing humanity outside Earth's realm lets us see our own shadows and light more clearly. Sometimes, allowing a half-alien character to personify humanity's struggles allows us to glimpse our own challenges in becoming whole.

In the late 1960s, creator Gene Roddenberry's vision for *Star Trek* "was to show humanity what it might develop into, if it would learn from the lessons of the past, most specifically by ending violence." Spock's Vulcan nature ultimately held the wisdom that responding rather than reacting brings less drama to a situation, but many viewers also learned about empathy and deeper connections from Spock's human half.

In 1987, the first episode of *Star Trek: The Next Generation* introduced viewers to the character of Deanna Troi, a half-Betazoid and half-human crew member who is an empath, which she naturally gets from her Betazoid half. Even in the year 2355 when the storyline is set, the writers didn't imagine a human with empathic capabilities. Instead, humans were portrayed as unique specimens, viewed as weak by alien races because of our emotional nature or as endearing due to childlike sensitivities we were unable to master.

As I grew up, Spock became a pop culture figure, proving I wasn't alone in my adoration of the pointy-eared half alien. My relationship with science fiction and fantasy genres became more complicated as I aged, particularly after gaining self-awareness of my own sensitive empathic abilities and in raising my four uniquely sensitive children.

On one hand, I enjoyed transitioning from fairy tales and fables to romping through countless series of young adult books with my children at bedtime: from Jules Verne's journeys to Lois Lowry's *The Giver*, J.K. Rowling's Harry Potter series, and on to Tolkien's *The Hobbit*. These are grand stories rich in fantasy that undeniably relate to our real world of human conditions and challenges. But on the other hand, all of the special intuitive traits and extrasensory features were confined to the fantasy portion of these tales.

It was a comfort to recognize myself and identify with some of these characters, but I was conflicted that I felt more akin to fictional characters than I did to the society in which I lived. Furthermore, it's specifically these traits and features that aid the characters in learning about themselves and their environment, which ultimately progresses the plot toward some self-realization or authentic embodiment. This is the reality that intuitive and sensitive people can offer to society now—it no longer needs to be confined to the pages of fantasy novels.

A Line in the Sand

Like no other genres, science fiction and fantasy place a line in the sand between what is and is not real. No one argues with a science fiction or fantasy writer about the reality they create. By the time the book or movie is marketed as part of these genres and costumed fans across the globe appear at cosplay conventions, there's little room to lend credibility in mainstream consciousness to what are very real heightened sensory traits—like being an empath. The fertile playground for extraordinary plots and characters is also exactly what limits people from accepting that such traits exist, at least without being deemed miraculous or freakish.

If we're lucky in our young lives, we're encouraged to sense and feel the world around us, to engage with our imagination, and to question absolutes. But that isn't the case for most of us. From a very young age, we're told what to believe and given the standards of normal conduct for our culture. This is its own form of storytelling—an oral tradition of sorts that provides the guidelines for belonging and fitting in, as it shovels doubt on any views or experiences that don't fit the norm.

Perhaps as a counter to this pervasively rigid status quo mentality, fantasy and science fiction genres are more prolific than ever. Worlds and universes are created that honor intuition and higher sensory perception in races that are pitted against militant and rigid colonizing republics or corporations—*Avatar*, for example, or *The Word for World is Forest* by Ursula K. Le Guin.

The duality of us versus them—the cold calculating opportunist against the sentimental and creative naturalist—is projected onto other worlds. I believe this is to satisfy some internal longing that seeks resolution in our own lives as a result of feeling fractured and disempowered from our authentic selves. We hope, as an audience, that some race (alien or not) is capable of consciously evolving to honor what's truly in our human nature—a thinking, feeling, sensing, intuitive, creative life capable of harmony and peace with each other and our world.

My Unrequited Love for Science

It isn't just science fiction with which I have a conflicted relationship. I also feel conflicted about science itself, and I suspect, if you are an empath, you probably have questioned your sensitivities against a perceived normal, too. After all, science informs policies and carries the weight of an authority that guides and informs our collective consciousness.

I grew up loving science, but I was like a schoolgirl who didn't understand why her crush couldn't see her. I had a sense there was a place for me in the world when I read biographies of women in science—Madame Curie, Elizabeth Blackwell, and Florence Nightingale. But our society seemingly has an unwritten social contract in which anything observed or experienced must be confirmed as true by science and then baptized as fact. Since anything science can't confirm or explain is considered suspect, dubious, and paranormal, it seemed to outwardly deny what I came to know about myself.

Despite my conflicting feelings, science is one of the pillars of truth that I respect and revere because it provides traversing and intersecting road maps of study. It helps our collective understanding that nature is more than one thing—it is a unified field of multidisciplinary components and systems. There is a continuum of endless derivatives to any question, which is awe-inspiring and showcases that mystery is as much a muse to the scientist as it is to the mystic.

Therefore, science isn't infallible, as history reveals. Past scientific views have been amended and simply discarded as new revelations and advancements are made. Elements have been added to the periodic table. New galaxies have been mapped. New medicinal remedies have been found in the natural world. New understandings of our psyche and physiology have helped us discover how one impacts the other.

Yes, I've been waiting for science to catch up with what my body experiences and already knows about the energetic world around us. The convergence of science with science fiction lends some hope for those of us who are empaths, as does the convergence of science and spirituality.

Crossing Over: Science Fiction to Human Reality

Science fiction has certainly proven to be prophetic in many ways, and researchers have often turned the ideas of these writers into reality. Here are but a few science fiction technologies that are now part of our real lives: artificial intelligence, planes, video recorders, drones, satellite communication, space travel, virtual gaming, and driverless cars.

But perhaps the most iconic *Star Trek* technology that later became reality is the handheld communicator, which manifested in today's relic of the mobile flip phone. In a poignant tip of the hat, Martin Cooper, working for Motorola, cited Captain Kirk's communicator on *Star Trek* as an inspiration when he created the first personal cell phone.

Today's successful IT and digital companies encourage employees to explore and envision future applications, thinking outside the box to power their innovations with creativity along with scientific principles. Yet, while functional technology has a relatively free pass to cross the line from science fiction to reality via science and engineering, functional heightened sensory reception and intuition have been, for the most part, left on the side of fiction, the supernatural, or the mystical.

As a culture, we have a bias in favor of technology over biological function and human potential. Even dictionaries place the origin of the word "empath" in science fiction. (Oddly, the same isn't true for "rocket ship," though the term was first mentioned in J. J. Astor's science fiction novel, *A Journey in Other Worlds*, in 1894, nearly seventy years before the first rocket was launched into space.)

Science fiction is where I've felt my sensitivities most reflected as a reality that can exist, but it's also where I've felt hemmed in. Ironically, when science and technology manage to cross over from fiction to reality, the writers are praised for being intuitive and knowing—ahead of their time. Yet it's too abstract for pure science to recognize that intuition and heightened sensory reception inform our sense of connection to our world.

This awareness has been slow in coming, and even the academics who venture into the nebulous arena of intuition are careful not to sound too "woo-woo." CUNY professor of philosophy Massimo Pigliucci highlights this caution in his chapter on intuition in *Answers for Aristotle: How Science and Philosophy Can Lead Us to a More Meaningful Life*:

> *Until recently, intuition, like consciousness, was the sort of thing that self-respecting scientists stayed clear of, on penalty of being accused of engaging in New Age woo-woo rather than serious science. Heck, even most philosophers—who historically had been very happy to talk about consciousness, far ahead of the rise of neurobiology—found themselves with not much to say about intuition.*

Why is this? What trips up academics and the scientific communities when looking at this field of intuition and empathic traits? Usually, the mere mention of a sixth sense or intuition conjures up images of seeing ghosts and paranormal activity, which then inevitably enters into a field of perception between *heaven and hell* and/or *good and evil.* I suspect this is why science steers clear of endorsing such studies—because too many other cultural authorities lay claim to examining the human spirit and conscience (i.e., religion and morality, history and humanities, and so on).

When it comes to the human experience, we simply don't seem so eager to move beyond the standard five senses of smell, sight, touch, hearing, and taste to understand our world or ourselves. Aristotle is credited with classifying these five sense organs more than two thousand years ago, and even today, that's all most people care to know about their senses.

Mirror Neurons: Monkey See, Monkey Do

Fortunately, scientific research is now promoting the relationship between the mind and body, including the revolutionary understanding that organ function can include perception. The awareness that both the heart and the gut have neural cells redefines the conventional wisdom that our "mind" is exclusively housed in our brain. The research on mirror neurons has also brought a flurry of scientific inquiry into how we understand others through not just thinking but also feeling.

In the early 1990s, while examining the brain activity of monkeys as they grasped an object, Italian researchers discovered that a non-grasping monkey's brain was activated by merely watching the action performed by another. These neurons "mirror" the behavior of the other, as though the observer is performing the same action. I propose that this is one of the biological components to the Field of Reflection, which hardwires us to be intrinsically connected to our environment.

Scientists have since discovered that humans, as well as some birds, also have mirror neurons. According to science writer Susan Perry, this discovery "radically altered the way we think about our brains and ourselves, particularly our social selves." Researchers are busy contemplating and researching if mirror neurons are the key to empathy and conformity. V. S. Ramachandran, a distinguished professor of neuroscience at the University of California, San Diego, has even called them "the basis of civilization."

Monkeys aren't the only animals that are assisting researchers to understand sensory capabilities. Dogs are able to detect cancer in people through smelling what have been termed *volatile organic compounds* found in samples such as breath, plasma, urine, and sputum (saliva). InSitu Foundation, a leading nonprofit organization training cancer detection dogs, explains on its website that it takes over three hundred samples to train one dog. The awareness that a disease has a molecular presence that can be detected through odor has prompted investigations in how to create early detection devices, such as an electronic nose.

According to InSitu, a dog has three hundred million scent receptors, while a human only has five million. The part of the dog's brain dedicated to analyzing these odors is also forty times larger than ours. Surely, humans don't have such abilities. Or do we?

Joy Milne, a retired nurse from Perth, Scotland, has been made an honorary lecturer at Manchester University because of her ability to smell and detect Parkinson's disease. She registered a change in her husband's body odor—a musky smell—that preceded his diagnosis with the disease by nearly a decade.

To develop an early detection test, Milne worked for three years with researchers to identify the "volatile biomarkers" that are secreted in greater quantities by Parkinson's patients. The hope is that with earlier diagnosis, treatments can be offered before the symptoms appear.

As an empath, I had an experience with scent, too. I became aware of a very specific smell around certain cancers, along with an intense denseness that interacted with my hands. This awareness developed after I volunteered at a hospice in Houston during the mid-2000s. The proximity to late-stage terminal disease exposed me to many sensations I had to decipher.

I suspect many hospice workers and volunteers register the different smells associated with a declining body full of pharmaceuticals and disease. But when I detected it on an undiagnosed client in a session, it was, nonetheless, surreal. That client followed up with doctors and discovered she had breast cancer.

Exactly what are our human sensory capabilities and potentials? Do we limit ourselves because of outdated cultural programming that defers to Aristotle's five senses model?

The Emergence of Empathy in Scientific Inquiry

I'm pleased that empathy is finally a legitimate area of study that crosses between the cognitive sciences of psychology, neuroscience, and social sciences. We are at last experiencing a movement in our popular culture's tolerance and inclusion of emotional sensitivity and vulnerability. Disney and Pixar even dedicated their award-winning 2015 animated movie *Inside Out* to the importance of having a balanced spectrum of emotions from joy to sadness if we are to experience life fully.

The importance of empathy is now embedded in educational and social welfare programs, as they recognize that the well-being of the individual impacts the whole. Denmark has implemented a mandatory program called Step by Step, starting with children as young as preschool-age, that has been lauded as an example for other countries. It reduces bullying and creates an environment of sharing and support. In my home state of Colorado, some school districts have created Peacekeeping Circles, implementing programs designed to reduce stress and promote communication and tolerance.

Empathy is even touted as a desirable trait in corporate leadership, providing a different strength and connection for executives to conduct business. Vulnerability, which is necessary for empathy, took center stage in 2019 in social science scholar Brené Brown's highly successful Netflix documentary, *A Call to Courage*.

Mr. Spock would undoubtedly be surprised by the scientific validation of this human trait and its fuller function in developing emotional intelligence and healthy social networks. But maybe these developments are a precursor to more mainstream acceptance of the empath and empathic abilities.

The Age of the Empath

I applaud the open-mindedness of discovery. My hope is that as progress is made in understanding the mechanics of intuition and the receptors that aid these sensitivities, our higher sensory perception will be included as part of "common sense." It's time to retrieve this part of our human nature from science fiction and fantasy domains and learn who we truly are: as a species, we're equipped with heightened intuitive channels that connect us to each other and to our environment.

Those of us who are empathic may not yet have identified the physiological mechanism that accounts for what we experience via the nervous system, but I sense that breakthroughs are emerging. A growing number of us will hopefully shape conversations to guide science, religion, and other cultural authorities to finally reflect a full image of the human experience. We *can* unmask ourselves from fear and ignorance, as we untangle our experience from the occult or paranormal.

How do I sense this? Look at what's popular in general society and what has magnetism and pull. Look long enough at the registry of subtle shifts and movements, and you can witness long-held beliefs being broken up and dismantled. You can curiously watch who or what steps forward to present a new form of expression. For example, look at the more recent contemporary fantasy series—*Heroes* and *Divergent*, for example—that now include humans with heightened sensory traits. The inclusion of humans and not half-breed aliens or technically enhanced humans reflects a movement toward bringing these abilities closer to home—to Earth as we know it.

As I write this, there are more resources available for inquiry into human connections and the nature of consciousness than at any time in my life, indicating that more and more people like me are collecting mutual interests and support. Two organizations stand out that offer research, education, and development for growing understanding of our human capacity for connection and emotional resilience: The HeartMath Organization and The Science and Non-Duality organization. There are also collaborations between researchers and skilled intuitive professionals who are working to bridge the two fields of study and create cohesion and mutual awareness for the public, such as Carolyn Myss and Dr. Norman Shealy, and Donna Eden and David Feinstein. In addition to these notable collaborations, many energy intuitives including Myss, Eden, Dr. Sue Morter, Barbara Brennan, and Melaney Ryan are among a growing field that offers extensive training programs for individuals. (Please review the resources page at the back of the book.)

I hope, like me, you no longer need to wait for science or society to validate what you experience as an innate, hardwired feature of your physical reality. I'm sure you're also eager for the next age, and I don't mean the age of Deanna Troi. We no longer need science fiction and fantasy to use our human potential to enhance storylines. Instead, I hope you'll join me in holding space for the age of empowered and embodied human sensitivity, as well as the wisdom and intelligence that guide this larger receptivity.

Spock and the Enterprise still symbolize the quest "to boldly go where no man has gone before"—the final frontier. For me, uncovering the potential of our authentic human nature may be the final frontier, but it isn't finite. Self-discovery is a process to ultimately embody a consciousness of acceptance and authenticity. That, my friends, is an infinite and timeless journey.

Questions for Reflection

Take some time with your journal to write down your impressions and feelings in response to these questions. Then, reflect on how your experience in your answers may have affected you emotionally or affected your development as an empath.

1. Have you judged your empathic abilities and sensitivities based on what you've been taught by your family and society? How has this judgment affected the development of your heightened sensory abilities? How have your attempts to belong affected your abilities?

2. Are you a product of your generation? What would you say defines your generation, and how does it affect your own self-perception and the way you view the world?

3. Has this chapter helped you recognize any influences from science fiction or fantasy on your beliefs about your abilities as an empath? If so, what stories have influenced you the most, and how can this insight help you accept and understand yourself better as a *human* empath?

4. Have you looked to the scientific and medical communities for explanation and clarity about being empathic? What resources did you find, and did they help you gain self-awareness? Write about your efforts and results.

5. Where do you see yourself reflected in your community? In what groups or environments do you fit in easily? Are you

able to reveal your empathic sensitivities in these environments? How do you explain your sensitivities to others?

6. Have you been afraid to share your abilities, assuming that others would be afraid of you? Write about these fears, and envision a world where you can be open about your sensitivities while others are encouraged to develop their own.

Chapter Two

Lost and Found

Religion has been an odd cultural authority in my life, presenting in my childhood home precisely because of its lack of presence. Yet it was still a yardstick my parents felt compared to and judged by. Both of them grew up with the model that good Christian families go to church, something they continued when they moved to Colorado as newlyweds in the late 1950s. However, when I was about six, we abruptly stopped. Just like that.

I sensed my mother was conflicted about the consequence of breaking from the image that was reflected to her since childhood. There was a flood of self-doubt that circulated between my parents as to what we "should" do and an element of shame about what we weren't doing—namely, no longer going to church.

When my father announced we weren't going back to the local church because of some "hypocritical bullshit," as he called it, I was deeply relieved. I'm still surprised that even as a small child, I felt as though I'd been spared. I was typically a quiet and compliant child. But put me in a church pew, and my inner dialogue instantly found an impertinent channel that broadcast through all of my senses and nerves.

I felt overstimulated by a strong internal presence that came forth from within me. A litany of questions streamed through my mind like ticker tape: *Why do we need to be saved? Is everyone evil? How is the body sinful? Is suffering synonymous with worthiness? Can we lose the fear and keep the faith? Can we be kind and generous if there's no threat of damnation? Is wonder enough, or do we need miracles to keep us transfixed? Will there be cake afterward, as promised?*

To prevent myself from raising a hand to ask a question, I would thrust my hands under each butt cheek and let my weight press down, pinning my hands onto the bench. Or I would clench my hands together as if deep in prayer. I felt my body take on an urgent need to either engage or flee, which confused me. This put me at odds with the adults who sat beside me, seeing me only as a fidgety child. But it was as if my body wanted nothing to do with that setup.

The Body as a Messenger

My uncomfortable experiences in church aren't uncommon for children. No one likes to feel forced to participate in a ritual they don't fully understand. It also didn't help that I was surrounded by dusty hymn books and a somber repentant atmosphere, which contrasted drastically with the purity and innocence a child purportedly needed to get into heaven. For me, though, my internal resistance was visceral and righteous, if I may be so bold to use such a word in this context.

Before I understood that I had the ability to receive extrasensory impressions from the environment—or that my body had its own wisdom—I often felt something internal and magnetic that wanted to remove me from certain environments and hold me steady in others. It was like an innate guidance system. I usually went with the flow, trusting the feeling, because it felt as if my instinct and intuition were integrated into one purpose.

These memories stand out for two reasons—it's my earliest awareness that my body appeared to have its own "mind" and was communicating with me, and it's my earliest experience of what internal resistance feels like. It's a conflict between an external reflection of authority and an internal wisdom that doesn't hold the same truth. Have you ever experienced similar feelings of being at odds with what's expected of you? Or have you found yourself moving out of certain environments with a calm supported by a deep reservoir of knowingness that you didn't realize you had?

Learning my body's methods and language has made my life as an empath interesting. It's an ever-evolving relationship that contains some of the biggest personal lessons for people like you and me: how to respect our body's wisdom, embody self-love, and not silence the messenger. And most importantly, learning to find environments that promote the truth that you are more than you know, not less.

Gifted, Special, or Touched

Just as I recognize that my empathic reception cannot be fully explained by science to date, religion also offers me no clear reflection of this trait unless it's awkwardly labeled as a "gift." It's an interesting twist to go from dark historic periods marked by witch-burnings and religious persecution of anyone with an intuitive nature . . . to being told you're special and "have a gift" in present-day society.

Typically, when people discover you have these particular abilities, they want to put them in context with either their religious views or their science-minded leanings. *"Is she divinely connected, a freak of nature, or a bit of a nut job?"* That pretty much sums up all the reactions I've encountered when I've revealed my empathic sensitivities.

People tend to feel more comforted by the idea that they are gifts, awarded like a lottery or sprung from a family tree of generations of "gifted" healers or seers, meaning you're just fulfilling your destiny or have been rewarded for a deep devotional practice.

I can only share my personal experience and lifestyle. I don't practice any faith of an organized religion. I'm culturally aligned to Christianity because I was baptized and raised with those influences and references. All of my children were baptized in the state church of Norway, which at the time was Lutheran, and represents our family's cultural identity with Norway. Some may think this makes me a hypocrite, but I see it as being culturally nuanced and adept.

I take issue with labeling my empathic nature as a "gift" because from my life experiences, this trait is part of my sensory physiology. We all have senses; they're part of our human anatomy. As a car owner, do you feel your tires are a gift? No, not unless you have a flat and hope you have a functional spare in the trunk. Otherwise, tires are part of the overall concept of a car and how it functions.

Our senses are the same; they're part of a functioning physical body. Heightened sensory receptors and intuition are present in the wiring of our nervous system and cognitive processing. It truly is a matter of integrating them into your reality, and it's also an invitation to be fully in your body and engaged as a sensory being. Are you taking time to smell the roses, taste the coffee, feel the rainfall, hear the wind rustling in the leaves, and know the warmth of another human touch or a beloved pet's fur?

This is part of my message to everyone, empathic or not: Don't take your senses or your body for granted. Get off autopilot, which is an easy mode to be in if you only focus outwardly on what's reflected and dictated to you from society.

Lost and Found

I may have had an unexplainable aversion to organized religion since I was a young child, but I've always been drawn to the great teachers and mystics showcased upon their altars and as their icons—mystics who transcended dogma and embodied the spiritual teachings of oneness and unity. Even as a child, clearly agitated in a church pew, I found my gaze drawn past the preacher to the images of the haloed son of God depicted in the stained glass.

I'm profoundly moved—and my own spiritual development has been deeply influenced—by teachings from Jesus that emphasize putting love into action. I also feel an affinity to many other spiritual traditions, particularly the respect offered to the Earth and elements from Native American traditions, as well as the deeply enveloping peace and mindfulness within Buddhist practices. I'm likewise intrigued by the Aboriginal spiritual traditions of storytelling and song lines in the land. I'm drawn to the spiritual aesthetics of authenticity—truth, beauty, and balance—regardless of its form. I'm just leery of absolutes, oaths, or any institution claiming authority over my soul or seeking to limit how I experience my own nature.

When I was discovering my empathic sensitivities, I was filled with many questions and doubts, and I even wondered if I needed to subscribe to a religious order to receive more instruction, guidance, or even protection. Yet my private practice in Houston attracted more than a couple of clergy and devout church members who were seeking a deeper understanding of their intuitive and spiritual lives. I realized then that I wasn't alone in feeling the limitations of religion to guide me in understanding my own energy body and the expanded fields of energy that support the physical realm and express consciousness.

Dogma and the Empath

Science and religion both offer explanations about the world we live in. Science is the authority on the laws of nature, peering into space with a telescope and into cells with microscopes. Organized religion has been the counter-authority to science, attempting to command and guide humankind's conscience and offer a moral compass to navigate life even into the mysterious hereafter. The problem with this moral compass is that it tends to divide everything into classifications of good or bad.

From my perspective, this quick judgment of good or bad, saint or sinner is what the cultural authority of religion maintains in the collective conscience, and it can feel quite dense. The history of civilization, with all of its growing pains and sorrows, has been tilled and turned back into the earth, imprinting the dust and dirt of our human consciousness with religious and political dogma for centuries. This dogma is undeniably part of the soil and landscape of our conquering culture. It still presents in marketing, politics, and martyred suffering, and it's rooted in humankind's need to judge itself and others.

I'm not alone in sensing this denseness that struggles to maintain its control and power. It's everywhere except in nature. And once you recognize that you don't have to align your direct experience of life with an outdated compliance to belong or be controlled, you're free to choose how you perceive the world and your relationships. You're free to confirm your faith based on your own experiences and values.

I sense that religion may have entered the field of humankind to offer a framework—one that cultivated discipline, devotion, respect, and civility toward ourselves and others. This can be seen as training wheels for humanity as it familiarized itself with the neutrality of nature: offering the human spirit a framework to accept life's tests, challenges, and joys as opportunities for reflection and acceptance, with a promise of reward and salvation.

How long does it take then to grow a collective conscience? It has probably taken thousands of years for the human conscience to evolve into the present day, where human decency is now properly incorporating empathy and compassion regardless of a religious structure and a fear of hell. You can be unaware of the Ten Commandments or other holy scriptures and still be authentically altruistic toward your neighbor. You can see beauty and feel a sense of wonder and gratitude for all of creation. You can praise and pray to life itself and not offend any forgotten gods.

Nevertheless, the collective conscience of religious dogma has an impact on us whether we grow up religious or not. When I first recognized my sensitivities, I would have a knee-jerk reaction that assumed what I felt empathically was either good or bad—particularly if I couldn't immediately identify its source. I had to break myself of that habit. I think it's helpful to notice how you automatically respond to what you receive.

Do you find that good/bad thinking is your default stance whenever you encounter unfamiliar and vague sensations from a person or place? It takes practice to stay heart-centered when you receive information and not wobble into fear of the unknown. While this is equally true for everyday living, the particular path of an empath is to get to the middle—the space in between dualistic judgments.

Empathic Sensitivities Have No Religious Affiliation

In truth, my empathic experiences are void of religious undertones. They're generally physical and emotional sensations, such as when I was on a busy highway in Houston on my way to work one morning in 2008. I purposely left the house after rush hour so that I avoided the standard bumper-to-bumper lineup crawling into the city. I was comfortable and listening to the radio when a sudden surge of adrenaline hit my chest.

I instantly brought my awareness to my breathing and asked myself if I was having a heart attack. Then, almost as suddenly, every car in front, beside, and behind me hit their brakes to avoid a massive pileup.

An accident had just occurred up the road, and the ripple effect of everyone's heightened reactions as they took control of their vehicles created a massive group adrenaline rush. That's what I picked up moments before I, too, needed to react physically.

I took a moment to reflect on what the hit of adrenaline felt like and catalogued it in my working index of sensations. As a young teenager, I had suffered from a bout of severe asthma that needed medical attention, so I knew what a shot of adrenaline felt like as a therapeutic remedy.

As I sat in my car, radio now off to limit stimuli, I mulled over the experience and tried to distinguish the layers of sensation—much like trying to pick out the flavors of a mouthful of food. Was there any emotional content? No fear, no anxiety—just a surge of adrenaline, which was a biological warning that action would be required. Immediately. Urgently.

When my body informs me of energy expressions in my field of receptivity, it doesn't classify or catalogue what religious faith is attached to the sensation. The group adrenaline surge didn't distinguish who was Christian, atheist, or any other religious association, nor did it denote ethnicity or race. In that particular moment, among a highway full of other drivers, we were just human beings faced with the urgency to control our cars to avoid a life-threatening accident.

The body has a relationship with the environment where it's placed, and it communicates in terms of sensations and through a registry of pain, pleasure, or fear. But the story we give it, the cultural parameters we box it into, and the reasons for our suffering are constructed by the psyche. The body lives in the senses, and that's its vocabulary. This is true for everyone with a working sensory system, but this is also how the environment communicates with an empathic person—through our senses.

Finding a Source: An Aquifer of Truth

Throughout history, each collective of people sought to explain their world experience when they encountered an unexplained phenomenon, when they were threatened, when they were swept up by desire, or when their conscience troubled them. Science gives reason and logic to guide some, and religion offers faith and discipline to steady others. And some use a broad lens that receives input from both agents, offering balance through universal symbolism.

In the same way that every waterway, stream, or river is connected far beneath the surface to a common water source, science, religion, and systems of beliefs exist beneath and within each of us. This is true regardless of how we practice them, regardless of their traditions, and regardless of how they impact our lives.

It's my experience, though, that if we go to the tap root, down to our shared humanity, we find an aquifer—a source of what it means to be fully human, integrated with our senses and connected to our environment.

If we go deep enough below the surface and away from perceived authorities and entrenched politics, we can develop an intimate relationship with the teachings of *love*, *honor*, and *respect*. There, we find a common aquifer that's the source of pure wisdom and truth. This is the magnetic presence I sense when I pray and meditate, when I feel reverence and gratitude, and when I embrace stillness.

In Chapter 1, I noted that I sense my empathic nature is reflected in both science and science fiction. Here, I acknowledge that though I lost my need for religion to hold my spiritual sensibilities, my own devotional practice and spiritual well-being is still supported by teachings of great mystics, each of whom found their Beloved looking back at them. This has helped me embrace that my body is my Beloved in form.

Regardless of your religious leanings, I invite you to deepen your relationship with your body and your senses, so that you, too, know that its wisdom and devotion in supporting your life is unparalleled. It's the wick and the wax that allow the light of your consciousness to experience the physical world.

Questions for Reflection

Take some time with your journal to write down your impressions and feelings in response to these questions. Then, reflect on how your experience in your answers may have affected you emotionally or affected your development as an empath.

1. Describe what internal resistance feels like to you. Where do you feel it in your body? Describe the experience using only physical sensations. Let your body speak to you. In general, what is your relationship to your body and your senses?

2. Think of an internal conflict that you have experienced. Can you identify the external authority that was in conflict with your internal experience? What was the dynamic between the external and the internal? Can you pinpoint a truth that tipped the scales or will tip the scales to bring about resolution and harmony?

3. Are you comfortable claiming your empathic and sensitive traits and abilities? Does it help you to consider them as "gifts," or do others around you frame them in this way? How does identifying them as gifts make you feel? Do you think it's to your benefit to identify them as such?

4. How do you nourish your spiritual self? I lost my need for dogmatic control from religion, but I see the sacredness of gathering and cultivating a community based on love, respect, and fellowship. Do you have a community that serves you with a sense of belonging? Describe what it feels like to belong in a group energy.

5. Are you more of a *facts and evidence* person, trusting more empirical data for what's possible and true in the moment? Or are you more of a *beliefs and faith-oriented* person for supporting your perception of the world and your place in it? Are you comfortable with the unknown, allowing room for changes to your understanding of the world and yourself? Describe which operating system helps you connect with your environment and your sensitivities, contemplating whether your current way of being is serving you in the best possible way.

Chapter Three

The Space in Between—A Contact Point

My husband, Knut, and I have four children, born within nine years over two continents. My family accepts that I'm empathic and sensitive and that I can be vocal about it in the privacy of our home. We all realize that my experiences don't translate easily into the conventional world around us. They laugh about times when my efforts to keep the house cleared of noxious and toxic energy interfered with their desire to be engaged in normal kid stuff—like electronic gaming devices.

All of our children are now adults who return to the nest once a year during Christmas and New Year's celebrations. I eagerly await this time of year when we can be together. We're a multinational family—Knut is Norwegian, and I'm American. Our global lifestyle has been reinforced by living in various foreign lands and exploring surrounding areas. Our most recent foreign home was in the world's sunniest capital city of Perth, Western Australia. (It receives on average eight hours of sun daily.)

Our first family holiday in Australia was very different since it was summer and hot in December. People celebrate with swims in the ocean and food on the barbie, not crackling fires and warm woolen mittens, which had been our default memories of Christmases past. All the kids had journeyed from different points of the globe and were adjusting to the time zone and climate change. They were charmed by this part of the world, and I was thrilled to be domestic with all of my babes in the house.

Then, as I was tidying the entrance and picked up a swim cap from a side table, I was instantly hit with severe pain pushing up on my sit bone. The sensation was so painful that I rushed to sit on the corner edge of our sectional couch to counter the pressure. I was perplexed by it, as it didn't match the object in my hand. I looked to my husband, who swims twice a week in the Masters swim group. "What's going on with your swim cap that it has so much imprinted energy around the perennial area of the body?"

He didn't follow what I was going on about, but simply stated it wasn't his swim cap. I threw the cap away, set about clearing the energy off my "message board," as I call it, and went back to my tidying. Our son Finn appeared and asked if I'd seen his swim cap, which was now missing from the side table.

When I retrieved it from the trash, I asked him to help me understand what I'd experienced. He started laughing and explained that he used the cap to wrap around the handles of his road bike, which helped to secure his watch so he could see his stats. Finn lived in Europe and had been training up the long mountain ascents of the Swiss Alps, sitting hard on the saddle of his bike. That's what I picked up. The experience gave me a personal understanding of the pain and endurance his training was having on his physical body, though he may have purposely tuned it out with endorphins and determination. The pain and pressure were being communicated, not the activity.

My nature as an empath—feeling things while not seeing them—pulls me into spaces and places that are entered and not viewed. I hope any empathic person reading this description can relate to this aspect of immersive and experiential living. Empathic people are drawn beneath the surface and into a sensory experience of life.

When I empathically register an impression from the environment, I'm aware that whatever it is, it corresponds to something in the physical world like thoughts, emotions, or physical discomfort. Someone created them, so they have an origin. I may not always know the source or the relevancy of the object that holds the imprint, but I do know how it makes my body feel. That's my point of reference.

When I have a new experience that doesn't feel familiar, I need to sift and sort my way through until I can find a way to perceive it. If that isn't possible, I accept that I don't totally understand its form or intent. Balancing in this space of contact between an impression I've picked up and my own space can sound like an out-of-body state, but in fact, it's an *in-body* state for a functioning empath.

The body is the medium, or in other words, there's a sensory component that reflects the environment upon the body, not in it. This is one of the most important aspects that I want to present to you if you feel overwhelmed by your sensitivities. Feeling something doesn't equate to being possessed or occupied. Instead, imagine that this space in between has a center—a fulcrum from which acceptance is cultivated and action is intuited.

And it's here, in this space between a *me* and a *you*, that I sense my reflection as an empath—the reflection that neither science nor religion can offer fully to my experiences. Poems, however, have the ability to capture the profound presence of this space in the pairing and stringing together of words—eliciting, eluding, yet not quite naming a feeling that's experienced. Crafted words, metered and measured, that simultaneously reveal or contain a sense of mystery.

Poetry is the closest form of expression that I find in deciphering the native tongue of stillness. Well, that and the power of transcendent artwork and music—and nature, of course. If I'm honest, my relationships with nature and the arts are the closest forms of seduction that I have experienced in my life. They assure me that beyond the reflection of societal structures of power and control, another dimension exists that synthesizes and transmutes life's meaning and mystery into expressions of depth and courage, beauty and harmony. And, of course, they illuminate creativity and connections.

Do you know this feeling I'm referring to? Have you experienced this deep and subtle interconnective space in your life? Perhaps you feel it when you're creative, and a timelessness engulfs you as you create in a flow. Or when you experience something that moves you—art, music, literature, landscapes, kindness, and so on. It's a feeling of expansiveness and inclusion while imbued with stillness. This is the space in which a functional empath can center themselves when reflecting upon an impression they've picked up and when they clear their own energy from the reception.

Experiential Living with Senses Engaged

Come, said my Soul
Such verses for my Body let us write, (for we are one,)

—WALT WHITMAN

I adore silence, not pin-drop silence, but rather the stillness of the whole body's senses engaged and absorbing impressions from nature. A silence that's void of words and thoughts. An awareness that there's a breeze floating across my flesh, the tree boughs are shimmering in the morning sun, the creek is churning over the boulders. Sensations that require no words to be experienced, no investigation of what and why I'm feeling what I'm feeling. In this stillness, there's the liberty of experiencing without the need for deciphering and judging.

Nature is authentic and pure, and we experience it directly with our senses: I *know* wind and how it caresses my exposed skin and tosses my hair. I *know* temperature and weather and what responses it produces in me if I'm hot, cold, wet, or dry. I *know* sounds of birds, running water, thunder cracking, and the ground reverberating. I *know* the scent of pine trees and flowers. I *know* the taste of blueberries. This knowingness of the natural elements offers my senses peace and calm because they're engaged with the authenticity of nature.

Nature knows itself, and from that knowingness, there's a palpable presence that can be felt when you're in the wilderness. What do you experience when you're in nature? Do you feel as though you've entered into a space of its own dimension? What do you sense is reflected to you while you're in nature's presence?

My relationship with nature has a sacredness that reflects an unwavering truth about my senses and how they connect me to my environment and orient or ground me. This is particularly true when contrasted with the management of empathic feelings or sensations in a room where I may experience the temperature change within just a few feet. Or I might feel movement against my skin like a viscous fluid, particularly at my ankles, or the "pins and needles" feeling of a static field of energy filled with repetitive negative thoughts.

Perhaps the biggest challenge of feeling and sensing empathically is recognizing that you won't always get a full picture or understanding of what's present. It's very similar to the child's game of guessing what's in a bag. An object is placed inside a bag, and each child reaches one hand inside to feel and guess what it is. One child grabs what feels like a furry tail and guesses cat, another feels large pointy ears and says dog, and so on and so forth. When the object is revealed to be a kangaroo, you can understand each child's guess. It has fur, a tail, and pointy ears. Yet it isn't a cat or dog. What they felt was accurate, but the guessing was faulty because they were unable to feel the entire object and match up a direct experience with it, especially if they'd never seen a kangaroo.

What we know about our physical world comes from direct experience and is enhanced with mindfulness and engagement. Empaths are like scientists doing field work; we must be discerning about what we pick up via our empathic reception—letting it reveal itself as fully as possible before presuming to know or understand what we're sensing. Sometimes, the energy of a room feels like a riddle to be solved, but most times, it's nuanced and simply needs discovery. How patient are you in letting things reveal themselves? If you aren't a very patient person, then I assure you, your empathic nature will cultivate this virtue.

It takes an openness and vulnerability to experience a poem's essence, and that's what it's like to be an empath. It also requires faith and trust that you're perfect as you are in this moment, and it requires the willingness to understand the authenticity of what that means—*as you are*.

We evolve from empathic to empath. Right now, your empathic nature might be limited by beliefs or perceived circumstances. But I sense that you know at your center that there's a depth to your own presence, which is intuitive and sensory by nature. It might even scare and intimidate you. If so, I invite you to look around you and see that you aren't alone. There are great masters in our presence who model acceptance and balance. They developed themselves from their center and expanded outward. So let those you respect embolden you to respect yourself where you are right now on your path, because it's perfect and uniquely yours.

Master Empath: Correcting a Reflection Back to Society

There are many empaths who consciously serve to support humanity. They have a mastery of themselves and their nature, and they don't need to seek attention. But the sheer magnetism of their depth of knowing attracts people who seek guidance. They have a way of shining the light on what's out of balance so that others can understand and reflect on it. I'm always delighted to hear the messages of masters, who typically speak in riddles, koans, or paradoxes. I know there will be teachings to uncover if I slow down long enough to listen and watch. Masters can speak on a specific event, but they will always use universal language. Don't be fooled that what they say is only meant for this moment in time.

For example, if I watch or read the news, I look for a broader reflection of what's seeking balance in society, how it's being presented, and who's stepping up to facilitate the change. Sometimes, themes present themselves, linking what some might consider unrelated articles.

On one particular morning, I automatically deconstructed stories that seemed unrelated but once reassembled, revealed their universality: stories into themes. An article entitled "Heyoka: The Most Powerful Type of Empath" caught my attention. Heyoka is a Native American word that means "sacred clown" or "fool." They act as an emotional mirror to individuals or groups to break down limitations and rigidity. I've had the great honor to watch a Heyoka healer work his medicine at a three-day sacred dance called the Naraya. His face was painted in black and white, the division between yin and yang, and the feminine and the masculine were exaggerated in his behavior and dress.

From the outside, looking at his methods was a hoot, but for the people involved, it was a teaching steeped in humility. The often outlandish behavior of the Heyoka healer pushes you to face what makes you uncomfortable, where your beliefs tie you up. A Heyoka wants to set you free by showing you the extreme version of yourself so that you might finally see what's hiding from you in plain sight. It takes a deep trust in yourself to know who you are, recognize when you're acting out someone else's drama, and untangle yourself from it.

That same morning, I watched a clip of the Dalai Lama speaking at the World Youth and Peace Conference in Washington, DC. At a press conference, in front of a panel of reporters and photographers, His Holiness sat between his ever-present translator and the conference director. He asked the group to take a moment of prayer for the recent shooting tragedy at an Orlando nightclub, which had taken fifty lives.

It took several attempts to quiet the room. The cacophony of camera shutters mimicked the sound of prayer flags whipping in the wind as he pressed his hands together in that universal gesture of prayer.

The moment lapsed with exactness—not too awkwardly long, not too short. It was a perfect moment of prayer for the news cycle. And then—God love him, the Dalai Lama chuckled and confessed to everyone that he was skeptical about the effects of prayer.

I laughed and nodded to the screen and whispered, "A total Heyoka move, Your Holiness!"

How many people in that room, upon witnessing his laughter and skepticism about prayer, had a momentary state of confusion as to what to think? The juxtaposition of the previous moment in silence with hands together in prayer with the next moment filled with laughter and skepticism was A Master at Work. His contrariness pushed his followers into thinking for themselves.

The Dalai Lama helped the audience out by explaining that "serious action" is what will have real effect: "Serious action, continuously, despite difficulties, and a lot of obstacles, we cannot lose our determination, our courage, and on top of that, some prayer is okay. No harm. Without action, it is just prayer." He was, among other things, invoking balance. Prayer alone is confined to the nonphysical world, and for it to impact the physical world, action is needed. He was present in the space between those two worlds, acting as a bridge.

How many of us hope a prayer is enough? Prayer is powerful, and it has creative powers to affirm and promote grace and mercy in the hearts of those who need hope. It creates a connection to a potential and promotes a sense of being heard. Most importantly, to form a prayer, you must put your hopes and intentions into words and define what you're asking to enter into your life. The Dalai Lama was asked to speak about a horrendous act of violence that was representative of the prejudice and hate that motivated the actions of the killer.

I have created both a prayer and meditation practice to support my awareness of being connected to my environment and to humanity. A prayer allows me to express some deeply felt awareness, while meditation allows me the stillness to be present without needs, wants, or words. This stillness resets my perspective and my nervous system, and it helps me integrate collective wisdom.

I keep a prayer journal that helps me express my awareness and intentions for those in need of comfort and in the midst of crisis, including myself and my loved ones. Here is the prayer that I added in the moments after watching the Dalai Lama:

For those individuals who died together in Orlando in fear and shock, abruptly and at the hands of hate and terror, I hold for you a space of healing so that your loved ones may honor your life, your body, your mind—to balance the gift of Life with the acceptance of Death. In this space that is outside of time and space, may you receive exactly the healing needed to continue your eternal presence in wholeness and in peace. I honor you and your life that you chose to live, however you began it and however it ended. In peace and with mercy, may your light be brightened by the love you knew and shared. Amen.

If you're inspired by a prayer or moved to compose your own prayer, that's a wonderful practice of expressing empathy, compassion, and awareness. But can you embody the sentiments of the prayer into a living actionable form? Be the integrated substance. Be the instrument. Be the change-maker.

Changing the Point of Reflection

I struggled from a young age to find a reflection in society that resonated with what I felt was fundamental to my sensory nature. Questioning and critiquing major aspects of society and cultural authorities is certainly not unique to me. Each one of us grows up, in part, by developing from a dependent, outwardly focused infant into a semi-independent teenager who is egocentric and looking for an identity.

Learning to shift our focus from the external world to our internal world is an important aspect of how we develop a relationship between ourselves and our surroundings. This process continues for the rest of our lives as we calibrate what we know about ourselves and how our environment reflects our sense of safety and belonging.

As I matured and embraced my inner landscape and honored my own sensibilities, it became easier to find external sources that were a truer reflection of my own inner life. These connections are like threads that knit together my outer and inner perceptions. They enrich and deepen my understanding of myself and the world around me.

There is so much intelligence, wisdom, and mystery present in nature, including human nature. This must certainly be the allure of exploring and discovering our inner and outer worlds and how they're linked as a continuum rather than separate fields of experience. As the late philosopher Alan Watts noted, "Really, the fundamental, ultimate mystery—the only thing you need to know to understand the deepest metaphysical secrets—is this: that for every outside there is an inside and for every inside there is an outside, and although they are different, they go together."

Change is upon us as a human race, and the external authorities that I once experienced as dogmatic and limiting are shifting into new expressions. In the last decade, there have been many inclusions in science and medicine that affirm what alternative health practitioners have known from their own studies and practices. Meditation reduces stress and anxiety. Trauma can alter DNA and cellular structures. Creating a non-victim narrative around pain and suffering can offer new perspectives. Empathy reduces isolation and forms connections while cultivating a sense of belonging.

We are at a time in human consciousness in which individuals like me—normal and ordinary people living their lives—are enriched by deeper connections and an understanding that oneness is actually the most expansive state of being. We no longer adhere to the belief that shamans, ordained mystical saints, and gifted geniuses touched by the hand of the divine are the only ones allowed to know greater depths and higher realms of understanding.

We're also experiencing young, driven, and innovative generations that are comfortable with technology while looking at the Earth as the focus of healing. They're bridging civilization and humanity toward inclusiveness and responsibility, careful not to let the mind outpace the heart or let technology completely replace our way of communicating with ourselves and our world. When diverse voices are allowed to express themselves in a safe and accepting environment, and we find that being reflected in society, it nourishes our sense of belonging and strengthens our community or nation as a whole.

Our intuitive and creative selves will guide each of us toward becoming more conscious creators, honoring balance and collaboration with each other and nature. This will lead us toward greater authenticity. If this sounds too idealistic or naïve, please consider that there's a field of oneness and intelligence that radiates truth and beauty. As Rumi said, "I'll meet you there."

Questions for Reflection

Take some time with your journal to write down your impressions and feelings in response to these questions. Then, reflect on how your experience in your answers may have affected you emotionally or affected your development as an empath.

1. Have you ever had to guess as you identified something from your environment that you sensed? If so, how do you feel when this happens? For me, I admit, it has been frustrating and confusing. Be honest with yourself if your empathic sensitivities bring up conflicts about how you feel in the world. Our receptive sensitivities don't come with a manual; we're all learning as we go.

2. What environments offer you the space to *just be* without an active comparing and processing mind? What is unique to these environments that supports your natural being? Have you ever experienced a suspension from the need to manage your thoughts and feelings—a stillness that comes from both inside and outside, like both halves melding into congruence with each other? If so, write about the experience. If not, I recommend practicing meditation and seeking environments that allow for this stillness.

3. What do your senses know from direct experience of the natural world? List five "knowns" in your sensory bank (like the ones I mentioned within the chapter), and create a poem or haiku to express how this knowingness inhabits you, bringing the inside and the outside together.

4. Do you have a prayer or meditation practice? If so, describe your intention with each one—what purpose do they serve in your life? Reflect how your practices have grown and developed over time as you feel more comfortable with your own traits and sensibilities. I encourage you to be creative and customize your practices as devotional expressions of connecting with your deepest soulful self and the greater unified field. If you don't yet have a prayer or meditation practice, explore creating them for yourself.

5. Thinking about the Heyoka, have you ever found yourself mirroring someone else's behavior in a weird acting-out episode that left you feeling unsettled and mystified by your behavior? If so, who is the person who has this effect on you? What is the behavior? What do you think it means when this happens?

6. Who or what in your life reflects an authentic nature that feels magnetic and still? It can be someone you know personally, or it can be a pet, place, respected statesperson, or notable humanitarian. Describe what their presence feels like and how it affects you.

Chapter Four

Breaking Down a Bias

Empathic receptivity is a subset of the sixth sense—or what I like to call our "knowing senses." For most people, this sounds like the stuff of science fiction and fantasy. And as I've said, that's indeed the origin that most dictionaries associate with "empath."

The dictionary's narrow inclusion of the word hints at the difficulties those of us with empathic sensitivities have when we try to communicate how we experience the world, whether to ourselves or to others. How can we effectively define ourselves when the common language of our society excludes or misrepresents a vital aspect of our reality?

What are the consequences of a vague and mostly dismissive definition in a standard resource like the dictionary? For one, it contributes to a real sense of alienation and isolation that presses in on empathic people, as we struggle to understand our sensitivities and our place in the world. It also leaves room for marginalized groups to create compensatory language to bolster self-acceptance, like declaring empathic sensitivity as a "gift" or a "power." This is perhaps framed as a consolation between sensitive people who struggle to understand the source of their sensitivities.

The dictionary's bias is revealed in the language used to define empaths, such as: "(chiefly found in science fiction) the paranormal ability to apprehend the mental and emotional state of another individual," as stated in my computer's own software.

The word "paranormal" implies that the ability of an empath isn't understood and is beyond the scope of normal scientific understanding. The use of "apprehend" shows an ignorance of how empathic sensory receptors function, while exposing how the general public's misperception is continually reinforced.

"Apprehend" can mean to appreciate, understand, or lay hold of, but the common use refers to grabbing at something that's fleeing. As an empathic person, do I reach out and grab the mental or emotional state of another individual? Do I pry into someone's thoughts and feelings to extract private intimate details? Not at all. And for the record, that behavior would fall under what I term *subversive psychic activity*.

I propose the verb "expose" as a replacement for "apprehend." It more accurately represents what empathic people experience. Higher sensory receptors receive information with exactly the same innate purpose as the standard physical senses of smell, sight, taste, feel, and hearing: to communicate environmental conditions. It's a one-way channel from the environment to the person, not the other way around.

An empathic person is exposed to other people's feelings—physical, emotional, and/or mental—in the same manner that your nose is exposed to smells wafting in the air. The more finely tuned your sense of smell, the more easily you can identify the essence of what's being impressed upon the senses. This doesn't necessarily mean that the source is identified. That requires more investigative measures.

For example, you may smell charcoal burning and know from your past experiences that it's from a barbeque, not a forest fire. You don't necessarily know who's grilling or where, but you could find out if you investigated further. For an empathic person, to go from the passive state of receiving an impression to an active state of investigating and/or engaging the impression involves more developed psychic and intuitive abilities.

Crossing this threshold from *passive* to *active* is a shift from being merely empathic to entering the domain of an empath. As empathically wired people, we each need to understand the difference between having an empathic nature and having the skills of an empath, and where we fall on that arc. Passive exposure is the default state where most of us find ourselves—which is why it can be so disorienting when we feel something from the environment interacting with our senses.

Sensory information is received; then, it's processed. This is true for standard and intuitive senses alike. No difference. Received sensory input is transmitted to a processing center via some aspect of the nervous system—and this communication makes us *think*, *feel*, or *know* something.

The Mind Has Three Brains

The mind is actually composed of the brain, the heart, and the gut. The vagus nerve, which is the longest cranial nerve, traverses the body and connects our brain to our heart and gut. All three have massive networks of neurons and very distinct roles in influencing our perception and decision-making. Isn't it a marvel that the wisdom of our physical anatomy includes an integrated sensory system of heart, mind, and body?

Spiritual practices and alternative wellness therapies have promoted these connections as innate intelligences that support the integrated Body-Mind-Spirit model. Melaney Ryan, founder of Melaney Ryan Institute of Applied Consciousness (MRIAC), explains that a person's higher intelligence or wisdom is accessed when each mind is aligned with each other. This view is supported by Marvin Oka, behavioral modeling expert, who said in an interview with the Australian Spinal Research Foundation, "Science is revealing that these massive neural networks exist. Now we just need to learn how to master them, learning to listen and interpret what each of the brains is saying so that we can get to the point of *wiser* decision-making."

In other words, intuition is wired into us—we just need to access and integrate the wisdom provided by our sensory nature. And to do that, we must accept that we're equipped with intuitive channels, which sense the realm of energy that animates our physical world. This is, in part, the issue I have with the dictionary's outdated position that an empath's abilities are paranormal. That position essentially blocks the growing awareness that empathic abilities are part of an intuitive sensory network and, more importantly, that intuition is a mechanism for expanding human intelligence.

Follow the Energy

In forensic accounting, the task is to "follow the money" and the truth will be revealed. In an integrated reality that senses everything as energy, the mantra is "follow the energy" to reveal the truth. Everything starts energetically and manifests physically. It's extremely easy to think you're only living in a three-dimensional physical world with concrete, tangible things before you. This is, in my view, the default mode that's programmed into each of us from our externally focused consumer-based society.

Everything in the physical world, however, has an energetic counterpart. All physical matter, stages of ideas, thoughts, dreams, fantasies, and concepts have an energy makeup even if they never materialize. It's all energy or vibration. Fundamentally, this is intuition's wheelhouse: the ability to sense patterns or situations that are holding in the energy fields around us, providing us with insights and guidance. I call intuition our *knowing senses* because it connects us to a knowingness that we're more than a three-dimensional body—it knows that we are energy.

How many of us can sense when the weather is going to change without consulting a weather channel? Or which route home will be quickest, which line in the grocery store is going to be slowest, or if your friend is about to call when you were just thinking of them? Or perhaps you've had a sudden creative insight that solves a problem you've been mulling over.

We tend to only hear people talk about their intuition when it saves them from a disastrous outcome or provides them with good fortune. Or conversely, we hear people regrettably state that they should have followed their intuition and didn't. In most instances, intuition is a quiet but distinguishable inner knowing or a gut feeling that offers us resolve to make decisions and steady our nerves. It's a subtle presence, like a design feature so cleverly integrated that you forget it's there until it remarkably presents you with a path forward.

Developing Intuition

Apple computer products and smart phones were originally marketed as intuitive tech because of their interactive features. Interactive software needs a level of intuitive design to be user-friendly. Knowing what you need before you know you need it is the endgame for most real-time processing entrepreneurs because that's the essence of intuition: to make life user-friendly. And though the Siris and Alexas of predictive software do their best at profiling our habits to create the illusion of intuition, particularly in the realm of shopping, intuition is not prescriptive. But like predictive software, it's developed and enhanced through experience and use.

When we lived in western Asia for a period of time, we were provided a local driver to help us navigate the city for errands and transportation. Valeh was an interesting local man who loved to begin our daily conversations by telling me how many people died the day before and how: stabbings, car accidents, electrocution by faulty water heater, and construction accidents were among the top reasons.

His motivation for sharing this somewhat morbid subject matter was varied, but at the crux of his character, he was a worrier. He worried about a great many things, but remarkably, he didn't let this influence his driving. He was an exceptionally intuitive and instinctive driver in what looked like sheer chaos to my foreign-born eyes. His ability to anticipate the movements of the cars surrounding us while still looking for an advantage in our forward progress was a skill that conjured up scenes of Luke being prompted to use "the Force" in *Star Wars*.

Valeh would look over at me as I grabbed my seat and occasionally placed my foot on the floor, reaching for the imaginary brake, and he laughed at my display of nerves and lack of trust. By the end of our four-year stay, I could sit calmly and knit or look out the window, unfazed by the bottleneck traffic and cars that were within inches of each other while bumping in and out of the transient potholes of our dusty neighborhood roads.

I learned to trust his driving style and skill. Intuition, you see, flows when there's a willingness to trust and surrender to your own wisdom, and part of wisdom is accrued through experience. I slowly recognized that driving was an area in Valeh's life that was reliant on his intuition and instinct, which were probably more freely developed in the absence of strict traffic rules. That is something to consider: Are you comfortable being spontaneous, or are you more comforted by rules? I have learned to be aided by both and to finesse a balance between them.

Intuition is both experience and potential. The potential is felt energetically, and the experience is built in as feedback. Developing intuition is really just developing trust in your own wisdom and allowing yourself to *not* be too predictive and rigid. So when you get that inner nudge to drive a different way home, approach someone with an idea for a new venture, or find a creative outlet, you won't dismiss it. You'll at least consider it as an option being offered to you with no other agenda than to place you in the direction of the most supportive energy.

I have found that intuition is the easiest point of entry to discuss the energetic realm with people. Most of us have had some personal experience with our own intuition, and many perceive it as guidance. Yet, in my early experiences discovering my empathic sensitivities, I didn't wrap it in a bow and call it my intuition. I had elevated intuition as this lofty sense of guidance that would arrive mysteriously, but not something capable of firing a pain receptor so that I would know the person beside me had back issues.

The Depth of Our Sixth Sense

The *sixth sense* is a familiar term used to denote a person's intuition and channels of higher sensory perception. If I were to ask you to identify any of the standard five senses, you could point to your eyes, ears, nose, tongue, or fingertips. If I asked you to point to your intuition, where would you point? "Intuition" and "sixth sense" are a bit like the kitchen junk drawer—catchalls of paranormal or mystical concepts that seemingly can't be placed elsewhere.

Each individual's sensory sensitivities have their own strengths, and this typically aligns with a learning style—visual, auditory, touch, or a combination of sensory inputs. The same is true for the intuitive channels. They inform a person through symbolic sight, imagery, or knowingness, or through engaging the physical components of the standard senses—seeing, hearing, tasting, smelling, or feeling—which all contribute to develop insight and intuition.

Clairvoyance (clear vision) is perhaps the most known intuitive channel because it utilizes sight as a means to receive information from the nonphysical realm. "I see dead people" has become an iconic film quote from the 1999 movie *The Sixth Sense*. It conjures images of supernatural proportions with unimaginable burdens. But not all clairvoyants see dead people or disincarnate beings. Some see aurically, meaning that they see the aura or bioelectromagnetic component of a person's physical body. In one extraordinary case after a head trauma, Jason Padgett could suddenly intuitively view the world through a lens of mathematical structures or fractals.

If you identify as an empath, you intuitively sense the space around you with your subtle energy bodies as the medium. I use myself as an example that intuitive channels are generally a composite, just like cognitive learning styles. My empathic receptivity includes hosting physical and emotional sensations and mental impressions, as well as a heightened sense of smell and taste. Occasionally, I have a faint registry of sounds, such as the chiming of my myofascial structure when I'm experiencing bodywork (massage), and the color of certain vibrations when I'm meditating.

My intuitive strengths come from automatic writing and meditative states, which present me with a sense of knowing relating to whatever I may be contemplating. All of this can also be described as clairsentience (feeling) and claircognizance (knowingness), with a touch of clairaudience (hearing) and clairvoyance (sight).

Here Be Dragons—The Boundaries of a Fearful Consensus

Throughout the book, I emphasize the statement "I was not born an empath, but I became one." I had to learn how to integrate my higher sensory reception in my daily life in order to find balance. I had to listen to and honor the wisdom of my body. I had to dismantle my perception that there were two different realities vying for my attention, as if my empathic senses and my physical senses were negotiating a timeshare for my nervous system. I now recognize that I have an integrated sensory system designed for one purpose: to receive impressions from the environment. The environment just happens to be more expansive than I'd been conditioned to believe.

In medieval times, map makers placed illustrations of dragons, sea monsters, or mythical creatures on the edges of uncharted territories as a warning. "Here be dragons" was a phrase that warned any traveler to take heed, as there was no firsthand knowledge to guide them farther afield. We can now look at these illustrations with amusement and appreciation at how much is known about our world, but in truth, a large percentage of the physical world is still unexplored, particularly the great depths of the oceans.

Collectively, though, we have enough personal experience and data points that we no longer need to issue warnings of dragons. Our perceived fear of what lies beyond our physical horizon can now be tempered with firsthand knowledge.

Beyond the veil is a popular metaphysical phrase used to identify a crossover point in the passage from one form to another. On one side, you're an incarnate soul, and on the other side, you're a disincarnate soul. On one side, you have a body that connects you to the physical realm, and on the other side, you're disembodied and part of the spiritual plane. It denotes a border between life and death and establishes a realm of mystery and unknown. We then fill in, with the help of our imagination and cultural beliefs, what we fear or hope may reside on the other side of the veil: judgment, heaven, hell, nothingness, eternity, and so on.

But before you and I cross this veil at death, moving from the physical to the ethereal, there are many subtle layers of energy that are accessible through our senses and consciousness. You are an energetic, dimensional being with an expansive network of connectivity. Can you sense this about yourself?

I feel the need to highlight this because there's an active misperception that tends to place the source of any nonphysical or non-ordinary sensations as coming from *beyond the veil*. Our higher sensory reception gets locked into an association with the "paranormal" and "mystical," when the sources are actually much closer in proximity to us energetically and physically. Our emotions and our thoughts are not *beyond the veil*; they're here attached to us. We can't escape our thoughts and feelings, but through self-awareness and the shifting of our perceptions, we can transform any that are harmful and unbalanced—particularly if they are impacting our environment and relationships.

An Integrative Reality of Energy and Matter

We live in a dimensional world of energy. Much like two sides of a coin that are made from the same metal, we tend to focus on the side that's faceup rather than recognize that it's simultaneously heads and tails. Our beliefs and conditioning—essentially our worldview—select what we accept as real. We then focus the majority of our attention on supporting that reality: an integrated oneness of energy that is both physical and nonphysical, or dualistic with each side separate from the other.

The dictionary's definition of an empath reveals more about collective mainstream beliefs and biases than it defines what an empath is. Recall that my onboard software dictionary offers the definition for empath as: "(chiefly in science fiction) a person with the paranormal ability to apprehend the mental or emotional state of another individual." This definition is delivered from the perception of a one-sided coin lying flat in a three-dimensional mindset, which shows its ignorance and hearsay. This is why it's important for those of us who identify as empathic to speak up and language our experiences and abilities as part of the intuitive spectrum that contributes to human intelligence. Otherwise, we'll forever be defined by a collective that repeats its limited understanding of something with no direct experience of it.

Because of my reverence for language, the challenge of confronting the dictionary's bias is complex for me. As an empath, language is a guide to give form to feelings, create boundaries, and construct relationships within my inner and outer worlds. In fact, a grand copy of the *Oxford English Dictionary (OED)* is one of the few family books I carried with me from my childhood home to university and across the Atlantic to my new home with my foreign husband.

I do take comfort in the fact that of all the dictionaries I've referenced, the *OED* is the one that at least stipulates that the term "originated" from science fiction and later expanded to "a person who can understand and appreciate another's feelings, emotions, etc." Yet even this definition is considerably off the mark—an empathic person can feel and know of another's physical pain, emotions, and thoughts, but that person doesn't necessarily understand any of them. To understand them, you need context and connection—you need empathy.

Questions for Reflection

Take some time with your journal to write down your impressions and feelings in response to these questions. Then, reflect on how your experience in your answers may have affected you emotionally or affected your development as an empath.

1. Have you ever experienced the effects of a bias—whether it's an institutional bias or from another person? Describe your awareness of what the bias represents and favors. How has this bias affected your own experience as an empathic person?

2. We all have biases to some degree. List a few of yours and what they might say about your view of the world. For example, confirmation bias is when we tend to favor information that confirms what we already believe.

3. Imagine that your preferred dictionary is taking submissions to update the definition of "empath" and "empathic." Write a definition based on your own experience that's representative of your reality. Make it no more than three sentences.

4. Have you experienced your intuition playing a decisive role in any aspect of your life? How did you receive the guidance? How was this like or unlike the way you experience your empathic sensitivities?

5. How would you differentiate between instinct and intuition?

Part Two

The FIELD of Definition

The FIELD of Definition

The beginning of wisdom is the definition of terms.
—Socrates

Not long ago, I went to bed with too many thoughts, each one centered on what to present in this book and how to best describe it. The frontrunners were obvious: What is an empath? What exactly does an empath sense? Others were more nuanced: Why do I feel so compelled to distinguish between an empathic person, an empath, and a Highly Sensitive Person (HSP)? How are empathy and an empathic nature similar, and how are they different? And somewhere in the deeper currents of my thoughts were edgier questions: Is this sensory feature a burden and a curse, or is it truly an authentic expression of a deeper knowing of oneness? Why am I so frustrated by the tone in articles written by people who identify as "suffering-for-their-gift" empaths?

I fell asleep and awoke in the morning, whispering the word "heuristic." I saw the word spelled out in front of me as I opened my eyes to the morning light. I bypassed making coffee and went straight to the dictionary for the following definition: "enabling a person to discover or learn something for themselves: *a 'hands-on' or interactive heuristic approach to learning*." I sighed and smiled. The dictionary, my complicated sidekick, had summed up what my intuition and empathic reception have exclusively presented to me—the hands-on ability to learn who I am.

No doubt, empathic reception is "hands-on" learning, as it presents felt sensations from the environment. We reach into the physical world with our hands—holding, touching, caressing, and controlling—in order to determine what's real. As empathic people, we must also learn to put into context our non-ordinary reception of thoughts, emotions, and physical sensations that don't emanate from us, yet feel real.

In questioning what I've learned from my empathic nature, I've discovered the nature of language and its essence related to Life, as well as the assistance it provides in creating and shaping personal boundaries.

In the physical world, there are boundaries, edges, and containment. Even a flowing river is defined by the banks that contain each particle of water, which has its own elemental boundaries. Gases and liquids appear loose and nebulous, formless to the eye, but in truth, they're also contained within their distinct chemical identifiers and molecular bonds.

Language mimics nature: in communication, there are also boundaries, edges, and containment. Words are particles of meaning, and strung together, they are powerful tools that can create clarity and identity. When we develop our vocabulary, find our unique voice, and construct an honest narrative to orient ourselves, we can navigate the world with greater ease.

The nature of our senses is to connect with the environment as a receiving channel. The nature of language is to communicate meaning, create comprehension, and provide connections. The nature of an empath is to sense what is out of balance in the space between denial and self-awareness and to operate as a witness.

Before any pattern or behavior can change, it needs awareness and acceptance. And a functional empath acts as a surrogate willing to feel and name what has been displaced into the environment. How these emotions and thoughts get displaced will be part of the discussion in the chapters that follow.

The space in between people, between thoughts and actions, between motivations and intentions—just at the edge of our sense of self—is rife with sensations and displaced thoughts, projections, and repressed emotions. It's here where a functional empath wades and supports the meeting between the muddy waters of disregard and the natural aquifer of innocence and truth.

When I began to question my empathic experiences, my cognitive brain only offered the possibility that it was my imagination. I had to push past that default cultural explanation to explore and define my experiences to give me context and meaning. The simple truth is that you can't define what an empath is, or what an empathic nature or intuition is, without talking about the realm of energy that supports the physical world and our own personal biology and psychology.

The *what*, *how*, and *why* of empathic sensitivities is contained within this energetic realm that correlates to our physical reality. And isn't it poignant and empowering that our own empathic nature invites us to expand our understanding of the world through direct experience? What do you suppose your empathic nature wants you to know about life that you wouldn't have understood without it? About boundaries and definition? About self-awareness? About connections?

In the Field of Definition, we will look at the mechanics and components that make up and define empathic reception. This section is dedicated to building awareness to support you in articulating and relating to your own life experiences. Hopefully, it will provide you with more context as to what it means to be empathic and an empath.

Chapter Five

The Empathic Blueprint

For everything in the physical world, there's an energetic counterpart—a template of patterns and pathways for energy to flow. When you recognize the complexity of the biological systems that sustain our life, you can also comprehend that our energy anatomy is equally complex because they are mirrors of each other. And both are still revealing their mystery and magnificence to the human mind.

For example, our physical form is made up of different systems: skeletal, cardiovascular, endocrine, respiratory, lymphatic, digestive, and connective tissue, to name a few. Our energy anatomy is comprised of some of the following structures: a central channel, chakras, meridians, auric layers, subtle bodies, and a weblike, egg-shaped casing.

We are bioenergetic beings, which means our form is both biological and electromagnetic. We are an integrated life form that is both energetic and physical. We're encased in tiny threads of energy or light that carry our thoughts, emotions, consciousness, intuition, senses, genetics, and much more. These threads cross, spiral, and form geometric shapes within our weblike structure, creating grids, chakras, meridians, and other aspects of our energy anatomy. Within yogic disciplines, these tiny threads are called *nadis*.

In general, every human being's aura is formed and assembled as a matrix that nestles energy fields and chakras as it is compressed into denser matter—our physical form. Consider the aura as our body's energetic protective field, much like the Earth's own magnetic field and atmosphere protects it from solar and cosmic radiation.

Each chakra is a spiraling vortex emerging from the central channel with access to each of the seven auric layers. Essentially, it's a seven-layer cake, with each layer flavored according to its filter or field. Chakras store and hold memories and themes relating to our life that can either block or open the flow of energy depending on how well we process the physical and psychological components that make up our perceptions: the physical, emotional, mental, and spiritual.

The seven chakras and auric fields relate to the totality of our physical reality and our operating consciousness in form. The first three chakras and auric fields specifically pertain to the physical plane and its composition of our physical body, emotions, and thoughts. The fourth chakra, the fourth auric field, and the spiritual subtle body are all part of what's called the astral plane, which bridges the physical and the spiritual plane at our heart. This plane offers us broader connections, empathy, love, and compassion. It's a balance point between our spiritual sensibilities and our physical reality—and how they match up or not.

Chakras five through seven and their corresponding auric fields are part of the spiritual plane and hold the energy for higher thinking, universal awareness, unity, and intuition, as well as our physical blueprint.

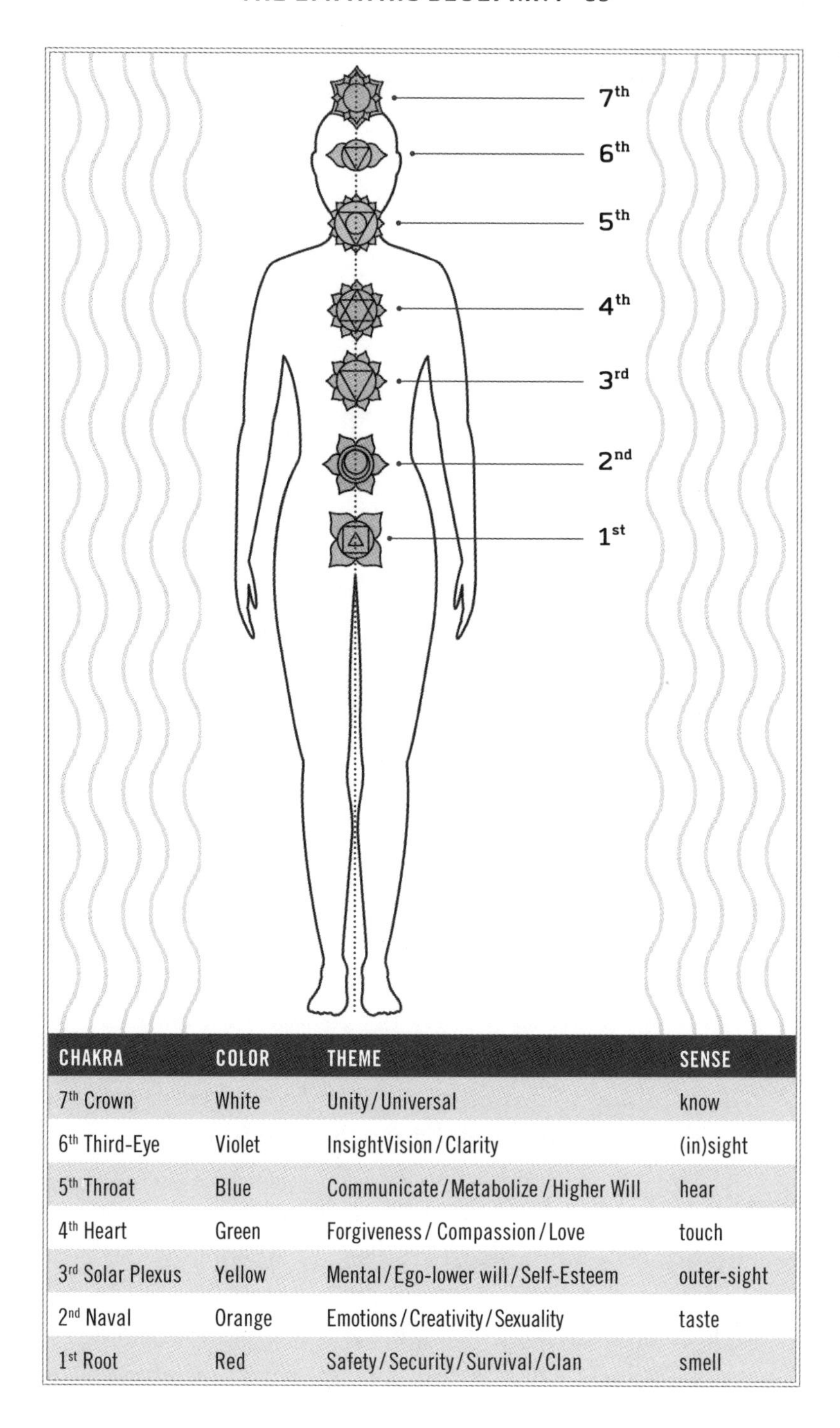

CHAKRA	COLOR	THEME	SENSE
7th Crown	White	Unity/Universal	know
6th Third-Eye	Violet	InsightVision/Clarity	(in)sight
5th Throat	Blue	Communicate/Metabolize/Higher Will	hear
4th Heart	Green	Forgiveness/Compassion/Love	touch
3rd Solar Plexus	Yellow	Mental/Ego-lower will/Self-Esteem	outer-sight
2nd Naval	Orange	Emotions/Creativity/Sexuality	taste
1st Root	Red	Safety/Security/Survival/Clan	smell

Ideally, the central channel connects the energy flowing from the top chakras down toward the Earth, and the energy from the Earth helps flow energy up to the higher chakras. Energy descending and ascending—just like our nervous system, our breath, and our blood circulation. The midpoint of the central channel is at the heart chakra. Therefore, the heart chakra stands out like a keystone in a bridge, supporting the energies that move down and up. This is why matters of the heart tend to be some of our biggest challenges and joys and why they offer us the biggest growth toward unity and connection.

Building resiliency at our center helps us to avoid wobbling too often or too far from our balance point. Our breath is representative of our life force, so central channel breathing to disperse energy with breath, sound, and movement is taught in many meditative and yogic practices as a way to unite the body, mind, and spirit.

Though the diagram I've provided is a silhouette, I want you to imagine that there are horizontal bands flowing around your body, as well as vertical flowing energy, and each chakra point is a vortex that spirals energy in and out. Ideally, there's an ebb and flow to your energy system, creating propulsion up and down, in and out. This may seem like a lot of commotion, but it's actually what provides you with motion and circulates your energy through your system. It also allows for expansion and growth as you become more self-aware, and your consciousness is embodied into a presence that emanates into and through your life choices.

The Energetic Blueprint of an Empath

I have come to appreciate that as empathic people, we have a heightened awareness of our environment through the *nadis* of light threads that support each of the four subtle energy bodies, which sense and perceive our physical

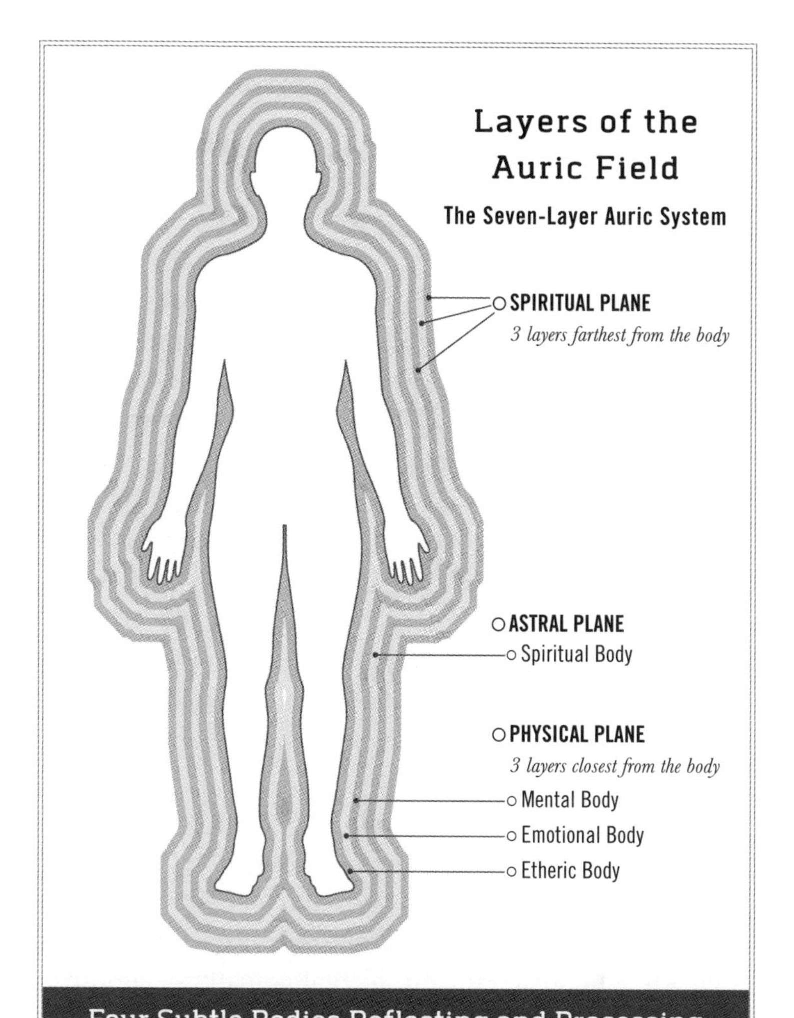

Four Subtle Bodies Reflecting and Processing

BODY	COLOR	PLACEMENT	ESSENCE
Spiritual Body	Pinkish tone	4th Auric Field: Astral Plane–The Bridge between the Spiritual and Physical	connects/accepts/knows/compassion
Mental Body	Yellowish/thoughts	3rd Auric Field/Physical Plane	mental/listens / thinks
Emotional Body	multi-color/emotions	2nd Auric Filed /Physical Plane	emotions/hears/believes
Physical /Etheric	blue / physical shape	1st Auric Field/Physical Planes	reflects/feels

reality. Our intuitive ability to tune into our environment happens with these subtle energy bodies—physical, emotional, mental, and spiritual. In a very abstract way, if you were an octopus, they would be your tentacles.

When you recognize that what you typically pick up empathically from the environment or from other people falls under one or more of these classifications—physical sensations, emotions, thoughts, or an extended presence of well-being—you can appreciate the direct benefits of building more awareness of these energetic aspects of yourself.

Intuitive senses operate from different energy centers within the energy body. For example, clairvoyance is associated with the sixth chakra. This doesn't mean that only clairvoyants can access the sixth chakra's intuitive channel. Each person's "third eye" gives access to many symbolic and universal insights, which aids intuition. And some intuitive reception, like being an empath, comes from utilizing more than one energy center. An empath's wheelhouse are the lower four chakras and subtle bodies.

One or more of your subtle bodies will be more sensitive to receiving impressions from the environment or another person. You can identify your empathic channel by narrowing to the field you are more attuned with: physical empath, emotional empath, mental empath, or intuitive empath. An intuitive empath is generally someone who can receive from all the fields and intuit broader information.

Boots on the Ground

Our connection to the physical, emotional, mental, and spiritual subtle realms is what identifies us as empathic. We are able to sense more directly energetic shifts that are occurring and moving toward physical expression because we have this rooted sensory connection to the physical plane. Former vice-president Al Gore's environmental movie *An Inconvenient Truth* featured an analogy about putting a frog in a pot of water and slowly turning up the heat, and the frog won't realize it is being cooked until it is too late. (Note: this is actually not true; experiments tend to show that the frog will eventually jump out of the pot when the temperature is raised.) The point was to showcase that we, modern civilization, may be in a pot of our own making, with the heat rising fast, and many of us remain ignorant and unaware that we are nearing a boiling point.

Empaths can sense the water warming, not just because we are more attuned to our surroundings but also because, in a way, we are "boots on the ground." Meaning, we can be agents, voices, and activists for what we are sensing is already present—or what is coming into form. Empaths who identify as physical and/or an Earth empath are particularly suited for sensing shifts emanating from the Earth's own energy system, as well as sensing what is forming energetically to come into manifestation. These are mostly subtle felt sensations, like a barometer reading, and once you have understood that is what you are picking up, it can begin to feel like a weather report. And what is the value of a weather report? Consistent reporting will show patterns and also lend flexibility to take action and to take care.

Our heightened sense of smell, taste, touch, and balance grounds us in the physical world in a manner that can seem all a bit too much, even at times as if we are being compressed and weighted down. Gravity is not impacting us any differently than anyone else, but it is important for an empathic person to learn to let go and not hold on to energy that is flowing to and from the Earth. A weather forecaster does not need to enter a hurricane to know it's a hurricane. And an empath can sense what is forming energetically in the subtle realms without needing to overidentify with the feeling.

The Not-So-Hidden Invitation to Become More

Many empathic people are spiritually attuned, which means we gravitate to the higher spiritual fields to find a truer reflection of who we innately know ourselves to be. We can easily be considered old souls—not only sensitive but wise beyond our years. Does this ring true for you? Have you been described in this way? Do social justice causes speak to you? Do you feel passionate about the environment, the animal kingdom, and human rights?

The challenge, however, for empathic people is how to embody the tenets of unity, love, and forgiveness and express them openly without reservations through our relationships—especially our relationship to ourselves. Our lower chakras and energy centers are where we hold self-esteem, self-acceptance, creativity, and a sense of safety. Therefore, it's often easier said than done to channel the unconditional love and total acceptance we recognize as truth from the higher energy centers down into our lower chakras, where life has presented us with opposite experiences.

The lower three chakras can be considered our relationship centers. The root chakra represents energies that make up our family's programming on safety and scarcity. The second chakra represents partnerships, one-to-one relationships, and how we're able to be creative and emotionally vulnerable. The third chakra, at our solar plexus, is our individual identity and our relationship with our self-esteem and self-worth.

Each of my lower chakras has required me to examine areas of my life where I've blocked energy from flowing because of stored childhood experiences and generational programming. I also, unintentionally, blocked the energy because of my own rather defiant and stubborn personality that my protective mind crafted early on to navigate the world.

I wish I could say I cleared my energy systems with earnest enthusiasm of my own accord, but it was the mastering of my empathic sensitivities that required I become more conscious and self-aware. Our empathic nature is intelligent and expansive, so if your system is locked down in self-doubt and limiting perceptions, there will undoubtedly be an awakening to the paradox that you expand outward by going inward.

I now find it rather ingenious that empathic people who want to gain authority over their energy and master their sensitivities must attend to what's out of balance within their own life, their lower chakras, and their subtle bodies. This is how they can engage their intuitive channels with accuracy and discernment.

Before I developed the skill of a functional empath, I really only cared that I got rid of the discomfort I felt. I cared only about how to stop feeling and experiencing what I termed "phantom pain." I would somehow push off the feeling, creating some space for myself, reacting rather than responding. I quickly learned that this reaction didn't give me the results I desired. The discomfort might have lifted, but it would be back minutes later. I certainly had moments when I felt my sensitivities were a curse—perhaps, I reasoned, even punishment for being an insensitive, narcissistic person in some past life.

We tend to trust that people who offer spiritual services must be wise, selfless, and altruistic, without fully understanding how they came to embody such a sense of purpose. Their paths to their center and their willingness to be of service surely brought them through painful landscapes that looked like a dark night of the soul. In these intense moments of feeling fragmented and lost, it's indeed hard to imagine offering a spiritual service or guidance. Yet, as empaths, this is innately our nature—to feel and sense what's out of balance in the space around us and to offer our presence. Each one of us must walk a path that reveals truths about why we hold certain patterns and how we can let them go, just as each of us will discover how our own story fuels the empathy we need to honor the balance that our sensitivities serve.

Questions for Reflection

Take some time with your journal to write down your impressions and feelings in response to these questions. Then, reflect on how your experience in your answers may have affected you emotionally or affected your development as an empath.

1. Write about your awareness of your energetic self. Is energy anatomy new to you? How integrated are you with regard to attending to your body, mind, and spirit?

2. The ideal for our health and well-being is to have energy flowing up and down the central channel connecting to the Earth and reaching upward above our crown chakra into higher energy fields of source. "But there is the ideal and then there is the real," as a yoga teacher once said in class. What do you sense about how your energy is flowing? Is there an area of your body that feels blocked or challenged? Do you find it hard to be grounded or even in your body? Do you prefer to be elevated and enveloped in spiritual principles and studies?

3. Have you had any experience with energy work, and if so, which modality/modalities have you experienced? Have you had any experience with a therapeutic modality that helped you integrate and understand your empathic sensitivities better?

4. Would you say you are someone who more readily senses balance or when things are out of balance? How good are you at sensing your own internal balance? Detail areas of

your life that you feel block your flow and indirectly impede the integration of your empathic nature.

5. Journal about any personal experiences that resonate with this chapter's material.

Chapter Six

The Essence of Language and Boundaries

Helen Keller, who was famously deaf, mute, and blind, demonstrated through her life how language played a profound role in connecting her to her own essence, as well as to the world of people and things. She said, "When I learned the meaning of 'I' and 'me' and found that I was something, I began to think. Then consciousness first existed for me." This quote has been a keystone in my own bridge to comprehending the power and sacredness of language to bring definition into my life. As empathic people, part of our journey is defining where the "I" begins and ends.

Language is one of the most important tools an empathic person has to navigate in the space between the physical and the nonphysical planes. And even though I refer to them as separate planes, they aren't truly separate because everything is energy.

Language carries energy between the planes. It does the work of expressing ourselves outwardly, and it does the internal work of building self-awareness and an identity. Language is both profound and subtle. We employ words to communicate with our world inside and out.

When accepting the 1993 Nobel Prize in Literature, the late author Toni Morrison said, "We die. That may be the meaning of life. But we do language. That may be the measure of our lives."

Indeed, we *do* language. Have you ever stopped to think how much words serve you? You ultimately have control over the words you use—the meaning, pitch, tone, delivery, and form. This is you as a creator, whether you're conscious of what you're creating or not. You create and craft your world and relationships through language, just as your body is in constant dialogue with its biochemistry to maintain homeostasis or balance. Just as your mind and psyche constantly receive information from society and culture, and just as your senses perceive and experience your environment. Every life form around you is involved with the activity of communication. It's the humming and buzzing of life.

Life's Mode of Operation: A Circuit of Three

This barrage of communication is Life. And for any form of communication to occur, you need three things: a transmitter, a receiver, and a message. These components create contact and connections, and every human is more or less outfitted with these components to connect with themselves, the environment, and others. It's a perpetual circuit that creates our reality.

Feel for yourself the essence of each of these components. What is it like to be a receiver with your arms wide open, standing in nature, taking in and receiving the natural wonder and beauty? Or sitting in a concert hall, receiving the music that reverberates through the space? Do you comprehend the importance of your senses in connecting you to your environment and your relationships? Likewise, what does it feel like to be a passive receiver of other people's emotions and feelings?

What is it like to be a transmitter, sending a signal to someone far away through your thoughts and prayers? How do you transmit the signal—through song, dance, art, poetry, spoken word, or meditation? What expressive channel are you using? What is it like to be a message, a messenger—the essence of what wants to be known and full of meaning?

Each part of this communication circuit plays a vital role in creating perception, comprehension, and expression of consciousness. When communication breaks down in the body for a sustained period of time, the result is typically disease. When communication breaks down in a relationship, the result is tension and stress that might lead to a breakup. When communication breaks down within yourself, life becomes a series of reactions and can feel like a boat that has lost its rudder, listlessly drifting with no direction.

Empathic people must learn to *do language* on multiple dimensions. Not only must we master language to understand ourselves within the context of our own lives, but we must learn to decipher energetic forms of communication that are part of our environment and culture. By our expanded sensory nature, we find ourselves in the role of a receiver of subtle energy transmissions in the space around us. Often, these transmissions aren't formed with a clear-cut message because they aren't intended for anyone but the person who thought them.

The energy impressions that unsuspecting empathic people pick up are typically thoughts and emotions that aren't registered by the person who created them. More than likely, the creator has no awareness that they're transmitting any messages beyond their own head space. These thoughts and feelings get displaced from the individual's center like a thread that has unraveled. They may have suppressed the emotions or thoughts out of denial, fear, or lack of awareness.

Language Offers a Container for Context

There is power in naming something and giving it form in order to break it down—not to destroy it, but to discover a buried truth. The unnamed and nebulous can haunt anyone's psyche and wreak havoc on the nervous system.

The nervous system is our communication system, which carries every bit of sensory and biochemical information to and fro, up and down, in and out. Imagine a communication system trying to pass along information that's intensely felt but not identified. It can quickly become a child's game of telephone:

> "It's scary!"
> "It's nauseating!"
> "It's cold!"

"But what is it?" asks the person on the other end of the call. "Am I sending out an ambulance, calling for a fire truck, or ordering takeout?"

To some, it might seem like flirting with fire to name what you fear, as if you're invoking it. But airing, witnessing, and ultimately integrating new attitudes can lead to radical shifts across the spectrum from the individual to the collective society. The recent #MeToo and #BlackLivesMatter movements demonstrate the cathartic nature of naming what had once been unmentionable or suppressed. It shifts the power to those with the courage to speak and allows for clarity and resolution, none of which can happen if everyone remains silent.

What holds me frozen and voiceless may not be the same for you. Therefore, each person gets to be the hero in their life, unmasking and naming what was once lurking in the shadows and syphoning energy like a tumor.

Expressions of Your Self

Look around you—all that you see and experience with your senses can be named. Find one thing where you are this moment that you can't name. More than likely, there's a table, window, chair, view of a tree or sky, and so on. Our cognitive abilities apply themselves in cooperation with our senses to define the environment through personal and learned experiences.

What can't be articulated or clearly defined by seeing and naming it has a difficult path to existence—which explains a surge in mindfulness practices such as journaling, affirmations, and vision boards. It's also why therapists ask how you're feeling to help you build self-awareness and learn to listen to your own self-talk.

The intrinsic power of language is that it's a tool: a paintbrush to create with, a looking glass to explore with, or a weapon to suppress with. Language isn't biased, but it will expose the user's bias. It's neutral but malleable, and it reflects its user: practical and pragmatic, poetic and obtuse, efficient and economical, rambling and incoherent, diminutive and controlling, and so on. What is your communication style? Does it reflect who you know yourself to be, or has it been molded by your environment and relationships, possibly even suppressed?

The Presence of Personal Space: Sovereignty

You are an enterprise that makes social contracts with the world around you. Your ability to stand in the center of your own personal sacred space to safeguard, protect, and develop well-being and health is paramount. It's the only way to maintain control and authority over your time and energy.

You must know yourself well enough to know what serves you and what doesn't. Part of this awareness involves the skill of tuning into the energy at your core and reviewing your capacity as a receiver to discern the messages you're receiving, as well as the messages you're creating and transmitting. This is something many of us aren't taught, but it's crucial in cultivating personal authority and boundaries.

The closest energy field to the body is also referred to as your "personal space." Within your energy system, your first field is critical to your ability to create healthy boundaries and a magnetic presence. It's a womblike structure, and its health and vitality are directly expressed as your physical well-being. If it isn't doing well, it may be because the fields above it aren't doing well—it's a trickle-down effect. And if it isn't doing well because of environmental reasons and physical stress, the fields above it will likewise be impacted.

We typically are more aware of our personal space when we're in public and someone gets too close. When this happens, it can feel intrusive and brash, particularly if the other person has done it purposely. I often feel proprietary about my space when I experience this, and it does produce a visceral sensation.

When someone tries to reduce you to nothing—a bully, for instance—it's this space they carve into, encroaching on its boundaries and leaving you with less of a sense of who you are. This may sound extreme unless, of course, you've experienced an abusive and dysfunctional dynamic. Then, you probably know what it feels like to be cut down and diminished. You feel vulnerable and weak.

If you're a caregiver or someone who tends to give too much of yourself, you may also feel a lack of energy, inspiration, or drive. We all have reserves of goodwill and

Energy Exercise

Here's an exercise that can demonstrate a person's first field: The person closes their eyes, and someone approaches them. They say "stop" when they don't want the approaching party to get any closer. The stopping point usually coordinates with the distance of the first energy field from their physical body.

Close friends and lovers often have a closer stopping point because when we're intimate with another person, our energy entrains together and feels familiar. I've always thought this would be a good exercise for couple's therapy, as it's an energetic clue as to how much distance each person needs and why intimacy may be compromised in the relationship.

stamina, but at some point, the only thing left to give comes from this space of personal energy. When overtaxed, this energy field quickly becomes out of balance and stressed. It's like a fetus developing while the amniotic fluid is leaking—it leads to the precarious state of managing your external world while leaving very little for yourself.

A person with a healthy, balanced lifestyle and mental/emotional well-being will typically extend their first field to just beyond their fingertips, as if their arms were outstretched. Have you seen DaVinci's Vitruvian Man drawing? It captures the first field's dimensions well. (Please look it up if you want a visual.)

Someone with a smaller first field kept inside the fingertips when arms are outstretched will likely feel exhausted, have a taxed immune system, and will base their sense of self on what they do for others. People who struggle with an identity can also have a smaller field, as they have little magnetic presence generated through self-awareness.

Conversely, a first level energy field that's well beyond the fingertips of outstretched arms can indicate a person who's very guarded and private. Or it can indicate a Highly Sensitive Person who doesn't feel safe within the environment and has created a larger energetic boundary to support their sensitivities.

Intentional Breathing Creates Space

At a recent presentation to staff at a local hospice, I helped demonstrate what happens when someone is overtaxed and gives too much of their energy without taking the time to give back to themselves. As a group exercise, we took a moment to breathe intentionally and deeply, centering ourselves and creating space for ourselves. A manager was nominated by the staff as someone who was available but perhaps overextending herself. She became the group model.

Before the exercise, her first field was well within her hands, nearly to her wrists. After intentional breathing of only a few minutes, her first field was just outside her fingertips. She shared with the room that she felt more centered and had more of a sense of space around her.

Breathing can be a quick fix on the spot, so I highly recommend incorporating a breathing practice into your self-care. But to transform chronic patterns of mismanaged energetic boundaries, it's important to do the inner work of defining and knowing who you are from the inside out. Holding and securing your own presence at your center is profoundly effective at creating healthy and respectful boundaries.

Why Unaware Empathic People Struggle with Boundaries

The first field placement of unaware empathic people tends to present at both ends of a spectrum—either too small or too big. Some are prone to let people get too close because they have a hard time distinguishing between their own boundaries and another's. This usually happens for two reasons: (1) it's particularly difficult to discern boundaries if you accept as your own all of the extrasensory thoughts and emotions that are displaced from others in the environment, and (2) a sense of familiarity makes empathic people more likely to accept thoughts and feelings as their own, especially when around close friends and family.

When an empathic person creates a large first field, it may be because they're at odds with their environment. Perhaps they haven't discovered the tools to understand their sensory reception. So they build walls and defenses because, paradoxically, there's a pervasive feeling of disconnection and not belonging while still feeling that everything in the room is attempting to connect to them. They retreat in order to feel safe, but this can also create hypersensitivity within them, while someone with a compromised smaller first field can feel overwhelmed to the point of numbness about their life and environment.

An Empath's Sense of Sovereignty: I AM

Building trust in yourself as an empathic person begins at the body and with the awareness of how to maintain healthy boundaries at the first field. To create your own sovereignty, language is your greatest tool to define and bring clarity. Just as you can name the objects in a room, you can apply the same technique to define yourself. Who are you? After all, you're also in physical form just like the chair or the tree. You create your magnetic center by affirming who you know yourself to be and living from this knowingness. This isn't a conjuring; it's a witnessing of your own nature standing in form.

In addition to impacting the first field, the following exercise will also strengthen all of the chakras but particularly the fifth chakra, which is at your throat and represents manifestation and speaking your truth. The strength and resilience of the first field becomes the beneficiary of your willingness to embody and speak your truth.

"I AM" declarations are held energetically within our center. Sound too simple? Try it. Be bold and honest. Choose a word to follow "I AM." Can you hold the vibration of your chosen word's energy? How does that word feel to each of your subtle bodies? Notice if there's any part of you that deflects or feels uncomfortable about your "I AM" declarations. Wobbles or self-doubts indicate areas where your subconscious mind is holding on to self-limiting patterns that you can work toward releasing.

Composing affirmations is easy, and consistently demonstrating them in your life solidifies them. When you declare yourself centered and present in your own sacred space, you're both the creator and the sovereign of that space. And the space around you will respond as you demonstrate and embody the energy.

Consider what you're declaring to the space around you when you state "I AM an empath." How does the energy around you respond? In my experience, this statement attracts energy that wants to be witnessed and balanced as I offer myself in service as an empath. It's especially important to understand this if you've been overwhelmed by your empathic nature because of your premature identification as an empath.

I'm not trying to discourage anyone who is empathic from aligning themselves to an empath's journey—far from it. The world and humanity need every functional empath to be present. But take time to invest in self-care strategies and honor the context of your own personal life in how it shaped and molded your sensitivities. Take the time to embody your "I AM" with presence. The world will take notice.

Questions for Reflection

Take some time with your journal to write down your impressions and feelings in response to these questions. Then, reflect on how your experience in your answers may have affected you emotionally or affected your development as an empath.

1. Write about how you feel as a receiver when your arms are wide open in nature or in a concert hall. Reflect on how it feels to receive other people's emotions and feelings. Then, write about how it feels to be a transmitter as you send a signal or message to someone else who is far away.

2. Language initiates a person into being a creator. Honor that power and reflect upon what you are creating in your life with your words. Take note of the essence of the way you communicate. Your voice and mouth are at your fifth chakra. I find it interesting that our manner of speaking can be described as tastes: salty, sweet, savory, rich, bitter, and so on. Describe how your words generally taste.

3. Write about a time when you have felt your personal space was compromised by someone else's behavior? How did it make you feel? How did you react/respond?

4. Write about a time when you felt your energy was overtaxed. How often have you felt this?

5. Try breathing intentionally and deeply, centering yourself and creating space for yourself. Breathe up from the Earth below you and up through the top of your crown. Now, breathe

down and through your center to the ground beneath. How does this exercise make you feel? Do you feel more centered with more space in the energy field around you? The next time you feel on the verge of giving away too much of your energy, try this breathing exercise.

6. Try the energy exercise within the chapter, in which someone approaches you while your eyes are closed. Say "stop" when you don't want them to get any closer. This is the distance of your first energy field from your physical body. Then, try it in reverse, as you approach them with their eyes closed. Make notes about the experience and what you observed.

7. When you work with the "I AM" declaration, write about how you feel as a result. How do you feel the energy around you responds? Do these words represent an "ideal" that you want to foster and introduce to your identity, or can you feel the words within you at your center looking for a way to be more present in your life?

Chapter Seven

An Honest Assessment

Here is my message for people who are in a perpetual cycle of emotional suffering and instability due to being an empath: *You may not be an empath*.

That may be my most controversial statement in this book. Let's take a deep breath and sit with it. Perhaps it's better to reframe it as "You may not be an empath *yet*." I offer this assessment as a means to liberate your sense of responsibility to feel everything around you and instead begin to feel what's *inside you*. Start there because that's where your essence and presence are generated from and where you'll learn to maintain balance.

Again, no one is born an empath; it's a transformation that happens, like going through puberty. For some exceptionally well-supported empathic people, self-awareness can develop without a lot of internal struggle. But for the majority of us, it's a messy and confusing process to navigate boundaries, crowded spaces, and vague visceral sensations without any context or real guidance from mainstream resources. This messiness is also related to our own self-perception—most notably, not trusting ourselves or our intuition. How messy is your inner world of thoughts and feelings? The state of your inner world will impact your abilities to receive and process accurately what you may be picking up empathically.

Much like the term Highly Sensitive Person, "empath" is a label that's loosely tossed around in forums of sensitive people looking for validation and direction. Many people use online self-assessment tests to help identify their sensitivities. But often, these assessments offer a label without further clarification or resources to understand what they actually mean.

Ask yourself: How did I come to use this identifier? What does it mean to be empathic or an empath—generally and personally? Do I use it as a scapegoat and justification to avoid people and places? Do I overly identify with it to give me a sense of identity and purpose?

Remember that being empathic isn't a condition or an ailment. It's an invitation to embody a deep level of self-awareness and connection to yourself, humanity, and the natural world. And, yes, it's pretty much a heuristic process—hands-on, learning through experience. This sensory feature requires you to shift from living your life on autopilot to becoming an engaged and attentive person. When you're on autopilot or living to conform, it's harder to learn heuristically.

The fine print missing from these self-assessment tests is important: not everyone who's empathic is an empath. As I've said, it isn't a foregone conclusion—just as everyone who can swim isn't inclined to become a lifeguard. And that's okay. Each step on your path that helps you experience your sensory nature and feel secure in the world will help you build trust and connections.

Your personal understanding of what your body feels like in different environments becomes useful information to build your own sensory index to assist you in the future. I'm an intuitive empath, but my primary reception is one of a physical empath, which means my body delivers messages to me from the environment, but I can also sense and tune into certain systems within myself.

For example, when I receive massage or bodywork from a skilled professional, I can hear my fascia release. It sounds like tiny high-pitched chimes. I can experience the gurgling of energy that may pop off or release from organs—particularly if I've been stagnant for a period of time. I can hear the static and buzzy sound of inflammation. I can feel a rush of adrenaline as pins and needles that move down my legs as I shake off jitters, such as when I first begin to play in a squash match. I can feel when my energy connects to the Earth as a settling and pulling feeling that drops from my perineum area. Knowing your own signature sensations will assist you in building a trusted relationship with yourself.

I've relied on the word "hear" quite a bit to describe what I experience about my own body, though I wouldn't say I'm clairaudient like someone who actually hears messages or voices. I do, however, tune into my body and the space I occupy. Language reveals connections in subtle ways, and "tuning" is an auditory feature. So it's poignant that when I tune in, I can hear sounds correlating to energy expressing itself through my flesh. This awareness about how my own body communicates to me didn't require anything outside of myself. It only required that I take notice.

When I advise you to start with yourself, I simply mean to take your extrasensory reception in-house and discover your own inner space. Do you feel spacious, or do you feel crowded and congested? Do some areas feel mysterious, as if you've landed on the shores of someplace unexplored?

When I took the time to do some inner development, the environment around me slowed down and demanded very little from me, even though I had previously perceived it as overwhelming with too many sensations and feelings. If I were to compare this sort of deep introspective learning to seasons, it would be like autumn and winter. The environment slows down from the business of expressing rebirth and regeneration. Instead, it burrows deep and goes inward.

When your awareness includes your own sensory vocabulary and what you associate with certain feelings, it will be much easier for you to relate to and empathize with a feeling that comes to you from outside your own life experience. This is how we develop empathy, by knowing firsthand what our life feels like for ourselves.

Being an Empath

When you identify as an empath, life will continually present opportunities to sharpen your awareness of yourself in multidimensional ways. How well do you know yourself as an individual, as part of a family, as part of society, and as part of humanity? How are you showing up in each of those relationships? Is there consistency? The people around you will feel the depth of your nature. Take notice of the moments when you witness others as they witness you.

For example, have you ever experienced a room or situation respond or change as a result of your presence? Have you seen someone else's presence impact a room? Or do people say they feel differently around you or find themselves acting differently, such as more honest and real? Do animals gravitate toward you, even ones who don't typically like strangers?

I've had interesting encounters that I now understand are because my energy presence can trigger people, in potentially good or bad ways. In one instance, the husband of an acquaintance apologized to me for his very strong unsolicited opinion at a dinner party. It didn't impact me, but his wife kept asking what I'd done to her husband, who'd never been known to retract or soften his strong views before. Plus, I was a stranger to him. Another writer in a writer's course was strongly triggered by an innocent question I posed about something she shared. The teacher was at a loss to understand the woman's reaction. I, on the other hand, suspected that she felt I'd invited her to examine something hidden in her life, and it freaked her out. Empathic people are so nuanced at sensing energy that even in the questions we pose to others, we can unwittingly support expressions in them to find balance.

As an empath, you need to be the embodiment of your own authority. Perhaps that's the question that needs to be put forth on self-assessment tests to help sensitive people identify where they are on the arc of development. Do you have authority over your own energy? Do you know how to take care of yourself without needing a crisis to signal that you're overextending yourself? Do you know how to ground yourself and why that's an essential component to developing sensory fluency? What do you typically do when you receive an impression from someone else, from a room, or from the Earth?

All of your responses to these kinds of questions will help you evaluate how you're doing with accepting and integrating your wider receptivity and if you feel aligned to the label of an empath. Part of the prerequisite work of empaths is cultivating self-love and acceptance. You can only get so far with understanding life—yours and others'—by using your head. Then, your heart needs to open you up for the last stretch.

Your heart has its own knowingness—an intelligence that transcends the ego. Embodying self-love and acceptance allows you to naturally enforce boundaries while also giving you the space to be available for others.

There are certain words that I will use often in this guidebook because they're fundamental to being self-actualized as a sensory empathic being: "integrated," "unified," "authentic," "grounded," "embody," "trust," and "compassionate." These are the equivalent of having the essential and necessary items in your backpack for an outing in the wilderness. A first aid kit is great to have with you, but you still need to understand how to apply a tourniquet or recognize shock, for example. Have you experienced and know what trust in yourself feels like? Or what being grounded feels like? Or being okay with the unknown?

Each fundamental word I've chosen is a process in understanding the composition that is you, your consciousness, and what shows up to animate your life. As you give yourself more love and acceptance, your life will unfold and prepare you so that you can feel complete even in the presence of more discovery and mystery.

Caution: Hold Labels Lightly

Philosopher Søren Kierkegaard once wrote these cautionary lines:

> *"If you name me, you negate me. By giving me a name, a label, you negate all the other things I could possibly be."*

I've stressed the power of language to name, define, and create a bridge between the energetic realm and the physical realm. It's one of the tools that an empathic person uses to implement balance and identify forms, but it's also important to recognize that there's an element of impermanence to life. It's constantly changing and shifting seasons and life cycles. We, too, shift and change, hopefully growing into our truer selves.

Honestly, I was reluctant to call myself an empath for many years. I sensed the responsibility and reverence instilled in the function and purpose of such an ability to feel beyond my own self. I didn't take it lightly to declare myself as such, but this is who I learned I AM, just as I learned that I AM many other unique expressions of my core self. So, if you do identify as an empath, remember that you, too, are also more than this label.

Questions for Reflection

Take some time with your journal to write down your impressions and feelings in response to these questions. Then, reflect on how your experience in your answers may have affected you emotionally or affected your development as an empath.

1. Based on what you've read so far, do you believe you're an empathic person or an empath at this point? What experiences cause you to make this determination?

2. What "messiness" have you observed in your inner world of thoughts and feelings that you want to work on balancing? Can you identify which lower chakra may be involved?

3. Have you ever taken a self-assessment test to identify your sensitivities? Note how you experienced the test and its value or lack of value. Did you feel differently about the test when you took it than you feel after having read this book so far?

4. What, if any, signature sensations have you noticed in yourself? As I mentioned in the chapter, I hear something like tiny high-pitched chimes during fascia release, for example. Have you had any similar experiences? If so, make note of them. Then, connect with each of your biological systems to the best of your ability, and let yourself imagine that you're flowing with the chain of communication that allows them to function optimally. (You might want to close your eyes for that process.)

5. Recount an experience in which your energy presence impacted a room or where you observed someone else's energy impacting a room.

6. Write down your answers to these questions that I posed in the chapter: Do you feel you have authority over your own energy? Do you know how to take care of yourself without needing a crisis to signal that you're overextending yourself? Do you know how to ground yourself and why that's an essential component to developing sensory fluency? What do you typically do when you receive an impression from someone else, from a room, or from the Earth? Please don't chastise yourself if you feel you have more work to do to reach these goals. By answering these questions honestly, you'll know what you want to cultivate within yourself to strengthen your empathic abilities.

Chapter Eight

Displacement in the Simplest of Terms

Empathic sensory reception involves building your awareness about spatial relationships and energy dynamics, but as a sense, it's focused on one relationship primarily. Do you know which one? Empathic senses provide you with a more pronounced relationship with the energetic and physical space around you, sensing and feeling the environment on a subtle level that also detects and registers balance.

As I've said, empathic sensory reception is a subset of the intuitive *sixth sense*, but there is one sense that seems to straddle being viewed as both a physiological and an intuitive sense: proprioception. Both camps claim it.

Proprioception is the sense of self-movement and body position—the body's ability to perceive its own position in space. Your ability to close your eyes and touch your nose is due to proprioception. Science has pinpointed that it takes multiple sensory inputs to generate this gyroscopic sense—namely, the inner ear, visual optics, stretch muscles known as spindle nerves, and, of course, the brain to process the information.

Again, our physical body and energetic body are mirror images of each other. If something exists in the physical, it's because that physical component exists energetically as well. Macro and micro—micro and macro.

The physical plane is one of form, tangible and touchable. Then, there are layers of energetic content that correlate with what's in physical form. Among the subtle energies are emotions, thoughts, and feelings, which superficially can be felt as variations of denseness or pressure. When someone says there is tension in the room, this is the level from which they are picking up that information.

In a physical room, we walk around a potted plant, clearly knowing it isn't part of us. But in the energetic space of the room where we encounter an emotion by feeling it, we have a harder time understanding it's just like the plant. We are not the plant, and we didn't create it, though we can appreciate it and take care not to harm it with our actions. In the energetic space, we must also learn to not identify ourselves as the creator of what we feel simply because we can feel it. However, we can have empathy and appreciate what that feeling may represent for the person who displaced it into the energetic plane.

Your physical senses have limits as to what they can perceive. Testing your eyesight and hearing involves measuring against a range. For eyesight, you're nearsighted or farsighted, and your eyes are designed to automatically adapt to what you focus on, whether the horizon or a text on your phone. The same is true for your hearing—there are low and high frequencies, and we all tend to lose higher frequencies as we age.

Likewise, empathic senses operate locally, registering foremost what's in the space and environment where you find yourself. But they, too, can sense events that are farther afield. It's a matter of magnitude. A large explosion, even far away, can still be heard, or a bright flash of light can be seen at a distance. And a great emission of collective grief can be detected in the ethers.

At times, when we experience something of great magnitude that happens on the physical plane, it can be keenly felt in the energetic planes. My personal experience with this was in experiencing, nearly in real-time, the massive Indonesian tsunami that took place in December 2004. We were driving through the Texas Panhandle in the middle of the night, with all four of the kids sleeping in the back seats, when I was overwhelmed with emotion and grief. Tears began streaming down my cheeks, and my husband looked over at me with concern. He was used to me needing a moment to discern feelings, but this was certainly out of character. I managed to articulate that something horrible had happened somewhere in the world, and the nonphysical realm was being flooded with the energies of disincarnate grief. Only later, when we heard the news of the tsunami halfway around the world in Southeast Asia, did I understand what I'd picked up. Approximately 230,000 people died in that natural disaster.

Conceptualizing Movement and Awareness in the Energetic Space

Let's say you're in a room right now. It's part of a larger building or house, but the room is contained and defined by the walls and door. This local environment primarily engages your senses. Perhaps there's not much going on in the room to register. If you're in a space with many people, the energy is busier. Other people's energies, plus any displaced emotions, thoughts, and physical discomfort, are now part of that environment, particularly if the people present aren't good at processing their thoughts and emotions.

In a tangential way, it's like what happens when you're in a crowded swimming pool filled with people, swimming equipment, and toys. When someone else or any of these objects is close to you, you can sense them through the movement of the water and not because they physically touch you. You're in direct contact with the water, and it's the water's movement that relays the information to you. (This is also why swimming pools use lane ropes to dampen the water's movement and aid swimmers.) In a similar fashion, your intuition detects energetic movement or transmissions, and it functions by giving you the information like radar.

This dynamic is a profound awareness that can help you understand what it means to be empathic. From my experience, when unaware and underdeveloped empathic people feel something from the environment, they tend to process it in three ways: (1) they believe it to be their own; (2) they believe they're being occupied by someone else's energy, so they feel displaced from their own space; or (3) they believe they have unwittingly trespassed into someone else's personal space. All of these are possible, but not by the design of your empathic senses. Of course, none of these perceptions necessarily fosters a sense of safety in public spaces.

Your empathic sensitivity may undoubtedly be more engaged in public places since more people equals more potential movement in the energetic planes. But you'll allow yourself to have a less reactive or defensive view of being out in the world if you incorporate the awareness that your empathic senses aren't trespassing on other people's energy. And other people are generally not trespassing on yours, either.

The ability to distinguish your thoughts, feelings, and emotions from those you receive from the space around you is an important skill in public spaces. Hopefully, this awareness will help you feel less entangled by the energy of others. It will also help you maintain boundaries and a sense of safety in public places.

Feeling Something to the Point of Naming It

The reality, though, is it's very easy to feel boundaries dissolve in public spaces when you can keenly feel both static and dynamic energy in the space. So I don't mean to diminish anyone's struggles to construct healthy boundaries.

If I continue with the pool analogy, I want to point out why it can be extra challenging for empathic people to feel safe in public places or even in relationships. In addition to detecting the movement of the water, we can also detect when something has actually entered the water itself—say, when a child involuntarily pees in the pool, when the ideal chemical balance is off, or when the temperature changes even subtly.

Our perception of the water as a safe environment is then put into question because it's the water that's the medium, and it's touching us. In the same manner, displaced emotions, projected thoughts, and physical pain can also involuntarily enter the space outside of the person's auric space. This is what's detected by our empathic senses. Think of it like a cargo ship with a breach in its hull, leaking contents and polluting the water, but the captain is unaware of the breach.

I came to this awareness many years ago when I was worn out from managing my negative perception of public spaces. I asked myself in all seriousness, "Where is a peaceful place to exist in society?" The answer was simple and idealistic: a place where people were capable and willing to process their own emotions and thoughts. A place where healthy self-awareness is promoted and encouraged to develop. Do you know where that place exists in our world? Can such a utopian place ever exist?

Once I recognized that what I primarily picked up from the environment was emotional and mental "stuff" that people hadn't processed themselves, it infused me with hope and compassion. These individuals were unaware that they were impacting the environment in any way. I began to understand that self-awareness and acceptance were the minimum requirements needed to clean up energetic spaces from emotional and mental debris. Sure, self-compassion and self-love would be the ideal, but to change anything, we need awareness first, followed by acceptance.

I admit that while I was empathic at the time and not yet an empath, I thought rather self-servingly, "If only everyone else could just pick up after themselves and self-reflect, my life would be so much easier." I went through a period of writing in my journal: "Dear Humanity, the goal is to be conscious and engaged, empowered, and authentic. Please contribute. Humbly yours." But like most imbalances that begin by laying blame outside of ourselves—what we see as an issue outside of us actually requires us to look within and address the issue within ourselves.

Empaths certainly aren't exempt from the need to do inner work. In fact, it's pretty much a prerequisite to transform from an empathic person to an empath. Before I ever considered myself a functional empath, I had to clear myself of the tangled web of projected thought-forms and displaced emotions that I had ignorantly accepted as my own over a lifetime. If I was feeling it, surely it was mine, right? This also meant I needed to understand my own content.

This is the reality of most sensitive empathic people. We must own and know our own emotional baggage and triggers so that when we enter a room or a crowded space, we can identify when something is out of sorts for us personally or when we're acting as a mirror for someone else's imbalance.

The Power of Self-Awareness

Fear and doubt are among the greatest intimidators and suppressors of self-awareness. They inhibit us from living consciously. Typically, when something is repressed, suppressed, and silenced in our psyche, it gets shelved or put at a distance.

We're like mini processing plants. We create, invest in, and manufacture our lives. Imagine you have a smoke stack atop your head like a cartoon character. How much debris and unfiltered emissions are you leaking into the environment from your unnamed fears? Are you unwittingly creating a toxic environment for yourself and others? Are you held hostage by dysfunctional patterns that don't seem to shift because you make them someone else's problem or someone else's fault? Are you moody, and do you find it hard to regulate your emotions?

Self-awareness, of course, is a lifelong endeavor and doesn't happen overnight with one fell swoop. But as more people seek self-awareness and harmony, fewer people will create fear and anxiety in the energetic realms. More people will disconnect from sources that promote drama and fear.

The by-product of self-awareness is cleaner emissions and a transparency that would pass a safety inspection. Being transparent doesn't imply there isn't trauma or private details that are safeguarded as deeply personal; it just means you've processed your life experience with enough thoughtfulness that it's held closer to your center. You're willing to own it. You've begun to integrate the experience, and you accept and value it at some level.

On the physical plane, you can see the effects when someone isn't self-aware, denying aspects of themselves. Their displaced emotions are expressed through their behavior. Anger and jealousy are two common examples of suppressed emotions that are acted out. When someone has anger issues but doesn't deal with them, displaced anger begins to surface through destructive and abusive behavior. The intense emotion looks for expression, and in lieu of self-awareness and acceptance, it may get channeled in an unhealthy way, such as passive-aggressive behavior.

Jealousy is a wily one, as we often don't realize we're jealous until we're already acting out and dramatizing our feelings (often to our own shock and horror). However, if you're aware that you're jealous of someone, you'll be much more likely to keep your behavior in check. You'll also be willing to examine what the jealousy is truly about. It isn't really about the other person; it's about your perception of what they have that you wish you had.

Think about times when you've seen behavior that wasn't particularly healthy in its expression. There's a sense that the person is oblivious to how they impact a room or conversation. They can seem quite selfish, entitled, and childish because this is an aspect of them that hasn't matured. It's stuck in the lower chakras.

Behavior can be a channel for displaced feelings, but that doesn't eliminate the root source of what fuels the behavior. And not everyone acts out what's suppressed and holding in their energy fields, which creates stress in their systems. Chronic stress may lead to the weakening of the overall energy field. It also makes aspects of the person's physical, emotional, and mental health more easily perceivable by others, but particularly to empathic people.

It's important to remember to not take it personally when you encounter someone's unprocessed emotions. They probably have no idea that they've impacted the space with their displaced energy.

Filtration Systems

Admittedly, discussing energetic components is abstract. As best I can, I try to use common and accessible descriptions. So far in this chapter, I've employed public swimming pools and factories to illustrate what happens in spaces energetically. These two examples also share an important component required to function optimally: a filtration system.

Yet there are subtle differences between how they operate. The factory's internal processing and filtration is evident by its outward emissions, while the swimming pool system filters out unhealthy substances in the water. In other words, one system processes what's yours so that you don't negatively impact the environment, while the other buffers toxic elements from the environment so they won't affect your perception of yourself and the world.

Self-awareness supports our ability to be in healthy relationships and avoid negatively affecting shared spaces. But what helps us filter out unhealthy and toxic substances from our environment like the swimming pool's system?

As sensitive and empathic people, we must be gentle with ourselves because our senses receive a double dose of whatever is seeking balance in the world. We see the physical effects of neglect in our environment and upon the Earth, and we also feel what's too painful, shameful, or fearful for others to process. This reflection of turmoil displayed in both the physical and energetic realms requires that we learn how to balance ourselves in a neutral space between the two.

Our ability to observe and witness without judgment, as well as our capacity to care, is paramount to sustaining boundaries in any environment. Both of these require trust, experience, and an integrated awareness that everything is connected.

Boundary Guards: Observe and Witness

Awareness is the by-product of both observing and witnessing. I see it as a special ops team—the mind observes and locates a dynamic, while the body and spirit witness it.

An *observer* acts like a pin drop on your phone's map app, registering your placement within an area. You are here, and you're experiencing this spot and observing the details, mundane and interesting alike. In the simplest terms, an observer is a variable in an environment—which, according to quantum physics, is all it takes to alter a reality. The role of the observer is the essence of the popular thought experiment "If a tree falls in a forest and no one is around to hear it, does it make a sound?"

When I was in college, I observed one of my roommates' strict relationship with food. She was slender, but not too thin. I merely observed this as a detail that I thought was a result of her interest in nutrition and fitness. Years later, as part of a counseling and treatment program, which required her to be honest with the people around her, she opened up to me about her eating disorder. I was surprised when she revealed that it was deeply embedded during the years we lived together. She was also surprised, assuming I had to have known since I'm generally perceptive and tend to notice miniscule details.

But since I was a variable in her living space, she needed to hide the truth from me. From my perspective, I merely observed her routines to learn how to cohabitate with her. I was preoccupied with my own internal upheavals and wasn't readily available to do more than just observe my surroundings.

A *witness*, on the other hand, participates. For example, a witness at a marriage ceremony must sign their name on the official document. They aren't just standing by, observing indifferently. A witness at a crime scene must interact with officials and give a statement. A roommate witnessing self-destructive behavior may ask questions out of concern. Witnessing invokes a level of compassion, empathy, and respect. Observing offers you the distance to be detached from the situation.

This is fundamentally what it means to be an empath: to witness someone else's displaced emotions and thoughts on the energetic plane. To feel and witness them with the intention of balance and self-awareness. This is a profound way to participate with the environment because it creates movement and space for new expressions and perspectives to form.

An empath doesn't process displaced feelings or emotions for the other person. They merely witness the feelings, perhaps naming the felt sensation and recognizing that someone is challenged by an aspect of life.

In the next section, I'll share an example of a house clearing to highlight the relationship between myself, the space, and the energies of the inhabitants. This scenario is a bit of a hybrid: I was empathically passive and let the impressions present to me, but I also energetically investigated the impressions as I worked with them to find a balanced expression.

Empaths who do this kind of work are also known as energy workers. We intentionally work with the energies, which requires intuitive abilities. This is why you need to be comfortable claiming that you're an empath because it indicates that you're able to cross boundaries from passive to active with clear intentions that ground and support your work in both the physical and the etheric.

The Energy of Feeling Trapped

The house for the property clearing was located in the prestigious neighborhood near Rice University in Houston, Texas. The owners were a middle-aged couple, and it was the second marriage for the husband, who had children from his previous marriage. It was a large home for a family of three, and most of the house had very small energy spots with nothing major. Then, I found myself sitting in the almost off-to-college-age daughter's room, sifting through the many jumbled thoughts and feelings that coated it. The daughter was the youngest of the husband's children and the only one living with them. She was independent, sporty, and quite active outside the home. Yet what I experienced in her room was the feeling of being held prisoner or trapped.

It took me some time to feel the essence of the energy, but once I identified and named it, the energy shifted as if the knot was untangling. I didn't just name the feeling or sensation; I also asked for an examination of the perception that created the feeling of being trapped. This was the inner work that still needed to be processed by the daughter.

To be clear, I communicated on an energetic level through my intuitive channels, not through a physical conversation. I didn't discuss what I felt with the daughter, who wasn't physically present in the room. I worked energetically through my sixth chakra, otherwise known as the third eye, with the room, the daughter, and her perception. If anyone had observed me, it would have simply looked as though I was meditating.

This example of the power of witnessing illustrates how an environment can allow for movement and the creation of new expressions. The feedback I received afterward from the parents mainly centered on how the daughter almost immediately came to them to talk about the challenges in her life. She was aware she'd been closed off to them—perhaps unfairly. She had indeed felt trapped by many aspects of her life, but once she admitted that, taking action to alleviate that feeling came more easily.

Honoring Collective Space

My kids liken me to a garbage collector, picking up displaced feelings and projected thoughts and then recycling them into expressions of balance and healing. They aren't far off, but I prefer to think of myself as a "spirit level"—yes, they are actually called that! I'm delighted that this carpentry tool already has such an appropriate name. It's also known as a bubble level that can detect horizontal and vertical plumb lines. Regardless, each time I pick up an impression, I feel it in order to name it. Then, I hold it up energetically for the person who created it and silently ask them to become aware of it so that they can try processing it themselves. I don't take responsibility, however, for whether the invitation is received and attended to—that would compromise boundaries and create an imbalance of grand proportions.

Humanity is a team effort. As an empath, I feel what's out of balance, what's not being said, and what's blocking the flow of energy. I'm not here to judge. After all, for me to know the impression, I have to have felt it myself at some point, whether it's shame, guilt, love, anger, peace, jealousy, or confusion. And the process goes on and on—feeling, naming, witnessing, and balancing.

Questions for Reflection

Take some time with your journal to write down your impressions and feelings in response to these questions. Then, reflect on how your experience in your answers may have affected you emotionally or affected your development as an empath.

1. Have you ever sensed a displaced emotion in an environment that you mistook for your own? If so, write about this experience and how you came to recognize it wasn't yours.

2. When you enter an environment or meet with people, I suggest practicing your ability to discern between your own feelings and those you pick up from others in the space. Take notes about what you experience.

3. Make note of displaced emotions or dysfunctional patterns within yourself that you have worked to heal, as well as others that you still need to clear. What can you do to begin to balance these issues?

4. What unhealthy behaviors have you observed in yourself or others that show a lack of self-awareness?

5. Have you had an experience of being an observer, as opposed to being a witness, and vice versa? Make notes about what you felt.

6. As you enter a new environment or meet with people, practice playing the role of observer and the role of witness separately in order to clearly feel the difference.

Chapter Nine

The Sponge Factor

My two youngest children, teenagers at the time and devoted Whovians, watched the episode of *Doctor Who* with me that revolved around an empath named Emma. When someone asks her what an "empathic psychic" is, she says that she senses feelings in the same way that a telepath senses thoughts. The Doctor then says that "empathics" are the most compassionate people you'll ever meet but that they're also the loneliest because they expose themselves to hidden feelings like guilt, pain, and sorrow.

Are we a lonely lot? Hmm . . . loneliness was a constant and pervasive undercurrent when I was *unaware* of my empathic nature, but not afterward. As a child feeling trapped in a lonely existence, I lived timidly. I was a keen watcher of life, sitting on the sidelines, convinced that life—or specifically, human dynamics—was a hardship and a burden. It took me years, as in decades, to understand why I preferred being in nature or reading books to interacting with large groups. For an empathically wired person, reading a book presents clear boundaries around interactions and drama without having to feel it through our senses—it can be totally confined to the imagination.

Ironically, or perhaps poignantly, it was the process of becoming aware of my empathic receptors and the practice of maintaining healthy personal boundaries that eventually humbled me to the point where I had to accept that I wasn't alone, nor would I ever be. I'm connected; we are connected. Everyone has the choice and the opportunity to discover this truth for themselves, whatever their life circumstances. And when you do, profound shifts happen to your sense of belonging, as well as your need to control and manage environments. Trust slowly develops within yourself about being okay with where you are, who you are, and the fact that everything will be revealed in its own time. Strangely, you begin to respect an unfolding to your life with more patience than you had in the past.

As to The Doctor's speculation about an empath exposing themselves to hidden feelings like guilt, pain, and sorrow, this is true (in part). As discussed in the previous chapter, the feelings an empath registers are typically hidden from the very person who's transmitting them. But empaths don't *expose themselves* to hidden feelings, as if wading through toxic waste without a hazmat suit. And not every impression received is from the "bleak and hopeless" basket of human emotions.

People are often surprised to learn that one of the most challenging environments I encounter is a room full of joy and exuberant pride. Imagine being present during a school's award ceremony, with all the families celebrating their child's accomplishments. For the buttoned-up patrons who rushed to get to the event on time and who may not be comfortable expressing or experiencing heartfelt emotions in public, the group energy creates a confusing physical and emotional cocktail that gets flushed out into the environment.

There's a tightness in the throat as people choke back tears, wanting to maintain an acceptable appearance. Or perhaps they hold their breath in anticipation. A fullness and richness sweep through my body in such settings. It typically requires me to do slow, deep breathing through the waves of excess emotions that move through the space around me and over me like a waterfall. A welling of tears inevitably follows, as my body acts as a transducer and expresses as best it can the excess emotional energy that isn't physically expressed by the audience members.

When the auditorium claps in appreciation, I also clap vigorously to help physically express the emotions. When I see audience members with full-on tears streaming down their beaming faces, I nod to them in admiration and appreciation for their willingness to be openly engaged. People who are accepting of their emotional responses, particularly from joy, will mingle smiles with their tears. But on occasion, people are so caught off guard by the public display of their joyful emotions that they look pained and embarrassed, perhaps even apologizing for what they consider inappropriate behavior.

I ride this wave of excess through my own emotions of joy and pride, which are also present. I'm not just an observer off to the side because I have my own responses to my life. Joy begets joy, love recognizes love, and pain can have profound depths when united with others' pain. This is part of the emotional broadband that we empathic people possess and learn to manage. I have learned to lean into these moments and physically express the emotions, if possible through actions like clapping, cheering, or crying.

Using energetic techniques can also help ring out the excess emotional content that I absorb from an event. Again, it begins with self-awareness and self-expression—identifying what's mine and what's from the environment that's hitching a ride. I also have to identify how to prevent whatever is hitching a ride from overwhelming my own experience, by redirecting the excess emotion to the Earth.

An Emotional Release Valve

As a young parent, before I truly understood how my empathic reception worked, a tragic accident occurred in our neighborhood. Stavanger, Norway, is a charming port town with historic clad wooden houses nestled together that form neighborhoods around schools and local shops. Children walk or bike to school. Classes spend many hours outside exploring nearby parks. It's routine and consistent, and groups of children meandering to and from the school building throughout the day become the backdrop of the weekdays with its own particular sounds filling the air.

The relatively predictable rhythm of the neighborhood was shattered one day by tragedy. A popular boy in our oldest son's fourth grade class was killed crossing a busy intersection close to the school. The parents of the class gathered together immediately to discuss how to best support the family and share the news with our own children. It began slowly with tears flowing down my face, as though a faucet had turned on and I didn't know where the shut-off valve was located. I had used up the few tissues I had in my pocket, dabbing at my eyes and wiping my nose. The tissues sat wadded in my palm, useless.

I experienced a nearly out-of-body sensation by the time the sobbing began in the midst of a room of fifteen dry-faced but somber adults. I cried as if it was my own son who'd died because I couldn't separate my reality from the enormous emotions that were being held in check by the rest of the parents—by the entire neighborhood. Faces turned toward me, pained in their own ways, but all contained and managed with notable Norwegian control.

Then, a few others reached for the tissue boxes that were placed on the tables and began to dab at their eyes.

My emotional display of grief was remarkable to everyone, including myself. I felt so overwhelmed, yet I tried to wrestle back control over my emotions. But the collective grief felt by each parent, which sat heavy in all hearts, overran the banks of my own emotional reservoir. Afterward, I internally chastised myself as the strange foreign wife who was unable to keep her emotions contained. I was embarrassed and exhausted, but this also marked a turning point in my own awareness that there was more to what was happening to me than just being "sensitive." I felt as if I were a canary in a coal mine, and I was determined to get out of that cage.

Your empathic sensitivities align you to this cathartic spiritual service: being an emotional sponge or release valve. It isn't unlike the person who's hired to laugh in an audience to get other people to laugh. An empathic person can express the emotions that are present—whether the people there understand that or not. It's an act of mirroring to others what's within them that they haven't noticed or have denied. When you understand this aspect of your sensitivities, you can be present and lend more direction to your emotional body as to how to process the excess emotional content, particularly in public events, as well as how to employ your spiritual body.

Do you, too, experience these emotional moments when in public that can seem disproportionate to your own emotions? As if you're the emotional release valve for a group or an event? How have these incidents impacted your self-image and how others may view you? Do you feel that your sensitivity has affected you negatively?

The Convergence of "Empath" and "Empathy"

Are you sensitive? Empathetic? Empathic? An empath? Social media and popular publications clump all of these identifiers together as if they're indistinguishable. They do have a relationship, but you can be empathic without feeling empathy. You can also have empathy without being empathic.

In the last few years, I have encountered many people who use the word "empathic" to convey that they're emotionally attuned and have a lot of empathy. As someone who is acutely aware of the tenuous status of the word "empath" in the dictionary to validate anyone's reality, I'm surprised by the prominent misuse of the word "empathic." For me, empathic is to empath as empathetic is to empathy.

Empathy is created by witnessing something on the physical plane that resonates with a similar personal experience. It's part of your emotional intelligence and psychological development as a human being. It unites an individual experience with a collective experience and helps foster supportive community around this common denominator. For example, in losing most of your personal belongings in a natural disaster, you may gain empathy for others who have dealt with similar losses.

An empath, however, senses and witnesses displaced thoughts and feelings on an energetic plane without visual clues. There is no "monkey see, monkey do" catalyst. Empathic reception is part of an intuitive sensory network that receives information, but it doesn't guarantee that the information or sensation will result in feeling empathy. Being empathic allows for heightened sensory reception and perception, while being empathetic produces a response of connection and reflection.

Consider this difference: An empathic person receives an energetic impression at the edge of their energy fields or aura, and they must intuit its message. An empathetic person, experiencing empathy for someone, uses something they've already experienced and processed to offer compassion and mutual understanding to the other person. Empathic is taking place in the energetic realm, while empathetic is taking place in the physical realm.

Empathy's Pathway—Personal Experience

We empathize with someone when we've felt similar physical pain, mental stresses, or emotional upset. Without empathy, we're isolated, experiencing the world purely as an individual. If empathy had a calling card, it would be something along the lines of "I *know* what you're going through; I can relate." Empathy expands with experience and self-awareness.

Successful support groups are formed from an alliance of empathy—not because misery loves company, but because healing is more easily facilitated when we don't feel alone, we're truly heard by our peers, and there's a level of accountability.

Politicians who have personal experience with social welfare and civil rights issues tend to promote equality and inclusion in the areas deemed "special interest" to them. The talking points of the politician resonate as truth-centered and grounded from personal experience. If the politician panders, their words feel hollow and false. This is partly why so many politicians borrow stories from their constituents—they must find a truth that resonates with the message.

When we align both our individual and universal sense of empathy, we connect to a massive potential for support and acceptance. Activism spawned from empathy unites not just one story but many stories. Part of the spectrum of empathy is how each individual worked through, healed, integrated, and embodied some personal truth to be part of the collective wisdom.

Empathic people don't lack empathy, but at the stage of being an unaware or undeveloped empath, they may feel as if the world is asking too much from them. It's understandable; they've probably had moments of feeling too much to the point of becoming numb. In contrast, with empathy, there's an element of trust and control. After all, it's our own emotional treasure trove that's activated when we feel empathy, not a random emotion from an outside source that we need to vet for its relevancy to our own life.

An Empath's Quick Study on Empathy

I'm intentional about my interactions with other people's energy. I offer compassion enhanced by empathy as a meeting place to listen to and witness what's out of balance, as well as to discern what I can do to help without interfering with someone else's personal work.

While empathy generally needs to be based in experience to be genuine, there appears to be an exception for empaths. When empaths pick up and momentarily experience another person's physical sensations or emotional distress, they can physically feel and comprehend to some degree what's happening to the person. Learning empathy in this manner without a personal reference point can be a bit surreal because it doesn't require knowing the person's story. It's oddly like getting a sudden dose of empathy, similar to getting a sudden dose of adrenaline. But rather than having a personal point of reference to connect with, an empath must simply rely on knowing what it feels like for them.

This is what happened to me with my son's swim cap that had so much imprinted discomfort on it. Another example of this from my own life involved a close friend's dad who was quite ill with terminal cancer. My friend Lars had asked me to support his father, who was hospitalized across the globe in Oslo while Lars and his family were living in Texas. This kind of support is known as remote energy work. I tune into the subject's energy while sitting in meditation, promoting a sense of peace for Lars's dad. As I did so, my head suddenly felt odd and pressured, as if it was being filled with liquid. I began to feel numb. I panicked, as anxiety flooded my chest, and struggled to compose myself. I cleared myself of my own reactions of shock and fright so that I could stay grounded and present with Lars's dad's energy. When I shared my impression with Lars and his wife, I told them that I discerned the sensations I experienced to be a stroke-like energy rather than cancer. A few days later, Lars's father died of a stroke.

I have never had a stroke, yet in that moment, I had a flash of what it might feel like. Experiencing it, even as a derivative of an energetic imprint, gave me a personal reference point for how to offer empathy to Lars's dad and his family.

Throw in the Sponge

More than a decade ago, I was standing at a checkout counter at the grocery store when I caught sight of the glossy cover of *O, The Oprah Magazine*. My eyes scanned the title of one of the articles: "The Sponge People." Sensitive and empathic people have long been referred to as "sponge people" due to the trait of absorbing other people's feelings and emotions. It isn't a sexy or empowering image, and it reinforces the idea that being sensitive comes at a cost. Nonetheless, I was intrigued and impressed to find this subject matter on the cover of a mainstream publication. I tossed the magazine in with my other items.

Not long afterward, I created the workshop "Sponge or Empath: Consciously Evolving Your Sensitivities," which I offered at The Spectrum Center, Houston's largest and oldest holistic resource center, where I worked as a spiritual counselor from 2003 to 2009 until my family moved overseas.

I began to notice that "sensitive people need to protect themselves" had become standard prescriptive advice in self-improvement and spiritual self-help columns. While there is merit to these practices, telling an empathic person to armor up is, for me, like telling a porcupine to put on an extra coat of quills. A sensitive person has already learned through their childhood and young adult life how to build defenses. Rather than insisting they need more armor and a smudge stick, I would say, "What makes you feel safe? Create that space inside you as best you can, and let's understand your sensitivities a bit better."

Highly Sensitive Person (HSP) or Empathic?

Understanding the source of your sensitivities is an important piece of self-awareness for everyone. It helps to look at how an empathic person and an HSP are similar yet different. Both empathic people and HSPs use the words "empathic," "sensitive," and "sponge" to describe their realities. HSPs are noted for "feeling too much" and "too deeply" when absorbing the details and subtleties of moods and body language. But an HSP doesn't usually question whether they're imagining their impressions or reactions, which an empathic person does on a regular basis.

The term HSP was popularized by Dr. Elaine Aron in 1997 and is accepted in psychology and counseling as identifying people who possess a genetic trait of sensory-processing sensitivity. It's estimated that as much as 20 percent of the population may be HSPs. Traits include, but are not limited to, processing information more thoroughly with detailed observational skills; having stronger emotional reactions and being overly sensitive to criticism and perfectionism; having strong environmental sensitivities, such as startling easily from noise, light, and chaotic places; seeking out quiet zones when overstimulated; and describing their inner life as rich and complex.

In contrast, a clairsentient or empathic person is characterized by their ability to experience contrary emotional states simultaneously, mirror another's behavior, experience phantom physical pain, possess strong empathetic sensibilities, and feel a deep relationship to nature/Earth.

Aron created a quick summary of HSP traits with the acronym DOES: Depth of processing, Overstimulation, Emotionally responsive/empathy, and Sensitive to subtleties. Though I have only taken a self-assessment test, not a genetic test, I identify with many HSP traits.

This leads me to the following question: Are empathic people just HSPs who are moving out of the fantasy and sci-fi realm and finally getting recognition in a mainstream forum? I'm personally cautious about labeling all HSPs as empathic or all empathic people as HSPs. Obviously, I'm not conducting studies and genetic tests. I offer my assessment based purely on my interpretation of what I experience as the difference between an empath's and an HSP's response to environmental stimuli. And it involves their shared mascot—the sponge.

From the Sponge's Perspective

Human energy fields aren't stagnant. They don't just drape over our physical body like a cape. They spin and rotate around each of us, and they have a subtle ebbing that mirrors our own breath moving in and out.

The sponge is actually a perfect analogy for what happens to an empathic person's energy fields when they encounter an impression. The edge of an empathic person's energy field expands by one to two feet when it senses something from the environment—just like a dry sponge increases its volume as it absorbs liquid. This expansion holds the information to be discerned and evaluated just outside of the person's energy fields in a space that resembles the expanding capabilities of modern-day suitcases.

This sensory feature of presenting information outside of someone's personal space is similar to how our standard five senses operate. Imagine if you had to wait to be on fire before making a decision about how to react. Instead, you smell smoke, feel heat, or see flames, which gives you time to respond appropriately. Similarly, the ability to hold information in the space between my personal space and the source that emitted the energy is what prompted me to put aside doubt and fear and embrace my empathic nature. I eventually recognized that my nature isn't designed to put me in a vulnerable position. Instead, it places me in a position of responsive connection and discerning control.

If the impression an empathic person absorbs goes unnoticed and is just accepted as part of their own thoughts and feelings, the message gets incorporated as part of their own self-image and perception. Or the person doesn't know how to clear their energy fields. This is how an unsuspecting empathic person can become bogged down and fatigued from large groups and social interactions. Basically, it's like a sponge that's oversaturated and stops working effectively. In contrast, an HSP who comes into contact with an environmental sensitivity will experience their energy fields contracting instead of expanding. I call it a "pulling up the moat bridge" reaction to a perceived threat in the environment or collapsing on themselves for protection.

HSPs can be taxed by being on constant alert. The environment is rife with variables they may react to: electromagnetics, sound, light, pollutants, motion, smells, food allergies, physical pressure, and so on. To manage their sensitivities and perceived threats, they pay attention to detail, which is a trait already attributed to HSPs. Often fatigued and exhausted in public places, they can feel as if they're constantly in survival mode. It's no wonder they're easily startled. The mental subtle body becomes extremely vigilant and dominant as it constantly assesses the environment. They may get headaches and stomach aches because the retracting energy fields constrict flow through the head area, while mental activity is more dominant. The tension between these two opposing reactions creates stress.

The HSP label gives a legitimate framework for both emotional and environmental sensitivities, but it doesn't highlight empathic sensitivities. I distinguish between an innate ability that *responds* to the energetic environment and an innate sensitivity that *reacts* to environmental conditions. And yes, there are HSPs who are also empathic, which creates the need for a lot of self-monitoring and self-care.

In fact, I count myself among this subset of HSPs, hosting both empathic and environmental sensitivities. I'm an avid squash player, for example, and recall one tournament in Dallas where I needed to change hotel rooms for various empathic and environmental reasons. I felt a density and stagnation from previous occupants, and I picked up a mildew smell from the carpet. Fortunately, my teammate took it in stride and didn't find me too "high maintenance" as we lugged our belongings from one room to another. I've learned what I can ignore and what will be too much to allow me to rest and feel comfortable. I can usually send compassion to an emotional encounter, but that doesn't work on environmental sensitivities like mildew or mold.

Why is it important to distinguish between non-empathic HSPs and empathic HSPs? A fellow empath, Alida, who lives in Perth, Australia, summed it up well by pointing out that an HSP's support is typically found in psychology and counseling, while an empath requires more specific mentoring and awareness to work with their clairsentient ability. But self-care and self-awareness are vital tools for both an empath and HSP.

Ask yourself if your sensitivities are more aligned to environmental elements that impact your five sensory networks—sight, hearing, touch, smell, and feeling—which can produce allergic-like reactions to the environment. This would indicate a sensory-processing sensitivity of an HSP. Do you notice and analyze fine details in the room and in people's behavior to build context and plausible outcomes and scenarios, which are often proven correct? This is also an HSP trait of sensitivity to subtleties. For your self-care, do you need to remove yourself from loud noises, bright lights, and busy/crowded places with too much stimuli to track?

Unifying the Human Experience through Compassion

While not everyone who is highly sensitive to their environment is *empathic*, everyone has the potential to be *empathetic* and host empathy for someone/something outside themselves based on similar personal experience.

Empathy naturally unites and fosters inclusion; it doesn't encourage manipulation or competitiveness. Empathy doesn't expire and isn't time-sensitive. There is some predictability to the seasons of life: from being a child, through the years of education, transitioning into adulthood, with an emphasis on employment and family, possibly children, and then aging, which moves us all closer to the end of life. At each stage, we experience life and form personal understanding through our relationships. This lends us the ability to empathize with others, even retroactively.

The world and national news are constant "trigger" zones since every day and nearly every second, someone is in danger somewhere. Wars, pandemics, pollution, poverty, greed, economic crisis, political pandering, social injustice, sexual mistreatment, mass extinctions, and on and on—a seemingly never-ending newscast of the horrors afflicting humanity. How can a sensitive person hear, feel, and experience all of this while continuing to live and breathe with hope for a better world? Quite simply, through compassion.

"Compassion walks into a bar—how did it get there?" Most likely through *sympathy* and *empathy*. Through both of those channels, we extend compassion toward others. Compassion is the deep endless well of care that we have in our hearts, and until we develop direct access to this awareness and presence, our life experiences allow sympathy and empathy to be the couriers. The more we can see ourselves in others' suffering, the more empathy and sympathy will grow until we can access compassion completely without the need for personal reference. We will no longer need to limit how we care about others based on our own life experiences.

Questions for Reflection

Take some time with your journal to write down your impressions and feelings in response to these questions. Then, reflect on how your experience in your answers may have affected you emotionally or affected your development as an empath.

1. Write about your childhood in terms of your sensitivities. Were you a watcher of life, and did you often feel lonely, as I did?

2. Have you had a similar experience as I have when at a public event where people are joyful or extremely sad? If so, write about what it was like for you. List any strategies you can use.

3. After having read this chapter, do you have a sense as to whether your sensitivities are rooted in being empathic or an HSP? Or both? Write about why you sense this about yourself—give examples that support your understanding.

4. As someone with empathic sensitivities, have you ever had an experience of empathy without a personal reference? If so, write about it.

5 Have you ever felt that your "sponge" was oversaturated, or have you felt taxed due to being on constant alert? If so, write about how that felt and how you handled the experience.

6. Write about the differences between sympathy and empathy. Write about something you once had sympathy for, but now you can empathize with it.

Chapter Ten

The Arc of an Empath

I sat in nervous anticipation, listening to Lys, my maid of honor and old college roommate, deliver her speech to the room full of our wedding guests. She framed the speech as helpful firsthand advice to Knut, so when she wished and hoped for us to have a large bed, I was uncertain where she was headed. Lys went on to describe an experiment she and some of our floormates had conducted one night. They placed my chair, a lamp, and other loose items on top of my twin bed to see if I would still crawl in and go to sleep. Indeed, I did.

I had come home late to our dorm room and gone straight to bed without turning on the light, dropping my clothes on the floor, sleeping in the shirt I'd worn all day. I instantly felt the bed was unusually overloaded. I was a bit peeved but recognized I was being "punked" by my dear roommate and didn't want to disappoint. So I removed only the chair and crawled in.

Lys and I had been like the Odd Couple. Our dorm room was a bizarre display of our differences. She marveled that I drank cold coffee from a cup that had been sitting on my desk overnight, or that I often crawled into a bed full of books, clothes, and my backpack. In contrast, her side of the room displayed order, style, and both natural and intentional beauty.

We were opposites, but also the same in many ways. With the lights out, we shared our imperfect backgrounds, worries, issues with self-esteem, and hopes. Then, we'd fall asleep in our own disorganized dreams.

As Knut and our wedding guests all laughed at the image, Lys continued to share her thoughts on what it had been like to be my roommate, pivoting to more endearing qualities she saw within me. I was adaptable, resourceful, and made room for a lot of people with whom I generously shared my love. For all of this, she hoped Knut and I had a large enough bed to hold everything I would bring to our marriage.

Signs of Overwhelmed Senses: Indifference

Obviously, I was indifferent to my living conditions when I was a college student. Looking back with the wisdom I've gained about my empathic sensitivities over the last fifteen to twenty years, I can see my younger self with compassion. I can register the warning signs of how disconnected I was to my center and true nature. I also look back with great regard for Lys, who saw past the chaos and connected with an aspect of me that was still friendship material.

When the waters recede from a flooded landscape, things are scattered and out of place, as the force of the water moved boulders, trees, and other objects. For an empathic person with emotional sensitivities that aren't quite grounded or felt with clarity, things tend to get swept up and shifted around. Living with this state of uncertainty can make you either indifferent to your surroundings or hypervigilant about controlling them.

It's easy to become indifferent or insensitive to your environment and relationships when stress and isolation press in or when your belief systems place limiting parameters around your field of experience and awareness. From my standpoint, the cause of insensitivity and oversensitivity comes down to numerous expressions involving *lack*—a lack of self-awareness, a lack of perspective, a general or specific lack of concern, and finally, a lack of empathy. Put a sensitive child in a *lacking* environment, and defenses will be constructed. Then, voilà, an introverted demeanor becomes a form of self-protection. Ironically, the sensitive child becomes insensitive to their own nature.

The Path of Transformation

Let me introduce you to Liz, Beth, and Elizabeth—who could just as easily be named Bob, Rob, and Robert. These three profiles represent the spectrum of development and self-awareness that most empathic people undergo on their path from being unaware and overwhelmed to being self-aware and accepting of their empathic nature. I've used a proper name and two of its derivations to indicate that there are varying stages of awareness in each person. Every empathic person will identify with some or all of these profiles.

Liz is completely unaware of her empathic nature, but she may consider herself an HSP to help her frame and navigate social situations and overstimulating environments. Beth has more awareness of being "spongey" but doesn't fully understand what this means with regard to proper boundaries or how her empathic senses work. Elizabeth has traversed each segment of the path to arrive at a place where she understands and accepts her empathic nature. It aligns with her spiritual sensibility that she is more than a physical body and that she's connected to the environment and the energetic space around her. This allows her the freedom to explore different conversations with life.

Innately, they're all good listeners, they have keen observational skills and are detail-oriented, they sympathize easily, and when appropriate, they can empathize with others. They all have similar empathic sensory responses that occur naturally and automatically by absorbing an impression from the environment. However, they diverge in how they process the received information based on their self-awareness, life experiences, and understanding of their empathic nature.

The Sensitive Child

Liz, Beth, and Elizabeth were likely all sensitive children who struggled in public places and found refuge in nature, books, and places of stillness. Imagine a child who unknowingly senses displaced emotions and feelings in the space around her. Most of her childhood is a barrage of unidentifiable emissions that she lacks the context and experience to understand or process. She feels the tension of what isn't spoken, the burden of loneliness in the living, the confusion of boundaries between her thoughts and feelings, and the depression that seeps around her feet and follows her footsteps. She feels her body as a great mysterious landscape: fluttering muscles, stitches in the gut, and sharp pains that come and go.

This extrasensory input can entrap the empathic child in hypersensitivity to her own physical pain and emotional isolation. This is particularly true if her home life is limited in recognizing her sensitivities or is its own field of trauma. Pain is amplified as every nerve is taxed, and her mental and emotional processes are filtered through a loop that's constantly assessing safety and self-worth.

How often do we hear that so-and-so is a "sensitive child" because she seemingly possesses the ability to pick up on the mood and temperament of others? These sensitive children are known to get upset easily and take offense quickly. They may be difficult to calm or reason with because they're so emotional, or conversely—so quiet and withdrawn. This all gets labeled as negative and creates the perception of a somewhat difficult child in an over-paced environment. But these children do what most children do—they adapt. This happens more subconsciously than consciously. The sensitive child tends to transform into the quiet and observant child who is then praised for her patience and maturity.

For sensitive children without emotional support and awareness, a survival instinct emerges. By late adolescence or young adulthood, various paths open to disconnect from the body's empathic functions. This is accomplished by numbing and desensitizing the nervous system. Among the defensive maneuvers is using substances such as alcohol, drugs, and food for numbing purposes. Another is giving more authority to mental processing, which buffers and deflects the necessity to feel. It's seemingly easier to judge something than to feel something. Emotional intelligence requires self-awareness and the ability to be present without judgment, or a cycle of self-loathing and cynicism will follow.

Most unaware empathic people who feel challenged by a room's environment or another person's demeanor will try to leave the area. If it isn't possible to physically leave, they'll withdraw inside themselves. This is an unaware empathic person's first attempt at creating boundaries, which becomes more of a barrier than a boundary.

Stages of Empathic Awareness

Both Liz and Beth are *unaware* of the mechanics of being empathic. They may manage their social interactions or be overly cautious in certain stimulating environments. Perhaps they comfortably identify themselves as being HSPs, and this label explains some of their environmental and social stresses, providing some support and self-advocacy.

The following stages outline how each person processes empathic reception differently based on their own self-awareness when detecting an emission of anger.

STAGE ONE: REACTIVE AND ISOLATED

Liz is unaware that she has an energetic component to her physical body and reality, so she doesn't realize she has empathically interacted with this "angry" energy. But she does feel uncomfortable, which is a feeling she often has in public. In this instance, the energy presents feelings of agitation and irritation, so she might likewise feel fidgety and anxious and want to leave the room.

As a protective measure, she reacts by withdrawing into herself. Since she's emotionally sensitive, she may want to be invisible and out of the way of any conflict and unpleasantness. She has probably done this time and again since early childhood, and now, it's an ingrained defense mechanism. She still has empathic and HSP traits of observing fine details and nuances, reading nonverbal cues, being a great listener, and understanding the dynamics at play. But she's often isolated and alone.

Even though she may feel protected by retreating within herself, she has no real support or resources. She is, more or less, in her own self-prescribed internal bunker, waiting to feel safe before she emerges. This undoubtedly affects her overall well-being, as well as her perception of the world.

She isn't aware that the moment her empathic receptors absorbed the emission of "annoyed, fidgety, and anxious" is approximately the same moment that she withdrew into herself. She feels the information, but she doesn't question why she feels that way—she judges herself rather than the feeling. Without skills of discernment, she'll either accept that these are her feelings, or she'll give up her space and leave. Additionally, her empathic sponge isn't cleared, so over time, its functioning is decreased and can create a heavy feeling in her aura. This further impacts her perception of self and the environment.

When Liz stops being passive with her environment, the catalyst for her to become self-aware of her empathic nature will unfold, and she'll gain more authority over her own energy.

If she can begin to notice when she withdraws inside herself, she can shift her knee-jerk reaction with strategies and building awareness of what triggers her defense mechanisms. This can help her to build resilience and trust in herself and her sensitivities.

STAGE TWO: TOO FEW BOUNDARIES EQUAL TOO GREAT A SENSE OF RESPONSIBILITY

Beth understands that she can sense things about people, but she doesn't necessarily understand the mechanics and the energetic aspects of her sensitivity. She will try to identify who is agitated and upset, and she may spend some time assessing if there's anything in the room causing this stress. Cause and effect is an awareness that empaths develop intuitively as they tune into the energy in the room's dynamics.

Beth takes too much responsibility for other people's emotions, however. She wants to connect and help shift the mood of the person who's experiencing something unsettling. She's the equivalent of an extension cord with accessible outlets for anyone to use, offering her own energy system as a source to support a situation outside of herself. The obvious result is that soon after any interaction or over-involvement, Beth is fatigued and drained. This is the classic symptom of being sponged off, and what has been almost singled out as a cautionary tale for people who are emotionally sensitive. She doesn't understand that witnessing the energy is enough.

Beth engages the emotional distress, which leaves her vulnerable. Perhaps she has been rewarded on occasion with praise and recognition for her ability to empathize and help, and this has created a motivation to be needed. Maybe focusing outward rather than inward gives her a feeling of control over an environment or situation.

Beth can begin to notice when her personal involvement in the problems of others becomes out of balance. Does she spend an excess amount of her own time and resources to help others process their emotional challenges?

STAGE THREE: THE FUNCTIONAL EMPATH

To contrast Beth and Liz, let me introduce you to Elizabeth, who is aware of her empathic nature and has evolved her sensitivities into self-realization as an empath. In that same room, she notices the shift in her own mood and has developed a working glossary of physical sensations that may accompany energetic impressions: a shivering in the skin, the heaviness of a body part, a smell that lingers just at her nose, an organ that feels warm, an achy joint, and a multitude of other signals.

Elizabeth tunes into the information that she registers. It's benign. Unlike Liz and Beth, she takes some moments to discern what to do with the information. She meets the energy and possibly interacts with it in the space outside of the physical realm rather than directly with the person.

She doesn't assume that because she feels something in her immediate surroundings that it automatically means it was emitted from someone in that room. She doesn't try to create a story for it or the person who created it.

Perhaps on this occasion, the emotional and mental content that's emitted has something to do with the individual feeling frustrated and angry. Elizabeth offers the energy an opportunity to be witnessed (seen, felt, known) and then observed as it shifts. She isn't responsible for "fixing" this person; she merely brings attention to an aspect that's out of balance and is reflected in the space. If she does intuit that it's from someone in the room, she may choose to say something to the individual in a lighthearted way to lift the moment.

Lastly, and most importantly, she clears her energy fields from the collection of information. She rings out her sponge, or as I do, cleans her message board. This is done most effectively by simply acknowledging the message. (For good measure, I usually tense up all of my muscles at once and take a deep cleansing breath to give my nervous system the message to reset.)

Elizabeth has found and cultivated her center with self-awareness. This took time, patience, and a willingness to explore. She understands her sensitivities and can easily discern her thoughts and feelings from impressions that are communicated from the space around her. This centeredness within herself is a resource that she continually updates and expands with each new experience. She understands that her body is a cipher, and it adds to the "in-house" databank of what emotional states and accompanying physical states feel like in her body. Elizabeth has learned that these sensations aren't invading her own center. They're outside of her personal space, though it doesn't necessarily feel that way when her body mimics the physical sensations of another or if she's challenged with multiple sensations from multiple sources.

Finding Balance: The Key to Integrating Self-Awareness

Liz, Beth, and Elizabeth all have empathic functions informing and affecting their daily lives. There are many scenarios that produce the reactions from empathic people like Liz and Beth—withdrawn or overextending. At one time or another, fully aware empaths can humbly recognize themselves in both versions. I certainly can.

Elizabeth matured in how she responds to these interactions. She lives her life unafraid, willing to tune into what serves her own sense of balance. She also recognizes that she has authority over her own energy, and the wisest stance when encountering an energetic impression is to simply ask, "Is this mine? Is it an aspect of my own thoughts and feelings that I'm registering, or is it my work to witness and balance the expression I feel displaced in the space around me?" Not all encounters have to be attended to, as in actively interacting with the energy to create balance. At times, it's as simple as acknowledging the reception and releasing the residue from our own receptors.

"Is this mine?" is a particularly relevant prompt for physical empaths who almost instantly feel the sensation communicate upon the body. They need to discern if the ache they're experiencing is directly related to their life experiences or from someone else.

At some level, Elizabeth has accepted that there's a component of Mystery to being an empath. Rather than resisting what's evidently hardwired in her nature, she finds comfort and support in the interconnectedness. The capacity to be present and witness each other's vulnerability creates depth and intimacy to life.

Questions for Reflection

Take some time with your journal to write down your impressions and feelings in response to these questions. Then, reflect on how your experience in your answers may have affected you emotionally or affected your development as an empath.

1. Have you ever noticed that you were or are indifferent to your living conditions? If so, check in with yourself to determine if it's a result of overwhelmed senses, as was true of me when I was younger. If so, write about your experience.

2. Are you introverted and overwhelmed in public spaces or groups of people? Write about these feelings, and ask yourself if it's a result of your empathic nature or being an HSP.

3. Write about your experiences as a "sensitive child." What do you recall from those years that you can now better understand through the lens of your empathic abilities?

4. What would you like to have been different in your childhood home? What was the communication style or dynamic in your home?

5. How did you adapt to your environment in order to survive? Did you create a default pattern of shutting down and going inward, or taking control of your environment?

6. Do you believe you're currently a Liz, a Beth, or an Elizabeth? Wherever you currently fall on the spectrum, when have you felt like a Liz or a Beth? Write about some of those experiences.

Chapter Eleven

An Empath's True Boundary

Establishing healthy personal boundaries is sound advice for everyone—whether you're an empath or not. These are the boundaries we create by fortifying our personal space with "I AM" statements, which I detailed in Chapter 6. Healthy boundaries reflect our ability to embody our own authority and direct our lives without shutting down or giving away our own space. Everyone, empath or not, thrives in their environments and life when this is attended to.

Empaths, though, require a second boundary—one that safeguards their sense of balance and responsibility. Developing empaths need to create strategies that give them control and authority in how they respond to what they sense from the environment. In order to preserve the donor's well-being, even blood centers have limits on how much blood someone can donate. This is true for empathic people as well—you aren't singularly responsible to absorb and witness everything in your vicinity.

My own early mentor was quick to point out to her students that "responsibility" just means the ability to respond.

We may sense peripheral activity in our energetic environment, but we aren't meant to neglect our own life.

When you're driving a car or walking down a sidewalk, you'll notice the periphery activity around you with small side glances. If you took time to take in everything that could come into focus from all directions, you'd consume so much time and energy. On the other hand, when you're driving or walking down the street, and something from your periphery catches your attention, you adjust in that moment to take in more details because there's an aspect that requires your attention—say a ball rolling toward the road, someone absent-mindedly cutting in front of you, or a strong intuitive pull to notice some detail. You automatically slow down and take notice. This is how your empathic senses present impressions to you as well, but it still requires your awareness and attention, which are both dependent on your availability.

The Capacity to Care

Our availability to our surroundings is also linked to our capacity to care, and our resilience is built through trust and respect in ourselves to attend to self-care and our own inner well-being first and foremost. As in airline presentations, the safety instruction to put your oxygen mask on first before helping others is applicable here. There isn't, however, a mandate that says once you have your mask on that you have to look around and help others. Some people will naturally possess this altruistic outreach, while others may need to spend their energy regulating their own fears in order to stay calm. Some may be so consumed by fear and unable to focus on the task at hand that they require assistance, and others may simply not even consider that it's their responsibility to do more than what's instructed in the safety presentation. Many scenarios are possible, and how someone responds or reacts one day doesn't mean that's how they'll respond another day under a different set of circumstances.

How much stress you're holding in your system will affect how much capacity and attention you have to give to others and yourself. Consider that if you're *holding* stress or energy, it means you're a container that's closed on one end, blocking the flow to release. This is a very simple image, but visualize a beaker with volume capacity of a unit of ten. If your stress is at an eight, you only have about two units available to assist you in dealing with what's presently before you. Pain of various means—physical, emotional, mental—takes a lot of space within your energy systems and doesn't leave much room for other impressions to be communicated.

I offer this example from my own life about how pain can impact your ability to respond compassionately to your environment. My nerves are extra-sensitive to pain. I suspect this is a trait of empathic sensitivity due to the fact that our nervous system processes information from both the physical and energetic planes. But anyone in constant and chronic pain can transform into a needy and highly agitated mess. Crushing pain can suppress our humanity—I know because I've experienced it.

I had a prolapsed disc when I was three months pregnant with my youngest child. The Norwegian doctors advised against any medical treatment or pain meds, hoping it would resolve itself. It didn't. I lived in constant, debilitating knife-stabbing pain down my right leg until I started to drag the leg and couldn't feel myself urinate.

The doctors decided that at six months, the fetus was developed enough that I could have an MRI to locate the disc. Then, we would discuss my options. So that I could lie still for the imaging, they mercifully gave me a shot of morphine. After three months of unimaginable pain, while being pregnant and still having three young sons to mother and routines to keep, I can't describe the mercy I felt when that painkiller eased my pain even slightly. My body, which had been clenched and tight in applying some version of an internal tourniquet to try and distance myself from the pain, relaxed enough for me to cry.

The doctors decided they'd try to microscopically attend to the prolapse. In the meantime, they placed me in the high-risk pregnancy ward until the surgery, where I received timed pain meds to help me get some much-needed rest. My roommate was a woman whose pregnancy was in a precarious condition. She was about twenty-eight weeks along and at risk of going into early labor. Full term is forty weeks, and even though pregnant women feel responsible to get as close to that marker as possible, we have no control over when labor naturally begins.

I didn't think about anything remotely related to being pregnant or about my roommate's legitimate worries. I watched the clock and calculated when my pain meds would be delivered. It was thirty minutes until my next dose. I went for a walk in the hallway because without the pain meds, it was difficult for me to lie down. As I was returning to my room to make sure I didn't miss the nurse, I saw a flurry of activity.

One of the nurses registered that I'd returned to the room and made eye contact with me. It was obvious my roommate was going into early labor. I understood the seriousness of what was unfolding, but I had the nurse's attention and couldn't help myself. All I knew was that I was barely managing my own existence. I looked directly at the nurse, pointed to the clock on the wall, and said, "It's time for my pain medicine." She turned away and pulled the curtain, not bothering to hide her disgust, just as I was unable to hide my desperation.

My experience with this unimaginable pain solidified my opinion that the only people deserving to be called saints are those who don't lose their capacity to care for others even in the midst of staggering pain. Pain took away my appetite, patience, focus, humor, and finally, my capacity to care. I contrast that with the version of me that sat cross-legged in my hospital bed forty-eight hours after the surgery, only feeling sore in my throat from being intubated. I had a remarkable recovery, and three months later, I delivered a healthy baby girl, whom I carried for thirty-eight weeks. My nerve sensations to my leg and foot returned within a few months.

I wasn't proud of my behavior during my roommate's emergency birth, but I have compassion for the part of me that was overwhelmed on multiple levels. Moreover, I gained empathy for anyone who deals with constant pain. While I wasn't available to give much during this time period, I recognized how much I received. I experienced mercy and grace with the relief of pain, and a community of friends and strangers reached out to our family to help while I recovered. This was a teaching steeped in balance.

The Empath's True Boundary: "Is This Mine?"

I'm a physical empath, and having personally experienced intense levels of pain has primed me to go straight to asking "Is this mine?" when I feel a sudden and random pain. In general, we human beings are great at storing pain in the body, especially if it was a code of conduct in our upbringing. My right leg that was affected by my prolapsed disc has consistently brought messages to me about being out of balance. I'm still building up its resilience, and it's still teaching me about letting go. Does a part of your body act like a barometer to let you know that your stress or balance is compromised?

This prompt of "Is this mine?" honors self-awareness while being somewhat of a passcode for you to employ the skills of an empath. It truly is a trusted gatekeeper in keeping your connection to your empathic sponge engaged.

I discovered that if it isn't something created from myself, and I witness it with compassion, the sensation leaves my body with little effort. If it's my own pain, I do the inner work of introspection and apply self-care as described later in this chapter.

The functional empath knows the wisdom in asking "Is this mine?" at the moment of sensing something from the environment. This boundary/border is located at the edge of your energy fields where your spongelike reception temporarily holds the impression until you can discern your response. I admit that you'll need to cultivate trust that this empathic sponge feature exists, particularly when it feels as though what you've picked up is still at the surface or even within your body. Spatial relationships are a bit different in the energetic plane. On the physical plane, I can use dowsing rods to show you where your fields extend outward relative to your body, and we can measure them. The energetic level doesn't provide the same definition and distance. So while I say it's at the edge of your field, you may feel it's actually right at your physical body. This phenomenon is part of becoming an integrated self, experiencing yourself as both physical and energetic.

How you come to the awareness that you've picked up an impression is unique to you. For me, it varies but usually involves a sensation of pressure or a tingling sensation through my scalp. Emotions seem to sweep through me, which stand apart from how my own emotions present. This is also true for the random thoughts that present almost like a commercial. Investigate for yourself how you register an impression from the environment.

This boundary also requires self-care in the form of regularly clearing what's held in that space and keeping it resilient and functioning. Recall my maid of honor's description of the chaotic condition of my portion of our dorm room. Part of the reason my living environments were cluttered was because I wasn't aware of my energy system's sponge reception, which was overloaded from years of ignorance and ineffective functioning. Just like muscles can become tired and no longer fire properly, your empathic reception may need some intentional clearing and tender loving care to activate well.

Remarkably, when I started attending to the clearing of my empathic sponge field on a regular basis, like brushing my teeth, my living spaces became more clutter-free, and my sense of the space around me expanded in the loveliest way.

When you have the awareness that your energy sponge is holding something for your attention, intuit the contents by utilizing your subtle sensing bodies to identify whether it's an emotion, thought, or physical sensation. I hope the explanation helps reinforce that your own energy isn't moving outside of yourself to work with the information. Again, most empathic people are, by default, passively receiving impressions from the energetic space. And with patience and willingness, your empathic nature can express itself succinctly and precisely as the thirty-second exchange that I had with the guard at the airport in Angola (described in the Introduction). When you consider how much time our minds chatter and needlessly project our opinions all over the place, that's no time at all.

How to Support Empathic Boundaries

- Honor the wisdom of asking, "Is this mine?" Is the impression connecting to you because you have something similar going on in your life? Not everything you sense requires that you interact with it directly. Develop discernment between when your empathic abilities can assist in balancing and when it's enough to be aware of your own boundaries and sense of balance. Ask twice for clarity:

    - *"Is this mine?" as in, is it something created by me that my conscious mind is only becoming aware of?* If "no," ask it in the next context:
    - *"Is this mine?" as in, is it appropriate for me to witness and balance?* If "no," disconnect and just observe it like a peripheral detail.

- What brings balance? Typically, naming a sensation and witnessing it by offering a counter-expression of healing and balance for the person who created the energy emission. All of this can be done without trespassing onto the other person's energy system.

- Clear your empathic "message board" by disconnecting from the energy and clearing your energy fields in whatever way feels appropriate for you. I use the imagery of a chalk board or a water hose. Sometimes, I visualize squeezing excess water from a sponge. I also will tighten up my muscles with an inhale and then let go and exhale. Or I imagine letting honey or wax encase me and then peel it off. I stay with the visualization until I feel a shift in my body.

How to Support an Empathic Nature

Energy awareness is essential for empathic people, as is self-care. They kind of go hand in hand. When I was gaining awareness of my sensitivities in my twenties, most of the advice was about protecting myself from outside energies. But as more and more people have realized that we're both energy and physical bodies, there's less need to fear the energetic components of the physical realm that comprises our own thoughts and emotions.

Thankfully, today's advice has shifted from the fear of needing "protection" from something outside of us to a more embodied awareness of "regulation" within ourselves. How well can you regulate your emotions? How is your nervous system response? All of this relies on self-awareness and consistent application of self-care measures.

Creating healthy boundaries is a part of emotional and mental health promoted by both traditional and alternative wellness practices, as well as managing stress, which is directly linked to our resiliency and overall health. Adaptability and flexibility help us regulate our responses and perceptions. They symbolize the flow and fluidity needed in our energy fields to grow and expand as we become more self-realized.

Our energy systems are malleable and programmable. They reflect our physical, emotional, mental, and spiritual health—and health can be defined by how well our energy flows through our systems. They can also reflect our conditioning and conformity, such as whether we were raised in a stressful environment. Such an experience sets our nervous system on a more active alert and potentially chronic conditioning that needs to be repatterned to experience more harmony between our inner and outer worlds.

Self-Care Modalities for an Empath

Regardless of the level of self-awareness you may have about your empathic nature, you can benefit from certain lifestyle choices that support your nervous system and regulate your thoughts and emotions. Healing modalities such as bodywork, movement, meditation, and grounding exercises will all have a positive influence on your subtle energy bodies. These practices offer energy circulation and may unknowingly wring out your spongey layer, providing clearer reception and easier processing for you as an empath. They can help you maintain a healthy and functioning relationship with your body and mind, as well as help you create a deeper sense of connection with the environment.

BODYWORK

When stress is stored in the body, it affects many systems—muscles, tendons, nerves, joints, fascia, lymphatics, connective tissues, hormones, and so on. Anyone who has experienced an effective traditional or remedial massage usually feels lighter immediately afterward. An overload of messages from the nervous system to the muscles, which are trying to create stability in the body, locks the muscles into a bracing pattern. When this happens, it thickens the muscles and puts more load on the nerves. When a masseuse releases this bracing pattern, it allows the nerves to glide easily through the muscles, thereby decreasing the load on the nervous system. This is why you get a lighter feeling. Acupuncture, stretching, yoga, energy work, and meditation likewise work to release bracing patterns, which is why you can feel lighter physically, mentally, and emotionally after a session.

As an empath who receives extrasensory communication expressed through the body, my nervous system is where I center a lot of my self-care. I use healing modalities that help my nervous system regulate itself. I have personally benefitted from bodywork by practitioners trained in visceral and neural manipulation therapies from the Barral Institute and the Upledger Institute. Both of these release restrictions within internal organs and local nerves. I also value somatic therapies such as Rolfing, which work directly with the nervous system, muscle function, and body awareness. Creating space within the body itself allows for a sense of fluidity and movement, which mirrors the sense of space in between the physical and the nonphysical.

MOVEMENT

The body benefits from movement regardless of lifestyle or athletic prowess. Your creativity likewise benefits from exploring new ways to express itself. Both outlets create connections for your place in the world—inner and outer. Movement supports stillness, which may seem counterintuitive, but when people talk about being in the zone, it's because they're focused and aligned to their choices. Even if the movement feels more like effort than a state of Zen, it demonstrates a willingness to engage and experience the journey of Life.

We need the physical component of action to express ourselves, whether in words, deeds, or physical endeavors. We express kindness in the words we speak or the gestures we offer to others. Kindness needs a vehicle, just like anger and every other stimulated emotion. Sadness produces tears; joy produces a smile. Physical activity can also aid a stagnant mental state. Ideas need to be circulated, just as our muscles need to be stretched.

MEDITATION

Meditation is a practice, which means it gets better with practice. It's a marvel at rewiring the brain's neural network. Applying mindfulness in daily life is a way to eliminate or gain control of obtrusive thoughts and unhealthy habits. Meditation can help turn off or turn down the part of your mind that wants to endlessly cycle through negative self-talk or ruminate. Inner work, such as looking at limiting patterns and behaviors that obstruct your energy and dreams, is a vital component in gaining self-awareness. Giving yourself a chance to inhabit your body and mind without a deluge of mindless chatter will help you sense your presence more clearly. It's important to have this stillness and presence available at your center rather than the idle chatter that most people simply accept as background noise in their lives. There are many schools of meditation to choose from—silent meditation, chanting, yoga, guided meditations, and so on.

GROUNDING AS AN ACTIVE MEDITATION

Have you ever touched a live electrical wire or faulty appliance—hot, angry, and full of electrons wanting to be released? If you have, I hope it wasn't powerful enough to knock you out. An electrical circuit wants a grounding reference to cast off its excessive electrons—it wants to go to zero volts. It wants balance and equilibrium, and it wants the quickest path to the Earth.

When we have a stressful, excessive lifestyle or when we're overwhelmed with emotions, we're charged with a frenetic energy that can be felt by everyone around us. When we're too much in our head, we aren't fully in our body. A telltale sign of not being grounded in your body is feeling off balance: you knock into things, you're clumsy, you're restless, you're forgetful, you misplace things, and/or you feel that you're unable to accomplish anything.

When we experience someone as grounded, we say, "So-and-so is a *down-to-earth* person." It implies that the individual is reasonable, easy to communicate with, and easy to get along with. Being grounded also assists with the ability to be present, to listen, and to respond when needed.

Grounding is essential when working with energy therapies. I can't map my empathic impressions if I'm not grounded. If you aren't grounded, you'll also have a difficult time with the other modalities in this chapter. In any kind of movement, you'll feel off balance and clumsy. In meditation, you may experience loss of direction and become anxious before attempting to access higher states of being.

It's more difficult to process emotional material, too, when you aren't grounded. It can sweep over you in waves, taking you under and causing you to panic or hyperventilate. Mentally, it's harder to break out of worry or to be present in the moment.

If you create a daily practice of grounding your energy beneath you into the Earth, it will help you stay present. You'll diminish the tendency to stay stuck in the past or project fear and worry into the future. To feel with your senses, which are attached to your physical being, you need to be grounded. Otherwise, it will be challenging to grow your sensory awareness and intuition. The easiest form is just to imagine you're a tree with roots connected to the Earth with limbs reaching up toward the sky. Personalize it by choosing the type of tree you like and how deep the roots should be to support and nurture you.

I often think of a saying that honors the balance of being grounded while expanding into higher realms of knowingness: "*Feel* the Earth and *know* the heavens."

Questions for Reflection

Take some time with your journal to write down your impressions and feelings in response to these questions. Then, reflect on how your experience in your answers may have affected you emotionally or affected your development as an empath.

1. Can you describe the distinction I've made between the two boundaries that benefit an empath (creating boundaries for personal space and for empathic boundaries)?

2. How available are you to respond with your empathic nature? What's your current level of stress on a scale from one to ten?

3. How is your living environment? Do you find that there's a correlation between your living space and how attentive you are to self-care, healthy boundaries, and especially the state of your empathic sponge?

4. How do you register that you have received an impression from someone or, more generally, from the space around you? Can you sense that the impression is held for you to discern a response, even though you may feel its message?

5. What self-care modalities have you tried that you believe have supported you as an empathic person? After having read this chapter, look back on what you experienced after bodywork, meditation, or some other practice, and evaluate how it helped you.

Part Three

The FIELD of Sensing

The FIELD of Sensing

Whether we choose to or not, we will, in time,
wear the deeper part of who we are as a new skin.

—Mark Nepo, author

This quote by Mark Nepo may very well be the anthem of every empathic person who perhaps has felt they had no choice with regard to their sensitivities. Our sensitive nature exposes us, our underbellies, and our tendrils of nerve endings to so many aspects of life and humanity that we often feel perpetually turned inside out with the pinkish flush of new skin revealed, even more sensitive and receptive to the art of living.

In Part II, I highlighted how a person's ability to process their own emotions and thoughts contributes to healthier boundaries and less displaced emissions into the space around them. This is a crucial first step for anyone, empath or not, in taking ownership of their feelings and emotions and recognizing that their behavior and thoughts can impact their environment.

Not only is it draining to continually perceive the environment and your relationships as problems, but it's also a distraction from truly knowing the depth of your own nature. Undeniably, it's important to foster a sense of safety and know that as a reality. That's why establishing boundaries and embodying the central truths about your essence into your core perception are necessary first steps. When you master your own boundaries and know your own essence, you gain the skills and awareness to sense deeper, subtler energetic constructs and dynamics that may influence your own energy, as well as the collective energy that supports humanity.

The Field of Sensing is about your ability to sense the subtleties of the energetic structures that help form your world. For example, you may encounter energetic pathways that specifically carry energy between people. I refer to these as *projections* and *cording*. You may also encounter energy imprints emanating from people that influence how you unintentionally treat them.

The imprint phenomenon is truly unsettling because it illustrates that living on autopilot leaves no room for us to be authentic and present. Life on autopilot becomes an old record played over and over with everyone conforming to standardized roles, which entrenches stereotypes deeper into the psyche of society. Truthfully, the gift you give humanity by becoming self-aware and authentic is the vitality of new expressions of connectivity and creativity.

Sensing Your Own Dimensional Self

As empaths, we sense the energetic component of the physical plane with our subtle bodies. Our four subtle energy bodies—physical, emotional, mental, and spiritual—act like managers with executive-functioning capabilities. They hold our thoughts, emotions, beliefs, and states of being. But they also help us identify the essence or message of what we sense from the environment like energetic sieves:

Is it emotional, a thought, physical discomfort, or more expansive in nature?

I discovered that the more I engaged with subtle bodies, the more I connected to a deeper awareness of how their structure and alliances create the framework for empathy and consciousness to arise within a person's energy system. This awareness can help you determine the best application of self-care to create balance when life is stressful and you're unable to access the deeper aspects of your compassionate self. Which subtle body is muscling on and which are checked-out?

As an empath who functions in the space in between—experiencing both the energetic and physical sides of reality—you can witness the power of the human mind and heart as they direct the flow of someone's energy. You have the opportunity to witness and observe the collective interacting as humanity. You can apply your senses as narrowly or broadly as you choose, both internally and externally, moving beyond knee-jerk reactions, subconscious sabotage, and mental manipulations.

Regardless of what you sense—whether a displaced feeling, an institutional imprint, your awareness that you're often drained from a friend who's constantly involved in drama, or the sublime ecstasy of a mystical encounter—you'll still rely on the foundations of energy practices to ground, center, and embody your authority as a means of self-care and building your own presence. Each application of your empathic abilities is still just sensing energy and then identifying the parts of the communication circuit that is Life: transmitter, receiver, and what is the message.

Chapter Twelve

Artists in Residence— The Subtle Bodies

Our physical body provides us with a mirror to our health. Any disease will be evident in either subtle or not-so-subtle ways, whether through a blood sample or with the naked eye.

Trauma may also impact physical appearance and behavior. Some of us have better defenses to mask what's happening internally, but eventually, an unintended level of crisis will bring the truth of what's out of balance to the surface. And that surface is the physical body, which is a self-portrait on a living canvas.

Every moment, our body reflects the input of senses, perceptions, stresses, and movement. It's a masterpiece that's textured and layered as different aspects of ourselves come up to be the artist. Our four subtle energy bodies—physical, mental, emotional, and spiritual—are our primary artists in residence. The beauty is that each subtle body contributes to our physical expression—four painters sharing the same canvas and interpreting the same life.

Though subtle, they're distinct in how they interact with the canvas of our life. The physical body is the last messenger and the artist with the broadest strokes. When it takes over as the exclusive painter, it's sending a warning. It wants your attention, and it needs to be obvious. There's no time for subtlety. It sends a signal outward so that if you don't comprehend that you're in trouble, someone close to you hopefully will.

The physical body reflects our self-care and how well we're tending to each aspect of our well-being. Even though we may feel integrated, complete, and whole as a consciousness, we nonetheless express ourselves through the physical, emotional, mental, and spiritual channels. If our consciousness is a rug supporting our life, it potentially can be woven with any combination of these four threads, adding strength and texture. A flinch, a wince, a wink, a glare—who painted which and why?

These bodies are instrumental in supporting our developing consciousness that's expressed through our relationships and perceptions. They're the energetic containers that hold space for our growth. While each is distinctly individual and can only perform its own duties, their ability to assist each other signifies a consciousness willing to be integrative and flexible. When they work in harmony, it helps us progress as dimensional beings.

Outward Bound, the outdoor education program, which I participated in when I was a youth, has often used the saying that "you can only go as fast as your weakest member." This is also true for the subtle bodies. They all benefit from each other's processing and integration of your life experiences, but if one moves forward with a new epiphany, the others must integrate the wisdom within their function and framework. This is why personal growth can feel like two steps forward and one step back, as each part needs to keep up.

The spiritual body is related to the heart chakra, the mental body is related to the solar plexus chakra, the emotional body is related to the sacral or naval chakra, and the physical body (referred to as the etheric body) is related to the root or sacrum chakra.

The subtle bodies have the ability to come forward or fade into the background, depending on what your life needs at that moment. When taking a test, for example, you'd do well to have your mental body more active and present. If you're dealing with grief, your emotional body is front and center. If meditating, your spiritual body will come forward.

In a healthy, consciously engaged person, all four subtle bodies will function and work together without too much dominance of one over the other. Life, however, has a way of forcing reflection or a change of lifestyle if one subtle body is burdened by consistently processing our life without the input of the other subtle bodies. This can happen when a completely inconvenient injury puts us out of action, and suddenly, we see our life through another filter while recuperating on the couch. Or when a deep emotional purge brings us sudden and obvious clarity that we previously lacked.

Your consciousness is expressed through your relationships—emotionally, mentally, and physically—and how you spiritually connect your experiences with other sentient beings. The human body, the human mind, and the human spirit are all impressive and powerful in their own unique ways. A multidimensional consciousness arises when you put them all together with the awareness that they perform best as a whole, each aligned with the other.

Sensing your subtle bodies' health and vitality is another way to gain self-awareness and monitor how you're truly doing with regard to your emotional, mental, and physical health, as well as why it may be difficult for you to have empathy.

If you feel a bit numb and cut off from more generous aspects of yourself, such as empathy, ask yourself which of your subtle bodies is working harder than the others to process your life experiences. Which one has been center stage without a break? Again, self-awareness and self-care promote balance.

Let's take a look at how our subtle bodies work together to create different expressions of dimensional consciousness. This may help you see opportunities to clear perceptions and embrace more creative and unified expression.

Two-Dimensional: Duality

A two-dimensional consciousness is perhaps misleading. All four subtle bodies are present, but the spiritual body is basically dormant, as there isn't an expanding consciousness to engage it or activate its skillset. And the three lower subtle bodies aren't quite working with equanimity—either because the mental or emotional body has been diminished or not allowed to contribute due to a belief system that doesn't support the importance of emotions; or because the person's mental capacity is compromised, causing them to rely on the emotional and physical bodies to process their experiences.

Imagine a consciousness that's expressed predominantly by the physical and mental bodies, while the emotional body is either developmentally stunted or suppressed. Under this two-pillar operation of the subtle bodies, the ego, which is expressed through the mental body, tends to rule without being questioned or quieted. Therefore, a lot of judgment runs the program. In place of experiencing emotions, what develops is the distortion of projected thought-forms.

In today's society, we have become adept at monitoring and quickly assessing our mental states. Feeling stressed? Simply breathe with mindfulness. Feeling low on self-esteem? Compose an affirmation. But notice that most of this management comes from settling the *mind* into a noncombative frequency, as if asking for a truce. Ask someone how they feel, and you may be offered a wide variety of responses. The mental body can quickly rattle off disappointment, regret, irritation, contentment, worry, resentment, and so on. The physical body can just as easily answer hot, cold, sweaty, tense, or relaxed. The emotional body can respond with words like love, sorrow, and fear, while the spiritual body might offer states of being, such as grief, joy, love, peace, forgiveness, and compassion.

We may be one human being, but we're a composite of a mind that registers input from a spiritual/universal plane, a mental plane, an emotional plane, and a physical plane. So, when you're aware of a feeling, ask yourself which plane is generating and communicating that feeling. Take, as an example, a painful breakup. You can project upon yourself that "I'm obviously not good enough," which becomes a perception your psyche pivots around as acceptable. However, the emotional content from a sense of rejection and its connection to worthiness is a whole other level of emotional depth that's avoided by the declaration. It's easier to shove the unprocessed emotional content into a Ziploc bag, sealed, stored, and labeled "not good enough" with a Sharpie, adding it to other unprocessed emotions in the deep freezer of your emotional body.

Often, when I'm picking up impressions in a room or from a person, it's a combination of a thought-form-like bubble or cyst holding the essence of the emotion that's being avoided or suppressed. The subconscious rationalizes that it's too difficult to feel the painful emotions of rejection, while the mental appraisal of "I'm obviously not good enough for him/her" is easier to accept. When I recognize any impression with the word "not" in its description, I know it's a mental projection. The mental plane uses the concept of "not," while the emotional plane is more fluid and moves toward expressing itself rather than containing itself to mental constructs.

Under two-dimensional consciousness that operates through heavy-handed judgment, it's difficult to let empathy get a foothold because the emotional body is limited in how it can inform perceptions, self-awareness, and connections. This happens for many reasons, but somehow, the central programming has received input that emotions are a weakness, a liability, confusing, or stressful.

Three-Dimensional: The Power of Three

A three-dimensional consciousness is informed by three of the four subtle bodies—physical, mental, and emotional. The mental body is one of structure, and a lot of different personal components go into whether it's more rigid and controlling or flexible and resilient.

The emotional body is fluid. There's a reason that water is often used as a literary device to represent emotions. The states of solid, liquid, and gas have certainly reflected my experience of my emotional development. We need water as a living organism, and we need our emotions to be accessible and able to flow. If frozen, we're rigid and unmoving. If steaming, we're fraught with too many "unmanageable" emotions.

The dynamic between the mental and emotional bodies comes down to that term "unmanageable." Who or what manages your emotions? Obviously, you do, as the person experiencing the emotions, but within yourself, how are emotions managed? Examining this point highlights the relationship between these two bodies.

They're unique and have individual functions, but they also have an alliance. We need our mental body to offer us structure—not in an overbearing and controlling way, but by offering perspective and a sense of space or a container.

In the healthiest relationship between the mental and emotional bodies, each honors the other. The mental body doesn't rush in to try to "fix" anything while the emotional body experiences deep emotions. It offers space to the emotional body by keeping itself in check and not unleashing self-judgment to diminish the experience. The physical body is also a respected member of the team and can help by providing cathartic movement in crying, laughing, or anything else that expresses and shifts an emotional state.

When given the opportunity to be felt and expressed, an emotional state can change fairly rapidly. Notice how an intensely felt emotional state can ebb and fade until you somehow find yourself steadied and full of resolve. That's the gift of being present with your feelings and unencumbered by an overactive mental body wanting to put a lid on it.

In contrast, have you ever felt yourself settling down from an emotional wound, and just as you sense you're more or less going to be okay, you're flooded with thoughts that tell you otherwise? "Go for it—rip the bandage off, and see the pain and suffering that breakup is causing you. Don't forget." Well, that would be the work of the mental body making folly of the emotional body, manipulating it rather than giving it the space it needs. The physical body is then left to be the container, and this is when hysteria or shock can break out.

So, what does the emotional body offer the mental body? Creativity and connection. The mental body is the host of reason and logic, and overall cognition is enhanced by the input of the emotional body. Creative problem-solving isn't dependent upon emotions, but the connections that are made, knowingly or unknowingly, during a creative exercise make room for intuition and expansive thought processes. I always imagine a stubborn, but not too stubborn, mental body acquiescing to an emotional body that's eager to play. And play is what the emotional body is designed for—to have a creative and emotive sense of the world.

There's a beautiful relationship between the mental and emotional bodies when they're both honored and able to support each other. For example, the mental body can organize symmetry, while the emotional body feels the sensations of balance and the elegance of that symmetry. There's a profound difference between viewing and that of experiencing a piece of art. Allowing that additional sensory input to inform the experience creates more connections and develops more self-awareness. These impressions, no matter how small in scale, build a base of emotional awareness.

Empathy emerges as emotional awareness informs us how we feel, and we can then connect to others in a shared learning environment. Empathy in the third dimension, however, is somewhat limited to the personal experiences of the individual. It often looks like a shortsighted politician who can only apply understanding and compassion to the one group of individuals he most identifies with without the ability to apply it to other broader applications of the same issue.

An evolving emotional awareness fuels growth in a profound way, just as employing your mind as an ally rather than a constant critic grants freedom in accepting yourself and others. Empathy from the fourth dimension, however, can recognize more universality and less hypocritical limitations.

Four-Dimensional: The Freedom of Self-Love

Freedom from fear and doubt. Freedom from expectations and outcomes. Freedom from suffering and apathy. Freedom through self-love. The spiritual body transforms the ordinary into the extraordinary. It provides an expanded awareness that invites mystery, paradox, irony, and symbolism. Through the spiritual body, we can see the macro and the micro as one and the same without separation. This includes ourselves. We must sit ourselves down and dine with the divine with reverence and without hesitation about worthiness and shame. We must look to see all of humanity sitting down beside us. If one sits, all sit. As above, so below.

The spiritual body offers the foundation for the fourth dimension to provide expansion to our awareness and consciousness. It's dependent on our inner receptivity and willingness to process our life's experiences. It emanates states of being that are felt throughout our entire energy system. It can feel as if time stops. Joy, love, sadness, happiness, and bliss—the spiritual body is responsible for these timeless full-body moments of being. It develops and supports you in meditation, calmly absorbing the mental and emotional body. Even the physical body becomes less apparent and present in these deep states of oneness. Have you ever experienced this bodyless state?

If "spiritual body" sounds too New Age, consider another name for it. But for me and many other highly perceptive, sensitive people, "spiritual" and "spirituality" do not represent a brand or school of thought. There are no disciples or initiation. Spirituality just supports an awareness of unity and oneness. It's the overall intelligence and wisdom that every cell within our body is filled with purpose and connection to sustain life—each part respected and revered. Genuine altruism and innocence are the benefactors of linking all four subtle bodies together.

Fourth-dimensional consciousness is more prevalent in the world today. Empathy isn't a fringe application of being human; biases are less tolerated. The holistic view of respecting all parts of the whole is emerging. We know that if we have the right to express ourselves, we must extend the same rights to those around us who are still diminished by social conditioning and systemic discrimination.

Five-Dimensional: Singularity on the Physical Plane

If I were to describe what this state of being feels like energetically, the closest I can comprehend is that the subtle bodies are no longer separate. They're brought together into one unified operating system, synchronized and in harmony. I experienced this sublime knowingness once in my life and captured it as best as I could in a journal entry:

> *It's hot and muggy inside the swimming pool hall, contrasting the cold and dark of an autumn evening in Stavanger, Norway. I'm a mother of four, ages spanning between one and ten years old. My days are spent hectically juggling domestic affairs amid the backdrop of constantly being reminded that I'm still a foreigner in my husband's country.*
>
> *The noise is deafening; the echoes of children talking and splashing compete with instructors, parents, and accompanying siblings. Parents line the walls or outside the doors, peering in through port-like windows that are dripping with condensation. I'm sitting poolside in too many layers, surrounded by children I don't know, next to their mothers, who I also don't know, exhausted and slightly disinterested if my children are executing their swim strokes to the liking of their instructors.*
>
> *And totally unexpected, and unannounced, my whole body is swept over with a presence of energy, and I'm tingling from head to toe. I'm fully present in my body, but it's as if time has stopped. I look around the room, and I have the awareness that what I'm seeing is equal to what I'm feeling, as if there's no difference between the sensory*

input. Or rather, it's one sense completely gifting me this experience instead of several working simultaneously. The swimming pool shimmers with light and is radiating an aura. The people around me shimmer as well with a vibration, and everywhere in that space, I feel such profound and deep love for each and every person with absolutely no differential regard to whether they're my flesh and blood.

The intensity of the moment slips from my ordinary senses after a few minutes, and I attempt to hold on to it—eager to capture it, if only fleetingly wanting a few more moments of whatever this is. Now, I know what a truly expanded state of consciousness feels like. It's no longer confined to a theory in a book. In meditation and in communion with nature, I experience great peace and a detached sense of well-being, but this is different. In this poolside experience, I'm anything but detached. I feel the unifying field through each of us, and I'm also able to feel my own mind and consciousness operating in the background while the experience unfolds—meaning I don't suspend my reality, but I'm present with another dimension or expression of it simultaneously.

This experience, though hosted by my senses for a relatively short period of time, has nonetheless had a great impact on what I know to be possible in hosting an expanded consciousness while in physical form. It wasn't a theoretical proposition; it wasn't a delusional fantasy of escapism. It was a sampler, a teaser, a taste of a unified embodied consciousness, and it's that state of awareness and being that keeps me on my path.

Will I be able to cultivate this state of being in this lifetime? I don't know—perhaps tomorrow, next year, or not at all. If I'm honest with myself, I know I'm still untangling from belief systems that limit me. I'm still processing forgiveness, and life is still presenting me with tests and challenges that direct me toward my authentic self. I'm certainly more aware of the mechanics of energy and the nature of consciousness than I was that day more than twenty years ago. But there isn't a formula or substitute for doing the work of revising our narrative until we know the truth for ourselves—that acceptance, love, and innocence are the cocktail of enlightenment. We're also in an age that requires more than enlightenment—an age where we must embody these energies and be present with our presence.

What would it look like within the physical anatomy to host such a state of being and awareness? I typically earmark newspaper clippings that I've read, wanting to understand different aspects of the brain's mechanisms. I found one very interesting proposition by Christopher Bergland in an article called "The Cerebellum Deeply Influences Our Thoughts and Emotions: The Cerebellum Fine-Tunes Cognitive Function Like It Fine-Tunes Muscle Movement." He presents the concept of "superfluidity," whereby he suspects that "optimal brain function is obtained when all four brain hemispheres are working together in perfect harmony at an electrical, chemical, and architectural level. . . . I believe that a peak state of consciousness occurs when every nook and cranny of each of your brain's four hemispheres are working together in synchronicity. I call this a state of 'superfluidity' because it represents absolutely zero friction, zero entropy, and zero viscosity between thought, action, and emotion."

That is what it felt like for me on that day—not in an ashram, or in prayer, or on a bliss-filled run (haven't experienced that, but Mr. Bergland holds a word record for running on a treadmill). My experience involved feeling a bit frumpy and overdressed in a hot, humid public pool hall with a growing list of things I needed to take care of, when an energy slipped over and through me. It was my own senses and thoughts that were pronounced, not anything borrowed. It was a magical marvel, but it wasn't a miracle.

A miracle is when something occurs outside of your comprehension and understanding, and the only way you can accept it is to declare it as such. I do comprehend the significance of my experience and its invitation to expand toward a singularity.

When I set out to write this book, I made a conscious decision to write it from the experience of being an empath, which means that the body is my filter—the embodiment of the spiritual principles in my life and relationships. It would be wonderful to meditate and envision a beautiful world of bliss and nirvana, but while incarnated on the physical plane, the physical body needs movement, the mental body needs stimulation, the emotional body needs creativity and connections, and the spiritual body needs beauty and truth. All of this happens in your life with intention and awareness. Energy flows where you put your attention; this is the powerful invitation of being awake and self-aware.

Subtle Bodies in Action

As part of my training to be a spiritual counselor, my class had to bear witness as each member shared a painful and difficult experience from their life. It was a multifaceted experiential teaching. We were learning how to listen to graphic, traumatic details without taking them into our own personal space, how to hold space to support the individual who was speaking, and how to tune into what we heard to gauge an appropriate response.

The mental body listens while the emotional body hears. Are you listening? What do you hear? Listening procures details and facts. Hearing reveals the emotional tones of a person's sadness, grief, dismay, humiliation, shame, and so on. The mirroring effect of empathy may trigger your own emotional wounds, particularly if you try to process someone else's trauma as if it's your own. As a result of our own discomfort, many of us try to rush an emotional person to gain composure. An overactive and righteous mental body may lead to judgmental and critical listening, which can create projections toward the person without supporting them in feeling heard or witnessed.

Essentially, the exercise prompted each of us to consider: Can I offer compassion without stopping the person's process? Can I offer empathy without crossing boundaries or making it about my experience? Can I offer sympathy when needed without pity or projection?

Questions for Reflection

Rather than questions for reflection, this time, I offer you a meditation to try. Afterward, take some time with your journal to write down your impressions and feelings from the meditation.

1. Picture yourself outside on a bright, sunny day in a peaceful, safe setting. There's a clothesline on which you can pin up each of your subtle bodies as if they were sheets of fabric. Each is unique and distinguishable from the others. How do they look to you? Tune into each one, and sense its features and qualities. Is one heavier than another or more translucent like mesh? Compare and contrast them with your curiosity guiding you. Were they easy to place on the line, or did they feel tangled up with each other? Is one smaller than the others? What colors do you see or intuit?

2. Once you've stepped back to assess their form, consider if they would benefit from a clearing and cleaning. If so, imagine what feels most natural to you for cleaning any stagnant energy or for any repairs you sense would make them more functional. Attend to this, spending focused energy toward each subtle body, honoring the work they do as an extension of your processing powers for your life and their subtle sensing of the energetic realm.

3. Sometimes, I imagine I'm rinsing and refreshing them by placing them in a gentle stream. Other times, I feel as if I need a water pressure hose to blast and penetrate gunk attached to a subtle body, particularly if my mental body seems too rigid.

4. Imagine them all vibrant and purified, absorbing the freshness of the sunshine and the natural fragrances of the surroundings. Then, one by one, take them off the line and step into them. Breathe deeply, and stretch your body.

Chapter Thirteen

Ties That Bind or Bond

Many years ago while living in Texas, I attended a local drum circle, which was its own version of fellowship, infused with a small contemplative discussion by the leader. These discussions typically used some metaphor or wisdom from nature. At one particular meeting, the leader talked about flexibility and how we can be strengthened by challenging times.

He told of the practice of bending sapling trees, such as willows, like the one in his backyard that was tied down in a deep bow. The temporary bending and tying down of the top boughs, while the young tree is its most flexible, hopefully stimulates the roots into growing deeper and stronger to counter the forces felt at the surface. This is to condition the solitary tree to withstand hurricane winds.

The conversation naturally turned to the spiritual importance of staying balanced by connecting to the Earth, grounding for stability like roots while remaining flexible enough to sway with the wind or whatever challenges come our way. Each of us in attendance was asked to examine if we were flexible or rigid in our minds and hearts and to take note of what we sensed about our inner life—were we flexible or rigid in our perceptions? Did earlier struggles in our lives strengthen and ground us in our own wisdom rather than uproot us? When in our lives had we felt uprooted and unbalanced?

I find trees, in general, to be remarkable symbols of both resilience and resources. Their existence is dependent on rooting into the soil regardless of the terrain, which can appear very inhospitable on the surface. As I've hiked over the decades of my life, I've marveled at trees rooted precariously atop boulders, emerging from the sides of cliffs, or twisted by winds that whipped down the faces of summits at high altitude. Each tree uniquely reflects its environment and offers its presence within the landscape.

I still reflect on the central message from that drum circle evening: a rigid tree with shallow roots will always be easier to topple in a storm. How deep is your grounding, and how well can you sway with the winds?

Environments Can Condition and Mold Us

Historically, Native Americans have used bending trees as a way to signal directions to important points of interest in an area, as well as to indicate territory boundaries. "Marker trees" and "trail trees," as they're called, are peculiar looking, often with ninety-degree bends cultivated into the growing pattern of the tree. They resemble a suspended bench in some cases. The craft of molding a tree to grow unnaturally (while not killing it) is a skill in patience and respect. Nonetheless, the tree has been manipulated and molded for an external purpose, and its appearance is forever changed by the manipulation.

Our childhood environments also mold us and imprint us with beliefs and patterns that shape how we see ourselves and the world. Some of us endured dysfunctional and abusive childhoods, while others had more balanced and nurturing parenting. Then, there are those who grew up in institutions that attempted to control them by instilling a rigid and precise mold.

Our energy systems are malleable and programmable like the tree bending. Energy sensitivity shows that when we interact with someone, we might be influenced by an energetic imprint or environmental molding that tries to instruct us how to treat them. Just as a "marker tree" is bent to give a direction, rigid environmental molding or imprinting gives directions to both the individual and to those who interact with the individual.

For example, in 2010, I started volunteering at a local orphanage for a program sponsored by the International Women's Club of Baku, Azerbaijan. The women's group provided developmental toys and weekly stimulating physical movement for infants, aged newborn to four years old. Initially, there were many difficult days due to language and cultural obstacles. Slowly, however, volunteers and staff formed a somewhat mutual regard for each other.

My first awareness of the impact of institutional molding on a person's energy fields was a by-product of volunteering there. I had previously been aware that each person's childhood environment contributes to how they develop their perceptions and corresponding energy patterns. But what I discovered about institutional imprinting was how destructive it can be, particularly at a young age—like a double-edged knife.

Generally, an institution has rules and routines to obey. It operates most easily and efficiently on compliance. It wants to dictate not only who you are but also how others perceive you. It wants to bend and contort your sense of self into submission.

On my very first day at the orphanage, I encountered a nine-month-old baby girl with a gaping smile and a chasm of a cleft palate. For our purposes, I'll simply call her M. She was placed out of sight, away from the other babies. As I approached her playpen, she rolled over to face me, and I was met with such radiance, joy, and magnetism that I barely noticed her disfigurement. Surrounded by institutional smells, depressing decor, and a profound hierarchy of power within the staff, I ignored the number-one rule we were given—"Don't pick up a baby."

As hard as it is to imagine, this rule was put in place to safeguard the staff, who could not, in their perception, cater to the cries of all of the children. If volunteers started picking up children and comforting them, they worried it would impact their workload once we left. Yet, for some reason, if we were sitting on the ground, and a child came into our lap, we could engage in a bit of a cuddle. The staff seemed to be so amused by the fact that grown women were playing on the floor that they overlooked the lingering lap time.

As I held this small package of joy up to my chest, her head instantly lay against my breastbone, and she relaxed as if she'd always been there. Ultimately, a parent's role in a child's life is to show them the wonder of the world and how they can fit into that world with respect and worth.

A parent's first coo to their child, nestled in their arms, is for me what Samuel Coleridge's poem "Answer to a Child's Question" speaks of—the lark so "brimful of gladness and love, the green fields below him, the blue sky above, That he sings, and he sings; and forever sings he—'I love my Love, and my Love loves me!'" To nurture the child so that even in the winter of bare darkness and howling winds, the warmth of unconditional love assures the child that the world is still safe and welcoming and that the songs of birds will return.

Institutional orphans may not encounter a caretaker consistent enough to imprint this message of love and safety. An entire industry of adoption advocacy and education attempts to prepare prospective international adoptive parents to overcome this deficiency within an orphan's perception of the world. The formative years are still the formative years regardless of a child's residence, so it's understandable that most orphans lag behind in developmental milestones. They simply lack the exposure that comes with an attentive parent/caregiver modeling and encouraging them to grow and explore.

There are obvious exceptions, as many countries are working to provide more stable and enriching home environments for orphans. I also understand that my time volunteering at the orphanage afforded me exposure to a portion of the Azeri culture. As a foreigner, I needed to be careful not to project my opinions of social welfare on a system that was based on a different political and religious platform than I was raised with. Though rich in history and culture, Azerbaijan was still a young nation that only received its independence from Soviet rule in 1991.

I volunteered at the orphanage twice a week. While I couldn't dote on M. exclusively, as I had to make myself available to all the children, I saw her learn to crawl and walk. I watched her take in the world as a toddler as she tried to speak through a mouth that was cavernous and unable to guide her tongue. I tuned into the room's energy and tried to lift whatever I felt was appropriate and supportive to the children's living environment.

Over time, however, I noticed something odd in my interactions with M. When she was in my lap, I found myself wanting to squeeze her firmly—not in a kind and nurturing way, and not because she had done anything in particular. It startled me, and I quickly turned to play with another child.

She would eventually come back, and I would welcome her. Yet the feeling was still there. I was aware of the impulse to *squeeze until it hurts*.

I noticed that this energy was present in other children as well—not all, but definitely some. That was when I experienced firsthand that an environment can create a mold that integrates with a person's fields like an instructional code that indicates how they "should" be treated. M.'s imprint read like some dark perversion of humanity: treat harshly or shake until content's will is broken.

Had I not known my own nature—that I could never physically harm a child—I may have easily been pulled into the pattern, acting it out to fit the mold. Instead, I disconnected from the energy. I even tried to lift this imprint from M. to safeguard her from mistreatment from others.

The imprint would weaken, but by the time of my next visit, it was back. If I hadn't known of her energy signature as a younger baby and my devotion to bringing her out of that environment, I might not have noticed this change.

We attempted to adopt her, but after much heartache and bureaucracy, we were unsuccessful. Months later, as she turned two, she was moved to the toddler room. She no longer wanted cuddles and instead focused on being part of a pack. When frustrated, she would rock and hit her head against things. Sadly, the energy I detected as an early imprint/molding had become part of her energy.

Discerning Your Behavior Toward Others

Have you ever experienced something like I did with M.? Feeling a pull to treat someone in a manner that doesn't truly reflect who you are? If you find yourself being pulled into behavior toward someone else that's unlike your usual behavior, step back and ask yourself if you're interacting with a noxious imprint/molding. Any institutional confinement with a debilitating element of suppression will want to mold a person and break their will to make them compliant. If you find yourself aware of an "instructional imprint" that wants to modify your nature toward someone, tell the energy you aren't willing to play a part in keeping someone down. Don't add to any additional harm that comes to the person. Challenge yourself to see beyond the entrapment of the molding, and see the person without these limitations. When you truly see them and reflect this acceptance, they may also be reminded of their true self.

What other institutional mindsets have you interacted with in your life? Do you know someone who was raised in a foster system? Incarcerated? In a cult or military setting? What other aspects of society can be experienced as its own institution—poverty, racism, and so on? Can you identify for yourself how these environments have imprinted with the individual's personality and affected their view of themselves and the world? Does it influence how you treat them?

Perhaps you were raised in such an environment. If so, have you worked yourself free from the limitations imposed upon your sense of self? Have you sensed, at your core, that you're more than what can be contained by an experience and a story?

The Power of Projections

The subtlety of energy that an empath can register gives us a glimpse as to how the mind directs energy. The Body-Mind-Spirit triad is constructed with the mind in the middle for this reason. The mind bridges the physical and energetic planes. Language and sensory perception assist the mind in packaging thoughts and feelings. Empathic people can more easily pick up displaced thoughts and emotions from other people because, as I explained in Part II, that person hasn't consciously processed the emotions or thoughts.

Projections, though, are thoughts that are *directed* by the mind. (Of course, a "mind" doesn't have to be contained to an individual; it can be an organization or institution. Oaths, pledges, and vows are all pathways to align minds and intentions to a singular expression. When you hear the statement "We are of one mind . . . ," it represents a shared intention.)

We project thoughts all the time. Our internal dialogue is made up of mindless chatter of opinions and projections. Where do our thoughts go? Where our mind directs them. "The cashier has funny teeth" might be an unexpressed thought, but it nonetheless contains a subject and a message. The energy of such thoughts follows the path to the subject: "They are such snobs!" "I'm so fat." He can't do anything right." We're both receiving and transmitting channels, after all.

When I conduct space clearings for houses or offices, it's very revealing to register which objects are dusted with projections. Bathroom mirrors, which seem to be headquarters for self-projections, typically need a good clearing. This is one of the many reasons that a lot of self-help therapies promote mirror work for self-compassion. Looking at yourself while giving compliments will quickly reveal if you have self-image issues that run belief programs in the background of your daily life. How do you feel if you look yourself squarely in the eyes? Do you look lovingly at yourself, or are you an instant critic? Practice some of your "I AM" statements in front of a mirror, and notice how you feel and where you feel it.

The weight of carrying your own weary self-esteem can be compounded by the projections of others. I remember one such clearing where the diplomas and certificates were covered in layers of projections. I cleared them away and directed my client's attention to why this might be. She was aware that she had been bad-mouthed by a particular group of people. These projections had landed on her credentials, which were extensions of her profession and identity.

Anyone with low or fragile self-esteem is dealing with self-projections, and this is where healing needs to be focused. We're like radios, able to receive transmissions that correspond with our range of receptivity. If you have a lot of negative self-perceptions, it will be easy for you to receive transmissions similar to your own thoughts. Therefore, the best way to avoid projections is to not entertain the thoughts yourself.

Take, for example, the opinion that "the cashier has funny teeth." If the cashier is self-conscious about her teeth, there's a similar thought that can easily receive what the shopper transmitted to her. The cashier may suddenly feel more self-conscious during their interaction. If the cashier doesn't believe there's anything wrong with her teeth or has come to accept them as they are, it won't matter what the shopper or anyone else thinks or projects toward her.

Self-love or, at the very least, acceptance and respect for where you are in your life protects the health of your personal space. Self-love gives your energy fields a Teflon coating from projections that other people or a group consciousness may direct at you, knowingly or unknowingly. It also hopefully moves you past the point of projecting negative thoughts upon yourself.

Anyone who has been in a car accident is rudely awakened to the force and power in a moving vehicle. The physical world is energy contained in form, and that power is still present as potential. A canyon is carved by water, and a piece of grit creates a pearl—just add time and pressure, and a landscape is changed by subtle means. Projections contain the same power and force and can have just as profound an effect. Projections that are relentlessly cast toward an individual or group can gain enough form to become an imprint that limits a person's self-perception.

What's the impact of a projection or, on a larger scale, an imprint? They can create distortions and blocks in how our energy flows, depending on which energy center or chakra the projection/imprint settles within. Cleaning up our thoughts will automatically clear off projections. The importance of kindness and compassion to ourselves and one another cannot be overstated.

Clearing Projections

My nightly practice before bed is to do an honest accounting of my thoughts and my day. When I feel a wayward thought toward myself or someone else, I ask: "Please lift and remove any projections that I may have consciously or unknowingly cast toward myself or others. I intend no harm to anyone, myself included." I ask myself to be more mindful and respectful of my energy and that of others. By engaging my mind, I bring in my awareness to create intention and action aligned to my consciousness. By extending compassion to myself and others, I bring in my heart intelligence, which honors that we're all connected.

Why would something this simple work? Because energy is programmable, and your energy will follow your focus. You created the thought in the first place, so by taking responsibility for it, you free up the space between you and the other person. Or you free up the space within you. The Lord's Prayer is essentially a lesson in projections. "Forgive me for my trespasses as I forgive those who have trespassed against me." That's essentially what a projection does—it trespasses into and onto another person's perception of themselves with the effect of diminishing them in some manner.

When someone annoys or frustrates me, I describe the behavior in my journal. I make it less about the person and more about the behavior. It helps me take control of my thoughts and any wayward projections that might have been launched before I had a chance to review the situation. It also helps me assess if I need to limit my contact or communicate my awareness about what's out of balance in our relationship.

Prayer and Praise as a Means to Counter Mindless Projections

Thoughts generated from our head space tend to go the pathway of a projection and negatively impact our own energy systems, as well as the other person's. We do it more often when we're stressed, frustrated, worried, and ungrounded.

Of course, sincere and genuine praise and prayers are uplifting and have the opposite effect. I stipulated "sincere and genuine prayers and praise" because interestingly, I've experienced prayer groups that felt more like a group of people judging and projecting upon another. And I've experienced praise that was more like flattery, which has the energetic dynamic of someone wanting something in exchange for giving nothing. It's a manipulation.

There is humility and reverence embedded in a prayer, and there's joy and respect instilled in true praise. In both prayer and praise, the energy moves through the connection at the heart through the central channel that grounds the energy in the physical world and the expanded unified field. It's why deeply felt prayers and exaltations have an emotive and embodied experience beyond mental activity.

A client of mine experienced a profound transformation when she shared my workshop material about projections with her husband. She recognized that they had both projected carelessly upon their teenage son, who'd been very challenging to raise. They were collectively tired and frustrated, but committed to changing their knee-jerk projections. They constructed this praiseworthy practice on their own, each writing down only positive statements and sincere wishes about their son, creating a master list to guide them back to honoring him and his life. When they found themselves headed toward projecting negative thoughts, they instead reached for this master list and felt the truth of the statements until the negative thought no longer presented. Several months after initiating this practice, the results had transformed their relationship with their son in beautiful ways.

Projections are subtle depending on how conscious you are about your thoughts and what motivates you to have such thoughts. Mainly, they're a sign of a lazy mind that hasn't been examined or made to mature.

Meanwhile, the practice of meditation and mindfulness can help you take notice of your thoughts. If you have a projecting mind toward yourself and others with nonstop commentary, you're energetically tying yourself up with the mundanity of judgment. It's my sincere hope that you come to understand that the subtle energy realm of thoughts and feelings, which you can sense more easily than others, is just the transportation of energy directed by many minds, including your own.

Questions for Reflection

Take some time with your journal to write down your impressions and feelings in response to these questions. Then, reflect on how your experience in your answers may have affected you emotionally or affected your development as an empath.

1. Reflect on whether you were imprinted or molded in your childhood or other environments to be treated in a certain way. Write about your experience of this phenomenon and how it has affected you in your life.

2. Think about people in your life whom you believe were imprinted or molded to be treated in a certain way. Write about your experience of this phenomenon in them. Have you been seduced into treating them negatively based on the imprint? Have you been successful in resisting the imprint/mold?

3. Reflect on projections from others that may have affected you because you held similar beliefs about yourself. What are you self-conscious about?

4. Devise your own nightly practice to review your day and let go of any projections toward yourself and others. How does it impact your sleep?

5. Assess the degree to which you're energetically tied to judgments, and commit to changing this condition within yourself.

What do you think would work best for you to ease these judgments toward yourself and/or others? As I said in the chapter, meditation is a great way to foster more self-awareness of your thoughts.

6. If there's someone you harbor judgments toward, try making a master list of positive statements about the person that you'll review whenever you have a negative thought about them. Keep track in your journal of how your efforts alter your relationship with this person.

Chapter Fourteen

Holding Space

I love a story full of coincidences. It makes for good storytelling and challenges the listener to consider what they believe is possible. We tend to think of chance encounters as fun and endearing stories about our good fortune at being in the right place at the right time. But what about larger scale coincidences, such as a historic geographical imprint from one culture influencing the next?

When living in Perth, Western Australia, our family took several city tours with a local tour guide named Adie, who walked us for hours through the downtown streets, filling us with amusing stories of past politicians and their influences on the architecture. She also showcased the amazing street art that's featured on many buildings in the lively Northbridge area.

We took equally as many walking tours with an Aboriginal guide company to learn about the indigenous culture from the region. Our guide Greg briefly told us some of the history of the Nyoongar people as we walked around King's Park overlooking the gentle, winding Swan River. Perth's original people are the Wadjuk tribe, "the guardians of the link between the land and the sea," which is the Swan River.

Pointing south down the river toward Claremont township, Greg described how once a year, Wadjuk men initiated the boys into manhood through a ritual that required healing from a deep cut on the arm before wading across the Swan River. Once the cuts had healed, they headed over to the south side of the river, where the women prepared a feast, timed to coincide with the arrival of the men coming across from the north of the river. The story was textured with layers of how the season, land, "bush tucker" (crops), and women and men of the Wadjuk tribe coordinated the events succinctly and in harmony. Listening to Greg was like having a basket weaver thread and braid the elements of time and place. We climbed into that space and let it hold our attention.

Greg ended the story with an interesting note that in the same area of Claremont today, there's a hospital, which he added is a well-known symbol for healing. On the south side is "Freo," more formally known as Freemantle, which is notorious for its free-spirited festivals and celebrations. Could the land, imprinted by the First Nation's rituals and traditions, influence how the future dwellers also used the land?

Our subtle sensing informs us, even guides us—often without our conscious awareness. Sensitivity to the environment and its energy around us is another form of communication and connection to different times and cultures. We can impact the land and the environment, but the land can also influence us—even so subtly that we don't recognize it.

Land can become a sacred container that holds space for ceremonies and rituals, and it has the bonus feature of naturally grounding the intentions of the facilitator. How long the ceremonial energy remains active in the area is dependent on a connection or link to someone who still holds the knowledge and intention to fuel it—just as shrines stay active as devotees pray and extend offerings. Otherwise, it will fade over time, becoming less perceptible to subtle sensing. I would love to interview archeologists to hear how often their own intuition helped lead them to discover ruins and artifacts.

A labyrinth holds space for those who walk the bending and winding path that circles back upon itself. Its structure and design secure the path and support the meditative walker to receive what they seek as they reach the "centering" stone.

Holding space is an energetic container that's created to safeguard a vision or creative intention from negative projections or naysayers—much like a mother's womb, which protects the unborn child from external pathogens while it develops and grows.

Holding Energy Versus Holding Space

We hold energy within our system in the form of beliefs and patterns from our family and culture. Holding energy isn't the same as holding space. Holding energy is just that—holding and static. Holding energy that isn't allowed to circulate tends to create blocks within your energy system and leads to stress in the overall system.

If I gave you a suitcase full of your family's negative generational programming—bigotry, racism, sexual abuse, and addiction, to name a few—and told you that you must carry it around without looking inside or trying to unpack the contents, you might become fatigued from the task. It might seem light at first, but over time, it would become heavier and heavier. You might start to question why you weren't allowed to examine what's inside. You might question why you have to submit to programming that's run by shame, guilt, and secrecy. Then, hopefully, you would set the suitcase down and decide for yourself if you wanted to be responsible for something that was simply handed to you. This is how a healing journey of self-discovery often begins—with discerning what's yours because you are continuing to act out the patterns versus your awareness of potential patterns that you have chosen to shift and heal.

A secret is another example of what holds energy. It's chock-full of perceived potential energy by the person who has declared it a secret. Energy is just information, but it's our perception of what that information can cause or create if known by others that gives it importance. A secret becomes a placeholder of energy, boxed in various forms in a person's psyche.

I have fond memories of sharing a secret with my oldest son, Per, when he was nine. I told him I was pregnant with a girl and that no one else in the family knew but his father. He sensed that this was special news that I entrusted to him, and I asked him to keep it to himself until I was ready to tell the rest of the family. His smile and the spark in his eyes were only matched by the look on his face when he held his little sister Grace for the first time. For a short time in his life, he held a space for her existence before there was even a nursery or a name.

For Per, holding the secret was an experience of holding energy, but knowing that Grace was coming into physical form was an experience of holding space for her. Holding space is an *active intention*. Like any space in your house, the space you hold needs to be refreshed, or it will become stale and stagnant. It needs to be fueled with intentions that support the life and energy it holds. What's in this space will grow and develop as it gains energy, and that's why it's important for the person or group who is "holding the space" to not be too rigid and outcome-oriented. The challenge of holding space for yourself is that any negative self-talk will erode the container and contaminate the vision with doubt and projections.

Ceremonies are created to hold space for connections and insights. They create a container to allow an interaction and integration to occur for those who participate. Business plans, vision boards, and prayer flags are visible examples in mainstream society of what holding space can look like. It's a matter of focus and intention, followed up with whatever action is needed to support the expression in the physical world. It's also a bit of an integrity test: can your discipline and actions match your intentions to continue the long course of holding space for something important to you?

Most energy-aware wellness practitioners set the intention for their office space to create an environment that promotes a sense of safety for their clients. When I visit someone for the first time, whether it's for a massage or energy session, I tune into the energy of the space and sense if it's active or stale. Does it have a vibrancy that comes from the practitioner practicing what they offer? Do they embody the wisdom of the modality and attend to the physical space?

Holding Space for Letting Go

Any workshop leader with a sense of energy awareness will create a container for the event to energetically preserve an environment that supports teaching or personal growth. If you walk into a space that was recently used for a retreat or healing modality, and the room is filled with displaced active energy, it's a telltale sign that the facilitator didn't attend to the space. I experience this as walking into a house party that no one cleaned up after.

At a Family Constellation session, I experienced a brilliant example of when "holding space" and "holding energy" created a profound healing moment for me and a group of attendees. I was fortunate to experience this modality when I visited my home state of Colorado just before Thanksgiving. What better time to look at your family legacy than Thanksgiving? Despite not knowing anything beyond the blurb written about Family Constellations on the facilitator's Facebook page, nor anyone at the event, my interest was piqued. I intentionally put myself in the company of people I hoped would have an interest in collective healing focused on family dynamics.

The main room was round with a vaulted ceiling, like a big yurt, and had approximately twenty chairs arranged in a large circle. I introduced myself to the facilitator, a middle-aged man named Stuart who had a soft-spoken manner that matched his sandy beard and kind eyes. I explained that I was new to this therapy model but would hopefully be a quick study, as I had some energy awareness. He seemed to appreciate that news, as I was the only newcomer that evening, and he hadn't planned on spending much time introducing the coursework. It would be an experiential teaching for me—baptism by fire, so to speak.

Family Constellation falls into the category of alternative therapeutic methods and was created by German psychotherapist Bert Hellinger in the 1990s. It explores how hidden dynamics in our family systems can negatively influence our thoughts, behaviors, and emotional experiences. The therapy relies on the concept of morphic-genetic fields and morphic resonance, which allows for the passage of past generational trauma to influence the well-being of present and future generations from a shared field source. Morphic resonance is a theory put forth by British biologist Rupert Sheldrake and presents "a process whereby self-organizing systems inherit a memory from previous similar systems."

This healing modality and the theory of morphic fields are both controversial by the standards of conventional psychology and science, and over the last several decades, there have been skeptics. However, time and research have produced more evidence that fields and systems can influence an individual's experience of life. Family Constellation's therapeutic approach is fascinating, especially in light of the recent findings by Rachel Yehuda, professor of psychiatry and neuroscience and director of the Traumatic Stress Studies Division at Mount Sinai. She is a pioneer in understanding how the effects of stress and trauma can transmit biologically, beyond cataclysmic events, to the next generation. There is now a field of study called epigenetics that researches this transference of heritable changes in a gene's expression.

Stuart welcomed us and directed each of us to place all of our life stresses and daily thoughts to the side in order to be present together. Everyone was asked to tune into the room's energy, to share what they were aware of, and to briefly state their intention for being there that evening—this is what is known as "checking in."

As you can imagine, this took some time, but I appreciated the pace. That's how a group connects—by interacting, sharing, and creating space. That's what I'd been missing in my life—opportunities to be accepted with my senses and sensibilities rather than being a silent observer in foreign cultures where my empathic nature seemed to always brush up against suspicious and rigid beliefs.

The room was quiet as each person tuned in and observed what they sensed and felt. The most prominent impression I received was that the room's energy was tilted. The back corner was heavy with what I call *disincarnate energy* or ancestors. They were packed in as if crowded together on a subway, waiting to spill out onto the platform once the door opened.

I listened as we went around the circle and the other attendees shared. "Oh, it's just so difficult to tune in. I'm just sooo empathic." A young woman repeated this declaration a couple of times in a tone that begged for attention. I found myself holding my thoughts in check, as she fit every sitcom stereotype about New Agers.

This is where compassion and patience serve a group's dynamics well. Everyone may not be at the same level of self-awareness and integration of their higher sensory receptors, but we all choose to participate in this group healing. This woman was being held in the space just as I was, and each participant contributed to the space with their thoughts and intentions. I reminded myself not to project upon myself or others, as I didn't want to make anyone feel diminished. What purpose would that serve?

Some may think "checking in" is just a way of introducing a group of people to each other. But in this particular therapy, which is reliant on energy techniques of sensing and intuiting, the facilitator was probably using each person's check-in to gauge who was grounded and who might need more assistance once the therapy session began. This is important information because someone ungrounded is more likely to be triggered by their own emotional issues in the midst of a group exchange. Each of us present represented our own interests, but we also served as surrogates for another individual. In the moment, we were there both as an individual and as part of the collective.

When my time came to share, I was brief, but I highlighted how the room was tilted and collecting energy in the corner. I was then told that the person whose Family Constellation would be the basis of the healing that night was sitting in that corner of the room. I can't go into specific details out of respect for privacy, but I can share that even though the night followed a script prescribed by someone who felt trapped in a family dynamic that flowed through several generations, each person in attendance could relate and empathize with similar traits in their own family structures. It was a perfect model for how one person can help heal the whole and vice versa by serving as the example for the group.

I drove home grateful for the timely healing opportunity. Small threads of discomfort still hang from the fabric of my childhood, and I understand that it impacts the family I've created as an adult. It's tempting to pull at the threads in a mindless, destructive way, which would unravel the fabric, but comprehensive healing mends what's out of alignment while still honoring the truth. I lean into these opportunities to release limiting perceptions and gain inner strength so that the work I do on myself can benefit my own children and my relations with my ancestors.

The truth is that humanity is a relay. Each generation hands off the baton to the next, imprinted with certain conditions and attitudes that were formed by the times in which they lived and how they managed their challenges. Undoubtedly, the hope is that the next generation will advance, honoring and respecting life in more sustaining and comprehensive ways.

The Capacity to Hold Space

As an empath, holding space can be a beautiful expression of supporting energy into form—of honoring your integrated nature as both energy and physical. You might not need to hold space for an office environment or workshop, but please consider how your first field placement (that I mentioned in Chapter 6) involves holding space for yourself and your well-being.

There are also valuable lessons for an empathic person who may overextend themselves if they feel responsible to hold space for everyone around them. Our capacity to care and support is admirable, but as I've said, it needs to be balanced. Otherwise, it can devolve into a Liz profile from Chapter 10.

Do all of your friends and family share their problems with you? What do you do with that information? Are you holding it? This can block your own systems because you're too focused on the issues of others. If, however, you hold space for elements of your friends' and family's lives, ask yourself if a prayer for them would suffice as support.

Questions for Reflection

Take some time with your journal to write down your impressions and feelings in response to these questions. Then, reflect on how your experience in your answers may have affected you emotionally or affected your development as an empath.

1. Write about any time that the land or a place influenced how you experienced it, or led you to entertain who else had been there before.

2. Write about your experiences of holding space or entering an environment in which the space is being held.

3. Have you entered environments where the space felt stagnant, stale, or unsafe? How does this compare to the energy of environments where the space is held with active intention?

4. Write about your experiences of holding energy. Have you caught yourself holding the energy of beliefs and patterns from your family? If so, how has holding this energy affected you?

5. Write about your experience of holding the energy of secrets, whether positive or negative.

6. Do you find that you hold on to the problems of others? If so, write about how you'll begin to disengage from this habit.

Chapter Fifteen

Authenticity and the Enlightened Ego

I am splayed open, organs spilling out; my center is gone, and my spine is exposed and glistening like bone china licked clean. I'm exhausted. I feel consumed. My eyes roll back in my head. Resigned, I implore, "Not this again. Just be quick about it."

A bit melodramatic, perhaps, but that's how I usually felt after visiting large, crowded places—from the time I was an adolescent to an adult, when I finally understood how to maintain energetic boundaries. Thankfully, I grew up in a time and place where letting your kid hang out in the car was permissible. My mom would give in and let me stay in our well-loved Oldsmobile and read a book while she and my sister shopped for our school clothes. As a college student, my roommates kindly did the supermarket shopping for me.

My childhood didn't reveal my empathic nature to me, apart from giving me the chance to learn early that nature was my go-to God and savior. It was there where I felt myself, my essence, in the symmetry of sparrows lining the wires strung from pole to pole along the dusty ranch road. Or in a cloud crossing the sky or the purr reverberating from my cat Sparkle's black-furred throat. But there were far too many times when I couldn't feel me within myself.

Oddly enough, my awareness of my own personal space came through my early reading consumption. My appetite for reading taught me to create a space where I could enter and be with what was on the page. Then, I suddenly wasn't preoccupied with what was happening around me. I gave myself over to books, as if each one was a lifeboat to transport me somewhere else.

I have been aware of the need to preserve my personal space since elementary school, when institutional lunchrooms and school assemblies presented me with a mixture of revulsion and boredom. I'd watch the kids around me for clues about how to survive—some kids fidgeted and jittered, poked and pestered, while others were still and obedient. Eventually, my eyes would focus on the floor. I would notice how the tiles came together with the pencil-thin grout crossing at every intersection. Essentially, turning inward became my default. I was a mini human turtle.

I was very much a "Liz" persona—the unaware empathic person from Chapter 10. The second I felt uncomfortable or challenged by the energy in a room, I started looking for my exit. I preferred to give up physical space rather than personal space, so I would leave abruptly. I suppose I "ghosted" people in the 1980s without realizing it—to my own detriment. I ghosted college classes, friends who invited me to family dinners, and my own family. All of this behavior impacted my ability to be present in my life. I was a one-foot-out-the-door kind of person.

I was a hard worker, and I was trustworthy. But admittedly, I was a bit flaky socially. I would like to think, however, that if someone needed me, I was there for them. After all, empathic people make excellent listeners, with the added bonus that we also sense what isn't being said. So the other person tends to feel witnessed and heard.

The problem with withdrawing as a defense strategy is that it creates multiple levels of internal stress. Not being present in your life has consequences. The classes I missed, as well as the friends and family members who were frustrated or perplexed by my social distancing, became yet more examples of my inability to express my experience in language. I felt deeply responsible for my behavior and that I needed to make up for what I missed, whether it was a lecture, dinner, or just being available.

Melting Point

When an ice cube transforms into liquid as it's exposed to temperatures above freezing, it crosses a melting point. Our Earth's last Ice Age lasted approximately eighty thousand years as it peaked and waned with climate cycles. I was very much like an ice cube for many years. My melting process was gradual as I exposed myself to teachings and readings that would help me make sense of my self-isolation. I explored topics that I would have considered fringe in the past and outside of my comfort level. My mental body had done a commendable job at keeping me functional in the world by doing what it thought was needed—mostly freezing out my emotional body as best it could with sarcastic and self-deprecating humor.

Once I registered that my primary relationship was with myself, I somewhat reluctantly accepted that I had to work with what I had—one last parting shot from my mental body. I became curious about my patterns and how to shift my defenses. As I gained energy and sensory awareness, as well as an awareness of the meaning of a unified self, I started to put together the language to guide me out of the nebulous landscapes that had kept me formless.

Many things became crystal clear to me that I had previously failed to note. I took notice when my abdomen felt bloated and uncomfortable, even though I hadn't eaten. I noticed when I held my breath, when my jaw tightened, or when my feet and legs got heavy and tired. I noticed if I had judgmental and self-effacing thoughts. This is how I learned to tune into my body and mind and let them inform me as to how well I was managing my own energy.

It's easy to believe that the environment is the problem or that your sensitivity is compromising your well-being, but that mindset continually reinforces that you don't feel safe anywhere—inside or outside of yourself. Anything that you pick up empathically will be assessed under the scrutiny and suspicion that it's a negative, only affirming that you don't feel safe. This is partly why different empathic people can register something in the environment and conclude different impressions. If you aren't centered, grounded, and in a neutral channel, your assessment is more or less processed by your lower self, and all the programming of fears and worries are on the "switchboard" interpreting the message.

Bodyguard Duties

Everyone has their own unique relationship with their physical body. It's how we experience the world and ourselves. It allows us a demarcation between what we perceive as outside of us and our inner world of thoughts, feelings, and sensations. But as empathic people, we also use the body as an intuitive channel, which makes our relationship with our bodies very special. I would even call that relationship sacred.

Energy awareness helps empathic people heighten their body awareness. It deepens the integrative nature between the two realms. The awareness of physical sensations, such as feeling bloated or muscle tightness, can be viewed in the context of how energy is flowing or constricted. There's a strong correlation between an empathic person's ability to stay grounded and centered and how well their lower three chakras are functioning. Safety, sex (create), and self-esteem are easy headers for these three energy chakras. There's much more to each one, but this is an easy alliteration to remember.

As I matured, I needed to upgrade my younger self's perception that my personal space was either a place I escaped to or it was nonexistent, leaving me feeling overexposed. Instead, I decided to see it as something that holds space for resilience and growth with the proper support provided by my focus and intention. I told the part of me that was easily martyred—giving away my energy—to get over it. I was done being an energetic meal, a feast, a victim. I was tired of the critical, constantly judging voice that kept me at a distance from others.

This declaration didn't come without effort and discipline. I had to train myself to be my own bodyguard and transform my knee-jerk withdrawal reaction into a conscious choice to stay present and discern a response.

I listened to the internal narrative I was using about my life experiences and my past. I questioned myself on my perceptions of safety and worth. I created a master list of traits and responsibilities that would instruct and guide me into respecting my body, energy, and mind—a flow chart and procedural manual of sorts, as in, "If this happens, do this until you feel centered. . . ." A confident and competent inner bodyguard helps you stay grounded, curious, and aware, even in a toxic environment—and if needed, directs you out of unhealthy environments without unnecessary drama.

So where do you find a bodyguard? Where did I find mine? In the very aspect of myself that formed my defenses in the first place—my ego, of course.

Your Bodyguard: Ergo Ego

As the self-appointed guardian of your esteem and worth, the ego is your biggest cheerleader or your biggest critic. Left unchecked, the ego will want to run the show, or rather, your life. The ego has been called the lower self, the shadow, and the subconscious mind. It operates from the base human consciousness of duality—black-and-white thinking. The ego is also the warehouse of your fears, and it helps you assign fear and doubt even to experiences and situations you have no prior experience with, such as death. It tries to prevent you from experiencing any future discomfort, and ironically, it does this by not letting you forget past pains and discomforts.

The ego is part of the physical realm, and its job is to keep your body safe by reviewing experiences and creating action plans based on memories and perceived dangers. It can stretch its reach into any arena in which you have personal interest. Imagine embarking on a spiritual journey of self-discovery and authenticity. How does your ego react to your desire to experience a neutral meditative mind or sublime mystical state of being? It may feel threatened at first. And once it gets a taste of the new skills that intuition and spiritual sensibilities can bring to your awareness, it's the same old routine: "Look at me—I'm special!" or "Who do you think you're fooling? You're incapable of being loved no matter how much you meditate."

The ego translates the conscience's principles into right and wrong. The conscience offers a prompt to self-reflect on behavior and attitudes to make room for adjustments. With the best intentions, the ego can take the bullhorn and throw in shame, guilt, worry, and despair to limit or modify your future behavior.

If you consider how much of your posture throughout your life has been spent navigating your sense of belonging and self-esteem, you can begin to understand the importance of self-awareness in gaining control of the inner dialogue while letting go of drama programming. We are all special and important, but not because our ego claims it so. Self-esteem propped up solely by the ego will eventually fall flat and feel unfulfilling. It's a constant hunger needing to be fed with more validations and praise until it becomes its own abusive structure with no conscience.

The ego and intuition, however, are parts of a whole, integrated self. We don't annihilate the ego in the pursuit of enlightenment. We create a collaboration that integrates our natural instincts and our intuition, along with our heart and mind intelligences. It's possible for the ego and intuition to have a harmonious relationship with each other, but it takes initiative. If my intuitive self doesn't have a clear understanding of the energetic impressions my body is registering from the environment, it isn't my ego's role to interpret it with a reaction (even though that's what it wants to do since it's part of the physical realm). When I became aware that the ego is only doing what it thinks is its job, I started to feel more compassion toward all of the aspects of my psyche.

The ego can be disciplined. It's essentially looking for a job, so give it one. For me, I've given it the role of my bodyguard, monitoring that I'm attending to self-care. You want to be able to be present in your environment, inner and outer, and not shut down or collapse on yourself. With my master list in hand, memos were issued to all parts of me to advise that my intention is to experience a centered, creative, and peaceful relationship with my environment and myself.

I have given my ego the message that self-care is important for my sense of safety and security. I emphasized that regulating my nervous system response *is* helping me feel safe and protected. So first and foremost, I want it to implement conscious breathing, centering, and grounding as a default response to stress. The knee-jerk reaction of retreating from environments was a chronic habit, created by a nervous system in a trauma pattern of *fight, flight, or freeze*. It was reinforced by what psychologists refer to as a negative bias that comes from registering and dwelling on negative events more than positive ones. Neuroscientific evidence has shown that there is greater neural processing in the brain in response to negative stimuli. This is why it can be challenging to reframe traumatic events from our past.

If you're someone who struggles with negative self-talk and still actively holds traumatic wounds, your relationship with your empathic reception will more than likely be complicated by these filters. Learning how to access your central and neutral channel gives perception a broader view and more room to be discovered. Remarkably your central channel is accessible regardless of how much perceived inner work you feel you need to attend to be whole. You are worthy to know your own greatness and stillness at your center.

It's vital to invest in self-awareness through conventional or alternative therapies with the goal of healing limiting perceptions and your sense of safety. This is how you become a resilient, integrated, intuitive person with empathic abilities. I suggest investigating trauma-focused therapy and somatic therapies that work with the nervous system's response, as well as energy anatomy programs that can help you understand your patterns and how they express themselves. As empaths, we use our body as a mediumship, so if your body doesn't feel safe, it will likely be difficult to be a centered and clear channel to receive intuitive input.

Keys to Resilience: Adaptive and Flexible

Current neuroscience indicates that our brain's health is tied to its plasticity—meaning how flexible and adaptive it is to new information and tasks. We're encouraged to be playful and challenge our thinking by playing word games, learning a new language, manipulating math and patterns, and even exercising physically. All of this is to avoid a decline in our mental faculties, such as our memory, as we age. A closed mind leans toward a rigid one.

Medical research is also emphasizing the importance of each individual's heart rate variability, or HRV, as an indication of how well the nervous system can reset itself after experiencing something unsettling. HRV measures the variation in time between your heart beats. The higher your HRV value, the better you are at self-regulating your nervous system out of a "flight, fight, or freeze" reaction. This monitoring of HRV has even entered into the realm of athletics to enhance training and recovery.

When you integrate bodyguard duties and understand that it's part of your authority to maintain self-care, you can develop a deep love and reverence for yourself. You truly haven't outsourced it to another, nor made any part of you feel subservient and separate. But your bodyguard is only as good as your discipline and your willingness to understand and tune into your own energy management.

Yes, you want to identify any compromising environments or situations, but not via the default of removing yourself from anywhere that's merely uncomfortable. When you do feel uncomfortable, be curious and understand the dynamics that have created that feeling. What can you learn about yourself?

Authenticity—An Inside Job

My dear friend Rose, who is now in her eighties and wise with tender strength, offered this compassionate thought on what it takes to become authentic: "You need to have a big ego to let go of the ego." That may sound counterintuitive, but there's much truth to it. I define authenticity as pure unimagining, which transcends the ego, as the ego relies on imagination to reign.

Authenticity is where self-empowerment dwells. Take a moment to consider what pure unimagining means. As we know, imagination is a powerful creative tool. We use it to envision and inspire new expressions and experiences for ourselves. It's part of a creative process. The famous Thoreau quote, "Life isn't about finding yourself; it's about creating yourself. So, live the life you imagined," is a rally cry to put into action what you've only allowed yourself to imagine in your mind.

However, I can assure you that I never imagined I would one day declare in public that I'm an empath. I don't recall thinking, *Oh, imagine if I could feel other people's emotional discomfort, displaced pain, and suffering*. No, it was more like, *Why am I feeling this stitch in my side? Is it my imagination, or does that person next to me in line feel cloaked in funkiness?*

Hiding your true nature creates tension and stress. Hiding from yourself creates isolation and loneliness. Acceptance, on the other hand, holds the energy of respect and creates space for you to honor yourself and who you are. The same is true when you offer acceptance to someone else. You give them space to be themselves—or to at least figure out who they are—by witnessing them with love and acceptance rather than projections and judgment.

Your authentic self already exists, just as all things in nature are authentic. A flower doesn't pretend to be something other than what it is. It isn't jealous of a tree. You don't need to create your authentic self; you create *from* your authentic self. This is why it's important to have a creative outlet in your life that nurtures expression of any kind.

Being authentic doesn't mean you've transcended living a physical reality or suddenly lack a personality with distinguishable likes and dislikes. Dishes will still need to be done, food prepared, and attention given to health and well-being. Relationships will need to be nurtured.

Being authentic doesn't mean you've evicted your ego, either. It means you find your strength, courage, tenderness, love, humor, and a multitude of states of being from an internal source that has no ambition or need to dominate or marginalize your environment or relationships. This lack of personal ambition isn't to be misinterpreted as passive—rather, an authentic person is fueled by passion, purpose, and presence.

Self-awareness creates the space for authenticity to emerge, and this happens when you come to know and identify all of the different aspects of your psyche—all of which help motivate or diminish your efforts to consciously create your life. So much of the journey of self-actualization is accepting yourself, your life's story, your creative powers, and all parts of yourself, including your ego, as part of the body's wisdom.

Questions for Reflection

Take some time with your journal to write down your impressions and feelings in response to these questions. Then, reflect on how your experience in your answers may have affected you emotionally or affected your development as an empath.

1. What do you need to reframe about your life that would assist your perception of wholeness? If I start to feel fearful about something in my environment, I go within and talk with this aspect of myself. It looks like journaling and role play all rolled up together—identifying when the memory or perception of my subconscious took hold, then getting myself to reframe it and work with me and my intentions for a centered and peaceful relationship with my environment.

2. In the chapter, I wrote: "As I matured, I needed to upgrade my younger self's perception that my personal space was either a place I escaped to or it was nonexistent, leaving me feeling overexposed. Instead, I decided to see it as something that holds space for resilience and growth with the proper support provided by my focus and attention." Reflect on these statements, and write about how they relate to you (if they do).

3. Create your own "master list" of traits and responsibilities that will instruct and guide you into respecting your body, energy, and mind: "If this happens, I will do ______ until I feel centered." Katie Byron, a well-known spiritual teacher, utilizes the question "Is it true?" as the premise of what she calls *The Work* of self-awareness. What part of your narrative may benefit from such scrutiny?

4. Write about how you experience your ego. Do you feel you have an awareness of it and relationship with it, or does it just currently exist without your conscious awareness?

5. Have you experienced authenticity? Or authentically expressing yourself? What does it feel like? What does pure unimagining produce in your sense of self? Does your self-image rely on your imagination?

Part Four

The FIELD of Experience and Awareness

The FIELD of Experience and Awareness

Nothing ever becomes real till it is experienced—
even a proverb is no proverb until your life has illustrated it.
—John Keats

My dad was fond of the quote "Life gives you the test first, then the lesson." My experiences brought me many tests early in life, and the lessons I learned, as well as the ones I continue to learn with hindsight, have been transformational. I'm certain I'm not alone in this regard. Tucked into any experience is an awareness waiting to be cultivated into a truth—one that expands the deeper your awareness grows until it finally reveals a truth that remains true no matter how you look at it. Stripped bare of any spin and victim narrative, it's a truth that can uphold an "I AM" statement at your center with no doubt.

Knowing knows no doubt is a phrase that encapsulates what your life's experiences provide to you. When you experience something firsthand, it's known to you, and your senses have recorded the experience. It isn't hearsay or imagination. What do you know about life from your own experiences? This treasure trove evolves your awareness and builds your perspective and empathy.

Our Family Tree

From the moment of our first breath and ability to sustain life, the clock starts on our unique story. It begins with a capital "I" and effectively ends at our death, when our first-person narrative concludes. Our story, however individualized and unique, is connected to other stories. Our backstory includes our parents' stories and how they were raised, the impact of their environment on their perception of the world as a safe place or not, and how this influenced their parenting. The family tree in story form makes up most of the content of our backstory, which is important for context up until the point it can dominate or overtake our front story—our own life.

Humanity has a universal theme that each of us examines in our life experience: the *sense of belonging*. Rejection, loneliness, unworthiness—who wants to admit to any of these feelings? These nicks and bruises that our senses register and record are like fascia that twist and fold from a physical impact. Even as children, we know how to go straight to the universal insecurity of not belonging to cause emotional pain and self-doubt to others. As many siblings do, mine teased me that I was adopted, and since I was the youngest, I couldn't really turn the tables on them. Where they might have thought they had the upper hand with the taunt, I secretly wished they were right. It would have explained why I felt at odds with my childhood environment.

The theme of belonging is embedded like a seed in each of us. What grows and reveals itself is dependent on where we place our focus and on what we fuel through our beliefs. But please trust that your life is continually presenting you with opportunities to embolden yourself to bloom, rooted in your own truth and essence.

Each of us has a story form of our life and a narrative that we create from our awareness. In fact, we have four versions if we consider that each of our subtle bodies can narrate from their point of view. What would our mental body's version read like? How might our emotional body wax poetic about the remains of our days? What spiritual insights would be revealed through our spiritual body?

We're dimensional beings, living in a dimensional timeline, and that creates a rich texture of experiences and awareness. In an average lifespan, we'll live alongside our grandparents, parents, and possibly our children and grandchildren. The intersection of the generations existing simultaneously on the physical plane allows for deeper perspective and compassion as we form our awareness and sense of belonging in the world. It's an opportunity to assess our contribution to future generations and examine family patterns that have been holding for several generations.

I'm delighted that the family unit is referred to as "nuclear" because it undeniably holds so much potential energy bound up by generational programming, limiting perception, and developmental trauma. Who wouldn't want access to that potential energy to propel and fuel movement in their life? That's the reward for attending to inner work—cultivating a space for peace, and creating a sense of freedom.

Experience, Awareness, and Sensibilities

When we clear what blocks our energy, we create propulsion in our life, which stimulates movement, inspiration, connections, creativity, and much more. It also reveals the depth of purity and innocence that naturally wants to be expressed from our heart's center. It clears the intuitive pathways for our inner wisdom, which can be easily masked by the "malware" of low self-esteem and chronic negative self-talk.

Depending on how we view the major events of our lives, our energy can be bound up, or it can be free and moving through our lower chakras and assisting to ground us into our lives. But even if our energies were to flow evenly and equally through our energy systems, we are all unique in what we experience and what's in our awareness. As empaths, we may share the same sensory mechanism for intuitive reception—our energetic sponge—but what I "pick up" in a space may not be what you would sense. Our reception and perception are customized to our sensibilities and field of awareness.

My awareness and your awareness of what's in a room may be different, and I'm not even talking about having an empathic awareness about the space. My spiritual sensibilities and empathic nature influence my awareness and perception by processing my experiences through the lens of cause and effect, intention and motivation, acceptance and growth, empathy and compassion—and ultimately, what is communicated, by whom or what, and why. Additionally, my unique life experiences have revealed my interests, passions, and a sense of purpose. This is the value of respecting that your life is designed by where you put your focus, and it will serve you if you allow it. So, what are your sensibilities, and how do they inform your sensitivities? What are you uniquely prone to pick up from your environment and relationships?

Life is a wondrous endeavor because there's a unique story in each of us that's emerging from a backstory into its own expression of wisdom and empowerment. My own path has resembled an internal labyrinth that traversed through the landscapes of belonging, longing, and balance and finally centered itself on mastering self-love. Each experience, trait, behavior, and belief will reveal your focus, your balance, and whether you feel comfortable with yourself. As I share stories of my life and how I brought intention to clear and heal, take note of your own.

Chapter Sixteen

To All My Relations

Our root chakra sits at the base of our spine. In Sanskrit, it's referred to as "muladhara," which combines the words for "root" and the "basis" of existence. I've also heard it simplified to the "root of all things." It's the first of seven chakras; therefore, it's the energetic base upon which we form our perceptions and sense of belonging in the physical world.

The root chakra is symbolized as a red four-petal lotus and a geometric square. I love symbolism, parallels, and paradoxes. The first color in a rainbow is also red, but it's seen as the top arch. All of the other rainbow colors create smaller arches beneath the red band. In our bioenergetic structure, the root chakra may be at the bottom of the stacked chakras, but it influences every chakra above it. And it partners with the seventh chakra, which represents our spiritual nature and universal unity. The saying "As above, so below" expresses how well these two chakras are talking with each other or if they're managing to talk with each other at all.

If you perceive that Life dealt you a bad hand, then it will certainly impact whether you accept and embody universal consciousness of oneness. This is how disparity starts within our energy systems. But the crown chakra can be a mentor to the root chakra, helping us grow up even with challenges.

The square and the number four are also symbolic for a base, a home, and the four cardinal directions of the physical plane. The issues of security and scarcity are themes of this chakra, as is the theme of abundance. As the "root" chakra, it will reveal exactly what you've rooted yourself into in order to feel safe, or conversely, why you don't have deep roots or a sense of belonging. All of these issues are largely formed through generational programming. As totally dependent infants, toddlers, and adolescents, we subconsciously root into our family's beliefs and their sense of safety about society and the world at large. Furthermore, our ability to feel rooted in our lives helps to stabilize our perceptions and sense of purpose.

Looking at Our Family's Past

The growing enthusiasm of genealogy as a hobby reveals a desire to understand who we are and where we come from. Often, it's motivated by the desire to understand our genetics and inheritance of traits. Sometimes, we do it out of a primal need to belong to something greater than just our immediate family—because once that umbilical cord is cut, baby, the world can be a lonely and disquieting place at times. This is particularly true if we never felt we truly belonged in our family in the first place. This has been one of my struggles in life, and my perception that I didn't fit in started very early.

But what would my blood tell me? Can we bleed into a cup and have the curandero or shaman read it like tea leaves? Would the dry droplets form a map of the cosmos, nebulas surrounded by faint lines of porcelain, traveling the edge of the cup like the universe bending back on itself? Would an arrow appear like a star in the northern sky to indicate the entrance of grace and destiny, colliding and announcing, "This is where you are, this is where you're from, and this is where you will return"? Would all points arrive at the same place—a place where my heart would quicken in recognition and, finally, a sense of belonging?

Rewrite Your Script

I moved out of the house when I was sixteen to live with another family when my family imploded from what is best described as a "failure to thrive." I was grateful to this neighborhood family but also extremely sensitive. I listened intently for any tension or tone that might imply I wasn't welcome. I interpreted any criticism or correction as evidence that they might want me to leave. It was its own form of mental and emotional exhaustion. Eventually, the mom, Sharon, took me aside to talk about my sensitivity. Her willingness to communicate with me, call me out, and give me assurance that I was okay was so unexpected.

This dynamic of communicating and clearing a field of confusion and conflict was new to me. Over the three years I lived with them, more or less full-time, it was Sharon's willingness and kindness in engaging me that pulled me out of my defensiveness and guardedness. She helped me to trust that life was okay—that I was okay. She never talked ill of my family, and she continually demonstrated how to be centered and present without projecting or judging them or me.

I have healed many of the fragmented parts that I carried with me from my childhood into adulthood. My relationships with my parents and siblings have mended and are nurturing today, for the most part. A large part of healing is hearing your own narrative and determining if it's waiting for someone else to do something to make your life presumably better: "If only this hadn't happened or that person would just apologize . . ."

Journaling is a great tool for self-reflection. It can hold space for you as you communicate with the different parts of yourself to discover what you might be holding on to. My own journaling revealed time and again how I longed to feel connected to a family tree that resonated with openness and joy.

I once bought a journal at the mineral springs Oja Caliente, north of Sante Fe, New Mexico. I held it, weighing it in my hands. Would it be filled with heavy thoughts, or would it be light and playful? It seemed like destiny: me, the aura of introspection and tranquility rising from the various healing mineral pools, and an irresistible soft, baby-blue, leather-bound journal that was embossed with the red-lettered prompt "Rewrite your script." And it was produced by none other than a company smartly named "the universe knows, inc."

This journal came branded with purpose: to rewrite my script. Blank pages followed that instruction. The potential not yet entangled and engaged, thoughts not written, realities not created, observations not noted, poems not scratched out and rewritten over and over like permutations to open a lock—all of this had yet to grace the pages. So many thoughts crowded my mind about my life, my immediate ancestors, and my family, knowing that my rewriting would also touch them. I would love to give them improved roles in their own lives, and in doing so, I would benefit from their new sense of worth.

When my son Michael was a junior in high school, he interviewed me for a psychology project about my views on parenting. I found myself emphasizing that of all the hopes I had for each of my children, my biggest was that they knew without a doubt that they were wanted and loved. I sense neither of my parents had that experience as children. They were both the youngest in their families and a somewhat surprise later pregnancy for their parents. Their older siblings were out of the house by the time they reached the age of ten. Therefore, they were both more or less raised like only children. They lived in western Pennsylvania and in an era that was still recovering from the Great Depression and the impact of World War II. These were undoubtedly stressful times for all families, which impacted my parents' home environments and their sense of scarcity and security.

Neither of them felt as though they fit into their families, which I didn't realize until I was an adult and had developed some empathy and perspective on their lives. I can understand them better now as an adult examining my own sense of familial alienation.

It's more common to think of generational programming as transferring addictions and abuse, but perceptions are also passed along. Many sensitive people hold on to feelings that they don't fit in and that conformity is the only way to survive or feel a semblance of acceptance. "If you could only know the depth of my soul" is a feeling that I rubbed against as I continually interacted with people in what felt like incredibly shallow depths of connection.

I think many of us have or have had this feeling that there's so much more to us than what's expressed or experienced in our relationships. This is the truth of our energetic, intuitive, sensitive, and authentic self at our center, which wants to emerge and integrate more fully with our life. We sense it, as probably others in our own family have felt the same way, and we either explore it or ignore it.

Finding My Place within a Do-Over

My father was the dreamer, and my mom followed as best she could. She moved west with my father from Pennsylvania to Colorado as a young bride, and she set to work as a teacher, even returning to work right after having each baby. She received her master's in education, and she was an honored and respected teacher in the county. My father worked multiple jobs, searching for a break that would give him a leg-up in the sales or marketing world. He was creative, funny, and undeniably moody.

I was thirteen when my parents divorced. Pursuing the American dream took a serious toll on my parents' ability to be present, to parent, or to attend to their own marriage. They weren't abusive, drunks, or any other version of derelict people. They were simply absent, working a multitude of jobs or commuting hours every day. By the time they came home, none of us kids wanted to bring them more stress, which was just another form of stress we had to manage for ourselves. Therefore, my siblings and I were left to conduct our own land-locked version of *The Lord of the Flies*, conveniently outside the watchful eye of a community or nearby neighbors. We were true latchkey kids.

After the divorce, I waited about three months before asking my mom for my dad's phone number. Apparently, he was uncertain as to what his role was to be in our lives. That's how little communication there was. I called, and we became regular movie and hiking buddies, as well as occasional pen pals when he moved to California and later to Alaska. I enjoyed spending time with him, though I learned to make exceptions for his moods, which came suddenly from any perceived slight or difficult memory.

I waited until I completed my ordination in spiritual counseling and set up my business in Houston before sharing this news with him. Dad was not necessarily an atheist, but he definitely had strong feelings about organized religion or belief systems that placed any authority in an all-knowing, disembodied realm. He always felt as though we were kindred spirits who found perfection in the great outdoors and needed nothing more. You can't go wrong in nature—no persecution, no judgment, just the wild untamed land to elevate or diminish your existence while still offering you freedom.

"Why don't you play the lottery, then?" he said, trying to hide his irritation when I finally made the phone call. I closed my eyes and breathed deeply, careful not to make an audible sigh. I had known this was going to be a difficult conversation. He'd never trusted anything or anyone in his life. The self-reliant man who gave to charities didn't tolerate any form of charity extended back to himself. It was the "then" that held his projections and irritation. *Where's the proof?* in other words.

In his view, I had obviously wandered from the safety of the wilderness and was being scammed by people selling bullshit from the self-help aisle. Upon hearing my news, I felt him lump me in one fell swoop with every carnival sideshow attraction that solicits séances or crystal ball readings. Worse, in his view, I had the audacity to put myself out into the world as a mediator or counselor, and for what—a New Age cult or mythology? If I indeed had the ear of God or the supernatural, why didn't I just go ahead and play the lottery and win big?

I reminded myself to breathe and extend an easy tone in my voice. "Well, Dad, I'm not really concerned with winning the lottery. Yes, I'd welcome the windfall of good fortune, but my services are more centered on cultivating balance and peace—in helping people find their voice, know their worth, and connect to consciously creating their life. I'm not a psychic; I'm an empath."

"Is this something you picked up in Norway? Did you come in contact with a missionary?" he asked, knowing how ludicrous he sounded. It was his schtick and backhanded humor. I suddenly imagined my dad placing me on an iceberg floating in the North Sea until I reached some rocky island inhabited by quarantined missionaries who had taken a wrong turn and, rather than ending up in Africa, had to settle on reforming the Norse gods.

I knew revealing my paranormal sensitivities wouldn't be easy for him to understand or accept. I listened with compassion because I knew he hadn't always been stuck in fear. As part of a document prepared years earlier by a hospital where my dad was having a treatment for his ankle that had been screwed together from his polio days, he was made to fill out "Five Wishes," a living will in case of any unforeseen medical crisis. His final wish is aptly stated: "My wish for what I want my loved ones to know. If anyone asks how I want to be remembered, please say the following about me: 'He was one of the men who didn't fit in.'" Even in this intimate declaration, he wrote in the third person about himself.

I would have loved to have had a functional and healthy childhood and what it would have afforded me on my own journey—less doubt and stress, certainly, as well as more of a sense of security and less survival-skill default. But my strongest desire is that my dad could sense the love that reached out to him and accept it willingly with a sense of worth. My desire is that he could have a do-over and that his parents could have a do-over. I'd love for that offer to then extend as far back as needed until we came upon two people who respected each other with deep abiding love, no matter the time, the place, or the conditions and responsibilities. And that each child born to them would be conceived with love, want, and hope and raised with laughter, joy, and wonder.

My hope is that they would have balanced praise and guidance with discipline and awareness. From such a foundation, each generation would express and expand this love and respect willingly and outwardly until the end of time—or at least until I was born.

Each generation is more or less the do-over I envisioned. We get the opportunity with fresh experiences to either recreate the past or release energy that has been bound in limited beliefs and create new realities and experiences.

Progressing Beyond Limited Perceptions

My father passed suddenly two weeks after his eighty-third birthday. Most of my adult life, I was troubled by the sense that I hadn't properly communicated with him how important he was to me and how I saw the world through music and nature due to his influence—something I am able to share with my own children. But I found letter after letter from me over the last forty years that Dad had saved. I was relieved to see that I had, to the best of my ability, expressed my love and admiration to him. But what he was able to hear, I don't know.

We can't control what another person hears, sees, or perceives. We can sense when there has been miscommunication or misperception and then try to express ourselves somewhat differently. But that takes willingness, dedication, and caring enough to readdress what lies between two people as an obstacle to real connection and intimacy.

I have come to have compassion for my parents and my ancestors. For too long, I judged them, conveniently forgetting that their life experiences were completely their own with their own parameters and frames of reference for what they were learning. Humanity evolves with each new generation tackling the social issues of the time, expanding when awareness is integrated as a common truth. My mom experienced what it was like to have a career in an era when many women stayed at home. My dad experienced the frustration of wanting to be a successful creative type in a world that didn't offer those opportunities if you wanted to have a family.

It's unfair to judge past and future generations. Yet this is what had me stuck for many years, wondering how my parents, who obviously craved to be loved and to belong, could not crack this commitment to be kind and gentle to themselves and each other. I suspect both of my parents are/were empathic, sensitive to their environment, and coped by shutting down these channels. Ironically, these sensitivities may have helped them feel more connected with a sense of belonging to at least themselves. Both were compassionate and generous, giving willingly of themselves to others, just not enough to themselves.

Honoring the Continuum of Humanity

Within Native American communities, there's a common invocation: "to all my relations." It's a reminder and awareness that as individuals, we're defined and connected to the world through our relationships in all directions. Your relationship with your ancestors, yourself, the Earth, and the Creator to the east, west, north, and south holds an aspect of your overall understanding of who you are in relation to everything, infused with the wisdom from each relation.

Imagine now the unbalanced posture of someone who's always looking back at past generations, wishing they could have been more aware and more conscious. Or looking forward to future generations, placing expectations and hope for salvation upon them. Yes, we look back to learn, and we look forward with hope and vision. But we must be willing to be present in the now, accept where we are, and create the change we want to experience. If the field of epigenetics has revealed anything to us, it's that stress and trauma can be passed on through our genes. Perhaps the HSP's gene variant evolved from our collective trauma.

Each and every one of us was handed a script that will influence us. It's in our biology, genes, attitudes, and biases. How will you create your own script from the pages you were born holding?

In 2005 at Brigid's Place in Houston, I taught a workshop examining how generational programming is a spiritual opportunity. A bias or prejudice from one generation is met by the next generation, and while it may feel tense at times with no common ground, the friction encourages dialogue and a willingness to grow together.

One participant shared a touching example of this dynamic in her family. Her father, she explained, was a bigot and racist most of her young life. She and her sister had partners who were Hispanic and African American, which was a huge struggle for him. Once grandchildren came into the world from these relationships, however, her father changed and had great love and acceptance for the mixed-raced children. When he passed away, their family found the grandchildren's photos were the only personal items in his wallet. This is the responsibility of one generation to the next: to clean up limiting patterns and do no intentional harm.

My own father, though never wanting to directly discuss what my empathic nature and intuitive guidance was all about, still allowed me to offer some energy work to him one day when we were sitting beside each other on a sofa. His knee was bothering him, so I placed my hand on it, moving energy around the joint as he watched the Broncos football game. He took note of the intense heat generated during the exchange and that the next day he walked more easily. Once he returned to Alaska, where he had lived on and off for the last twenty years, I started to receive books on the healing properties of plants and medicinal uses of herbs. In his own way, he was showing me that he was willing to accept my nature through our mutual interest in the land, and that's how he chose to interpret and respect it. I didn't need him to understand it as much as accept that this was how I experienced myself.

The more each generation takes responsibility for clearing the programming that inhibits, limits, and excludes, the more future generations will benefit and move forward in their lives, creatively exploring the world and their potential. Adversity can be a motivator, but it can also bind up our energy if we languish too long, focusing merely on our misfortune.

I accept that my path, in part, was about gaining a larger perspective and cultivating an enduring respect for all of the ancestors who got us this far in the evolution of humanity. We would not be here without them. They never needed my forgiveness; I only needed to mature and to forgive myself and my past tendency to look back and lay blame with the loaded "if only."

Questions for Reflection

Take some time with your journal to write down your impressions and feelings in response to these questions. Then, reflect on how your experience in your answers may have affected you emotionally or affected your development as an empath.

1. What do you know about your heritage? Write about how this knowledge informs your identity and sense of belonging.

2. Write about your relationship with your parents and how you've been affected by it. Have you developed more compassion toward them as you've grown older? Do you sense if other members of your family are also empathic?

3. What generational programming do you believe has been carried within your family, whether you label it as positive or negative?

4. How does your life reflect the themes of security, scarcity, and abundance?

5. If you've felt as though you haven't fit in, either with your family or your community, write about that feeling. Do you believe this feeling is at least in part due to your empathic abilities and your sense of deeper truths? How has it affected your journey as an empath?

6. Begin to "rewrite your script," writing your family history as you wish it had been. What would be different in your "do-over" for both you and those you love? What do you wish to do differently now in order to create your own script for your life?

Chapter Seventeen

Learning Balance

I've been asked on numerous occasions by curious and thoughtful people about how to raise and support sensitive children. This question is twofold: How have I raised my own somewhat sensitive and intuitive children, and having been a sensitive child, how would I suggest raising an empathic child?

To be honest, I was busy figuring out my own empathic sensitivities when my children were young. I didn't even know the word "empath" until I was in my late twenties, let alone understand how it related specifically to me and my personal reality. I didn't teach my children meditation or prayer in a traditional sense, but they had exposure to churches and sweat lodges. They weren't immersed in any particular tradition but taught to regard ceremony as something intentional to be respected. We did take them outside to explore nature, and we spent a lot of time reading aloud and discussing topics of interest.

My hope is that each of our children experienced a home environment that supported them and their interests—whether music, arts, sports, reading, or something else. I also tried to be a sounding board rather than an outright authority. Our children were encouraged to talk and share, so much so that all of them were comfortable talking to adults from an early age. The talking and sharing aspect of my parenting style is directly related to my own sense of what helps a sensitive child understand the emotional atmosphere of the environment.

Having children with speech difficulties taught me the importance of self-advocacy, which is a skill everyone needs to develop. Knowing how to ask for help isn't always easy even if you have the words. If you can openly name what you're experiencing, you're less likely to push it out in a displaced way and clutter the space we all share. If an adult can honestly say, "I'm feeling a bit sad because . . ." or "This situation made me upset because . . ." and give a brief discussion of the dynamic that caused the reaction, it models acceptance and taking responsibility for the child. Even stating, "I'm going to go to the local coffee shop to journal" or "I'm going for a walk to clear my head" communicates to a child how to engage strategies for inner balance.

Drop the Rope

My children and husband understand that I feel and process deeply. On the one hand, I can usually assess what's motivating someone's behavior—that they're lonely, need validation, or endless other derivatives of "need" that fuel certain subconscious behaviors. This awareness allows room for compassion, understanding, and empathy, which helps with patience and support.

On the other hand, I'm also a sensitive person with feelings, and it can be challenging to excuse and tolerate certain behaviors by friends, family, and others who seemingly have no awareness or desire to examine how they impact the environment, energetically or physically. Can you relate? I suspect you can.

I've been one of those parents who has required wrongs to be righted and who talked about deeper implications. This is true to such a degree that my kids have teased that to save my breath, I could just say, "Insert lecture number three or six," and they would get the message. I have a lot of patience until I don't, and I think each of them has seen me reach a point of intolerance when I create new boundaries in a relationship that's out of balance.

For example, my children picked up a phrase I overused when they bickered in the back seat of our minivan: "Drop the rope!" The reference was to the rope in a tug of war as they tried to win the honor of "being right" about something silly (but very meaningful to them in that moment). If each party was willing to drop the rope, peace had a chance. If one of the parties still held on to the rope, it became a burden to that person as they sulked and figuratively carried it around with them. If there was a follow-up comment starting with "but," the rope hadn't been dropped. "But that's not fair . . . but she said . . . but, but, but . . ."

Peace is wise, and it senses if you've truly dropped the rope. Peace needs the dust to settle and takes notice of what's in the hearts and minds of each party. Peace, compassion, and forgiveness work to loosen the grip, expand righteousness out of indignation, and sweeten bitterness. Our kids were quick studies, eager to point out when I didn't heed my own lectures. In difficult patches between Knut and I, as young parents who had our moments of heated positions, we would hear our youngest, Grace, say rather nonchalantly, "Drop the rope, Mama. Drop the rope, Papa."

Walking a Tightrope

My son Finn introduced me to the world of slacklining years ago when he was a freshman at university. He even has a few friends who are professional competitive slackliners, daring great heights across beautiful natural crevices the world over. Imagine securing a line between canyon walls or over jutting rock points and stepping off the edge onto an inch-wide webbing, even throwing in some yoga moves. It's impressive and exhilarating to witness this inner and outer balance, strength, focus, and flair in suspended motion above the ground.

Functional empaths, on occasion, traverse another kind of personal tightrope with their friends, family, and colleagues. It's the fine line that's laid down in a room filled with all the normal energetic pathways of interpersonal relationships, plus whatever unexpressed emotions and mindless projections may be present. The space can be experienced like a minefield, or rather a "mind-field." Each projected thought orbits the room with a gravity of its own narrative.

I admit it's harder to walk the tightrope and stay neutral when I encounter projected thoughts and feelings that are directed at me. Just because I'm aware that someone has projected in my direction, it doesn't mean *they* are aware of it. You have no doubt had the experience of trying to have a constructive conversation with someone who's unaware of their own thoughts or motivations. It goes nowhere fast, and it complicates your relationship even faster, as it sets the scene for unfolding drama. Sometimes, it's actually an opportunity to reflect on your own behavior and understand if you're being honest with yourself about your true feelings and intentions. It may also be an invitation to transform the relationship into something else.

It takes courage to voice your feelings and discipline to understand what part of you is expressing those feelings. Is it from a wounded aspect playing the victim, or is it from a genuine desire to clear and heal a limiting perception that stands in the way of growth and deeper connection? One posture holds the rope, while the other one is free. Do you need to be right, or are you looking for a deeper connection?

Not everyone is ready to be accountable for their thoughts and actions. Many don't even listen to their own thoughts, for they're on a loop so constant that it becomes white noise that's never examined. But every behavior needs a belief to support it, and behavior doesn't change without some awareness.

Because of our ability to sense and empathize with others, empathic and empathetic people may have more insight into another person's inner world than that person does. This creates some interesting pathways for our relationships. In some instances, it may appear easier to rationalize that someone behaves as they do because of their backstory and simply tolerate it, even if the behavior is imbalanced and draining. Have you experienced relationships like this?

Of course, you aren't responsible for someone else's degree of self-awareness, but consider if your willingness to tolerate certain behavior may prevent your friend from understanding how it affects the relationship. Or conversely, have you ever experienced a relationship ending or changing because of your own imbalanced behavior? Did the awareness that the relationship was changing prompt you to consider what you might need to change to restore it to a mutually beneficial relationship?

I have come to understand that my body's wisdom and intelligence will lead me toward either confrontation or nonengagement. It comes back to the dynamics of observing and witnessing. When you witness someone bully someone else, it generally prompts a response—a stomach wrenching, or wincing as if the sharp words have literally stung.

Your body is responding to the energy in a way that's made it personal, and you feel it. When I experience someone's voice being suppressed and power being abused, I feel my body respond, and if I don't speak up or take some kind of action, I'm left feeling a deeply reverent regret.

Courage and Discernment

One of the intuitive exchanges I had early in my spiritual journey while in meditation stated that a "master has no regret, for everything experienced serves the soul." In other words, accept your backstory. Make peace with it, and drop the rope. Integrate it in a healthy way with some perspective of what it has helped you understand about human nature. Even the feeling of regret will serve you to examine what was possibly missing in a situation.

Nevertheless, the feeling of regret at not using my voice in moments where someone is actively suppressing or interfering with another's, particularly if it involves a child or someone unable to communicate clearly for themselves, comes from some place deep within me—a soulful place. In those moments, with hindsight, I understood that fear got the better of me by way of an old childhood defense that equated being quiet with being "good." That defense overrode my ability to be present with courage and speak up for something I'm passionate about: the sacredness of language.

Many years ago, I found myself approaching a family member I heard mimic one of my children more than once. This child had an abundance of personality and charm. Yet he was innocent, exploring the world and becoming himself. This family member repeated what he said in a high-pitched cartoonish tone with the irritation bleeding through their voice. My son looked at them, puzzled, clearly not understanding the teasing. They would counter their abrasiveness with a hearty laugh afterward, the subtlety of passive-aggressiveness undercutting the exchange. But it wasn't funny; it was underhanded and fueled by feelings that were neither playful nor kind.

I'd been aware of these strained interactions during other visits. The obvious tension this person projected out toward him and toward me was confusing, as I still felt like an outsider in the country and the family. I had no manual or culture course when I arrived in Norway.

On the occasion when the family member mocked my son, I realized I'd been holding my breath. My balance slipping and my maternal instinct fueling me to shield my son, I stepped off my neutral stance and into a free fall as I found myself, in an almost out-of-body experience, asking out loud for the behavior to stop. The family member was shocked that I could think such a thing about them. And I was so mystified by my own courage that surfaced so boldly that the aftermath created more tension between us for many years. Each of us definitely held on to the rope rather than clearing the air.

I regretted that as well, but it taught me that if you plan to vocally call someone on their behavior when that person has no idea that you can pick up what they're feeling, you need to consider your motivation for bringing it forward, as well as your approach. As more people identify with being empathic and share their challenges and struggles with relationships due to their sensitive nature, I'm struck by some of the backlash that has surfaced. I have seen it in online comments and rebuttal pieces that accuse empaths of the purported hypocritical behavior of overstepping their own boundaries to manage another person's feelings. Have you ever found yourself forcing someone to examine their thoughts and feelings that you picked up energetically and then feeling vindicated that the problem lies with them (or some version of that)?

So why do I choose to walk the tightrope rather than just give voice to the feelings and thoughts I sense? Because the tightrope requires attention, focus, and compassion. We aren't at a stage in human evolution where everyone is aware that thoughts are energy and that energy is information that can be directed. Nor are we even at a stage where people are aware of what motivates their thoughts and actions.

Unfortunately, we are a civilization at varying degrees of awareness. Therefore, if you present an unsolicited message to someone who's unaware of their displaced thoughts, it isn't usually well received. They feel defensive, and the opportunity to discuss the issue dissolves.

The ideal healing modality is one in which each person processes their thoughts and feelings against their beliefs and perceptions and then takes responsibility for their own toxic and destructive behavior. An active approach to self-awareness promotes growth and balance. A person experiencing an internal epiphany shifts behavior and perception more effectively than an outside source putting demands in place. But the ideal is rare.

On the tightrope, you may find that it leads you to a person or situation where it's in the best interest of balance, healing, and clearing to prompt a conversation about the displaced emotions that fuel the disruptive behavior. But this takes discernment and a fair amount of courage, particularly if it's a relationship you want to save rather than end, like a marriage. Only you can determine if it's best to speak up or hold your tongue.

Balancing Act: Trust and Privacy

If you asked my husband what my being an empath means to him, he'd probably say it means I know what he's feeling before he does. This is true to some degree, but it's also because we've been married for nearly three decades. Our energies are entwined and working out lessons with each other—mainly intimacy, trust, and love. But it's also true that being empathic in a relationship can be challenging when one person is more in tune with the emotional environment.

We've had a lot to learn about ourselves and each other, and this is ongoing. Empathically, I can sense when he's wrestling with thoughts—not necessarily what the thoughts are, but that there is uncertainty. I've had to learn to let him have his privacy and not assume that it means something negative about our relationship. Being intuitive doesn't mean I get a free pass from taking responsibility for my own work about what throws me off balance, like jealousy and self-worth.

Being overly sensitive to the state of your relationships can create a neediness that's often felt by the other person. Is it your own emotional sensitivity infiltrating your ability to assess what you pick up empathically? Cultivating inner balance is a process of honest introspection about what's out of balance for you personally. If you have a tendency to be overly sensitive, it may be helpful to examine whether you're holding fear of abandonment and worthiness issues.

Ropes or cords are energetic pathways connecting two people. How the energy flows creates patterns within a person's psyche, and these patterns, which are generally created in childhood, influence how we connect with others. Codependency and attachment disorders are energetic patterns that can be examined and healed. Again, it begins with self-awareness and taking action to align with your center authority and empowerment.

Your empathic nature as a child may have created tendencies to feel responsible for someone else's behavior. And as a child, when you're naturally dependent on your environment to provide safety and security, you may have become hypervigilant. Examining your sense of safety and sense of belonging to yourself are very important in understanding your own patterns in relationships and, therefore, the balance and health of your connections.

Who can send you spiraling if their mood is off? Who do you need constant reassurance from that your relationship is okay? Do you need to be needed? These are hints that inner work might be beneficial to examine how you perceive yourself and manage your energy. This book is not to diagnose personalities and relationship disorders, but I merely want you to recognize that emotional oversensitivity reveals patterns that may cause chronic imbalances in your self-perception.

Connections are important, and just as a rope can help support and anchor a boat to a mooring in turbulent waters, a solid relationship filled with love, respect, and balance can be a reflection of the inner work and intentionality you've created. Learning the spiritual art form of inner balance will also grant you a slackliner's joy: inner and outer balance, strength, focus, and flair in suspended motion while still on the ground.

Questions for Reflection

Take some time with your journal to write down your impressions and feelings in response to these questions. Then, reflect on how your experience in your answers may have affected you emotionally or affected your development as an empath.

1. Reflect on times in your life when you've found it difficult to drop the rope. What was the consequence of holding on to it?

2. Write about times when you've dropped the rope, examining how doing so has affected the situation or relationship.

3. As an empath, when have you walked the tightrope, picking up on someone's displaced emotions and feeling that you couldn't or shouldn't mention it to them?

4. I presented how witnessing suppression of someone's voice activates a deep sense of activism within me. What draws out the activist in you? Write about a time when you wish you'd spoken up about someone's behavior but didn't. What caused you to hold back?

5. Write about a time when you spoke up about someone's behavior but wish you hadn't. What was the outcome of speaking up, and what do you think would have been different had you left it unspoken?

Chapter Eighteen

Self-Love Master Class

On the arc of becoming an empath, there will be moments that feel so profound it's as if the ground beneath you and the sky above you have shifted. It's a feeling of more expansion while feeling more connected to everything, but most importantly to your own life. The heroism of ordinary life is that we learn about ourselves and our nature through our life circumstances. Therefore, I'd like to share two such stories from my life in the hopes that you'll recognize some of your own such experiences.

A nodule appeared on the right side of my neck in 1998, about a year after recognizing I was still holding on to fears and perceptions from my childhood. At first, I thought it was just a swollen gland. When it became more pronounced, I brought it to the attention of my doctor, who sent me to an ENT specialist. The previous year, my doctor had tested me for lupus, taking a punch skin biopsy from my cheek, with inconclusive results. I had inflammation markers but in a borderline region. She said to wait and see how I felt.

Over a three-year period, my symptoms intermittently eased and intensified. My life was a series of taking care of children, restoring an old house, assimilating into a foreign culture, and more and more, dealing with vague and phantomlike pains in my body, still not aware that my own empathic sponge mechanism was overwhelmed and nearly out of order.

I went alone to my appointment at the ENT because we lived near the central hospital. The waiting room was filled with children's toys that were dated and sad looking. The institutional two-toned green walls didn't help the atmosphere.

I don't remember the doctor's name, but I remember his horrible bedside manner. I presented myself as an American married to a Norwegian. He was comfortable in English, so I didn't reveal that I was functional in Norwegian, but not fluent. I wanted to keep it in English so that I would be certain to understand everything.

He examined me with an attitude that I was a nuisance. He felt my nodule and took a history about how long it had been there. He was confident that it was just a cyst, but they would conduct a biopsy to make sure. Out came a horrifically long needle, and I was told to lie down on my side and remain still. I followed his orders and remained as calm as I could as I allowed the needle to aspirate the nodule.

Then, the arrogant tone of his voice suddenly changed, as did his language. He switched instantly to Norwegian to address his attending nurse. "This is not a cyst; this is a tumor." I understood what he said but stayed still and quiet. In a softer and more patient tone, he told me how long it would take for the lab results, when we'd have another appointment to discuss them. I walked home a bit numb, trying not to let my mind go into overdrive with worst-case scenarios.

When I returned to the doctor two weeks later, the results revealed a benign tumor composed of lymph and salivary gland cells. It was a great relief, apart from the fact that the mass had grown in the two weeks and was beginning to interfere with opening my jaw widely. The doctor presented his concern about operating, as the growth was located in a part of the neck where the nerves to the face run through. If there were any errors in removing the mass, I might experience paralysis on that side of my face. I went home not knowing what to do.

I began to pray—not in the imploring and apologetic way of a lapsed churchgoer wanting forgiveness or a deal. Instead, I found myself clearing a space in my mind, crawled into it, and allowed stillness to hold me. It was the same feeling I had when I would sit in the forest near my childhood home in Colorado. It was a new but familiar feeling, and it was magnetic.

One night, I had a dream that was very vivid and clear: I was to tell one of the members of my writers' group about my tumor. Her name was Sue, and as I came to find out, she was an energy healer. I had no understanding of what that was, but I was lost. This was the first time I had a feeling of being connected to something wise and knowing since my childhood refuge in the nearby forests that offered me sanctuary.

This was also a moment when my physical body was the only messenger left to get my attention, to bring me back to myself and engage with my true nature. My external life of kids, family, and finances had left little room for my own sense of worth beyond a manager and an administrator.

The tumor, the dream, and Sue's deft healing skills awakened me to understanding the difference between being a spectator and a creator of my life. It was one of those significant events that present us with the opportunity to shift how we perceive life and form a new philosophy on the meaning of our life—a mini personal paradigm shift.

I began to visit Sue weekly. I lay passively on her massage table as waves of energy coursed through my body. I felt hot, cold, twitches, pressure, and lightness. And I saw colors. It was all too unbelievable. Yet I craved it, and my body responded to it as though it had found an endless reservoir to quench a thirst I'd held at bay for a long time. Within the first month, my tumor shrank 75 percent.

When I returned to the specialist, he marveled at how the tumor had shrunk and said it was no longer necessary to make the difficult decision about surgery. I attempted to tell him I was seeing someone who did energy work using the meridians of the energy body, but then, I registered his face, posture, and scoffing disbelief. I stopped talking. It wasn't necessary. This was my journey and transformation. I didn't need his validation because I already had my body of proof. I was reconnected to my body, and I was ready to attend to my relationship with myself and the journey it would take me on.

Switching Off Automatic Pilot

The tumor woke me up, and my body's response to energy work brought me back to the helm of my life. My life changed, and my healing journey began when two things happened: I began to listen to myself without judgment, and I was able to hear myself with compassion. I had to look within and dismantle my emotional and mental defenses. I had to recognize the need to examine my "backstory" and the bleak narrative I had attached to my childhood, which was stunting my growth and blocking my forward path.

Most of my life, I experienced truly profound interactions from the nonphysical realm reaching in to get my attention. But I did what most ignorant people do—marveled at the interactions and considered them one-off wonders. On the timeline of my linear life, I was in survival mode from about the age of eleven until probably twenty-three, and that was followed by coping mode up until I was thirty. Yes, it took me some time to seriously untangle my inner resistance.

Part of the spiritual challenge that everyone must master is how to embody the theory of self-love. I had certainly mastered how to be present and giving for everyone else. That was my coping mode—if I was needed, I was relevant. On the arc of an empath, I had shifted from a Liz to a Beth, and that is mainly due to my children opening me up to the flow of unconditional love that poured from me without effort.

When we arrived as a family in Houston in 2000, after ten years in Norway, I stated my intentions clearly to Knut that I wanted to understand the energetic component of the human body. After experiencing how this therapy remarkably reduced my neck tumor to the point of no longer being a medical concern, he was supportive of my efforts to find my way into this field and receive the support he recognized he couldn't give me.

Dancing with Myself

One of the instrumental teachers I had early in my spiritual path was Janet Light, founder of Inward Resources Inc. in Houston. Janet had created an intensive spiritual course called Conscious Living Training. Before joining the program, I relied mostly on reading books about the human energy fields and attending a weekend workshop. The first energy awareness books I purchased while living in Norway were by Barbara Brennan and Rosalyn Bruyere. Next came Carolyn Myss and Donna Eden books. I knew I needed a guide in the physical world, and I was blessed to find Janet's school.

The program was challenging and required honest inquiry and accountability. It was designed to support us in gaining self-awareness and an expanded understanding of consciousness and its energetic representation. At the start of Conscious Living Training, I lacked confidence and struggled with not wanting to fail—or worse, presuming I was special.

The program gave each of us plenty of opportunities to be humbled while discovering and developing our higher sensory receptors. The coursework provided the necessary understanding to apply the teachings for individual use or to offer services to others. At the end, each student had the choice to apply for ordination from the Association for the Integration of the Whole Person, a national association.

My decision to study the nature of consciousness was motivated by a desire to become more self-aware and to integrate the parts of myself that were fragmented from childhood memories, as well as from being closed off to my empathic nature. The courage to look in the mirror and call out self-limiting beliefs and behaviors while staying compassionate became the model and discipline I needed.

Part of my spiritual journey incorporated Native American teachings, mainly because Janet was aligned to the "Red Road" from her Lakota heritage and her own instruction as a healer and counselor. As students of the three-year Conscious Living Training, we were introduced to many teachings and modalities that originated from Native American traditions: sweat lodges, medicine wheel, scrying, animal totems, and pipe ceremonies, in addition to other universal human energy anatomy teachings she had mastered and crafted into her own teachings.

Many of my mystical interactions in the program came in the form of concepts and images that were Native American. Perhaps this is because Janet's own path was aligned to the "Red Road" or because I have some distant Native American heritage or a natural affinity to nature. I would experience something in meditation—a vision or a viewing—and I would be confused and uncertain about its significance. I didn't know what the symbolism referred to or how to assign it meaning to my life specifically. Time and again, I approached Janet with the details I retained from the experience and ask for her interpretation.

I was in awe of Janet when I first met her—her confidence and centeredness in listening and witnessing and in facilitating energy shifts that were felt and experienced with so many of my senses. The reverence she exacted through ceremony humbled me, as it made me recognize how unintentionally I had been living my life. She was patient with me in the early days of the program. I may have been a doting puppy following her, watching her, and wanting her praise, attention, and guidance. I unknowingly turned her into my oracle and guru. She registered this, however. I was certainly not the first of her students to transfer my authority solidly onto her lap. She deftly shifted from supplying me with an easy answer or interpretation to holding me accountable to look inside myself for answers.

It was like training wheels for me as I gained confidence in who I was beyond the roles of mother, wife, and daughter. As a mentor and a spiritual teacher, Janet supported and held space for me to grow into the awareness that I'm an energy being with creative powers.

I protested a few times, claiming that I didn't understand what the Native symbols represented. I didn't want to get it wrong. There were no directions. Finally, on an occasion where I was again pulled into some trancelike state during class and found myself in the midst of an etheric Native dance, White Buffalo Calf Woman—who is identified as a cultural prophet, healer, teacher, and inspiration to the

Lakota and other tribes—stood beside me in the vision as we watched the dance. I sensed this was significant. Why else show me this? Why frustrate me again with an experience I couldn't put into context? Janet was aware the whole time that though I was physically sitting in my chair, I was having an out-of-body experience, and she acquiesced to the benevolent energy that was interacting with me.

Later, so as not to interrupt class, I asked Janet to help me understand the dance that I'd seen. She sighed and paused, discerning what to say to me. "You are the dance, Signe." And with that and some real introspection on my part, I recognized that the spiritual path isn't just joining the head and heart but also entering into the stream of Life instead of always being the observer on the sidelines. I learned over and over that there's a fine balance between seeking understanding and explanations from others and letting understanding and knowingness unfold with patience.

Have you ever seen a tea flower bud expand and unfold once hot water is added? It reveals the beauty and delicacy of its expanded form—opening quickly at first and then slowing down as certain leaves take longer to uncurl. It takes the time it needs to open up evenly. That's what it was like when I finally allowed myself the space to let go and surrender.

Step by step, encounter after encounter, I met parts of myself that were closed in and offered them a safe place to reveal and unfold. Some parts took longer to stretch out and uncurl, while others were like a spring release that had no problem letting go of the tension. The trust I'd gained in pursuing a spiritual path, the middle road of balance, brought me the strength to accept parts of myself that had previously intimidated me—the desperate parts and the pure and innocent parts.

That's perhaps the most surprising awareness I gained—that to build a stable base for the middle, you need to address how fear presents itself on both sides of the spectrum. Though we tend to think of our dark side or shadow side as where all of our fears sit, fear is actually wilier than that. It hides itself in plain sight in our lighter aspects as well. Joseph Campbell, the late scholar of mythology and comparative religion, said, "The cave you fear to enter holds the treasure you seek." I would add that a blinding light can also create a fear of what you can't see.

I graduated from the program, applied for my ordination, and started my own spiritual counseling practice in Houston, concentrating on, but not limited to, language as a spiritual tool. I owe Janet a public declaration of respect and gratitude for her patience and generous sharing of her teachings. She impressed upon each of her students the simple understanding that consciousness follows the rule "As above, so below," and that everything starts energetically and then manifests physically. Therefore, if there is something amiss in the physical world, there's something amiss in the underlying beliefs and perceptions.

The coursework she crafted relentlessly guided me through layer after layer of resistance, clogged with doubt and fear, and continually presented an invitation to open up and experience the vulnerability and profound depths of humility in learning to love myself. I hope you have found or will find such a teacher for your own journey.

Questions for Reflection

Take some time with your journal to write down your impressions and feelings in response to these questions. Then, reflect on how your experience in your answers may have affected you emotionally or affected your development as an empath.

1. Write about the two most profound moments of your life that have created your own personal paradigm shifts. How have they affected you? Have they opened you to your abilities as an empath?

2. Write about healers and teachers you've encountered who have guided you in your spiritual awakening.

3. Reflect on times when you have distrusted your own understanding and knowingness, instead seeking answers from someone else. Write about these experiences and how they've affected you.

4. Reflect on experiences when you allowed your own knowingness to unfold like a tea flower bud in its own time. Write about the difference between doing this versus relying on someone else for answers.

5. Journal about the Joseph Campbell quote: "The cave you fear to enter holds the treasure you seek." How has this quote's wisdom manifested in your own life?

Part Five

The FIELD of Mystery

The FIELD of Mystery

The possession of knowledge does not kill the sense of wonder and mystery. There is always more mystery.

—Anais Nin

I have a story I tell myself. It started many years ago when I was trying to fathom why my life was my life. Why female? Why Caucasian? Why my particular family? Why freckles and hazel eyes that can change color depending on my contemplations? Why my goofy enigma of a name? Why my difficult to explain sensitive nature? Why all of it, indeed?

In most great storytelling, there is nothing superfluous. Every detail serves a purpose. As an example, *A Prayer for Owen Meany*, the novel by John Irving, was written in such a way that the reader understands at the end of the book how many of the details were there from the beginning. In hindsight, we can appreciate the significance of each detail in how the story unfolds.

I have always liked to tinker and reverse-engineer a dynamic—to take things apart and understand their relationships with each other. This deep desire to understand the significance of my life experiences and the function of my sensitivities has led me to seek answers. And "why" is where I started because even if I outwardly have a straight face, my natural default inside has been to question external authorities, as in: "What's your agenda? Why do you care what I'm doing?"

Somewhere along my early sojourn in learning about my intuitive channels, I was told by spiritual teachers that the Universe/Cosmos/Spiritual realm doesn't answer "why" questions. Even using a pendulum, dowsing rods, or divination tools, you must formulate "yes/no" questions. There are no mouthpieces on these discernment tools. But if you think the presenting energy is just answering "yes" or "no," you're limiting yourself. More mystery and understanding are always present.

Humility and self-respect assist the channels of communication when you ask for clarity and guidance. Asking, "Why me?" only highlights that an immature temperament is asking the question, and this limits receptivity. This is why, I believe, most spiritual development teachings consider asking "why" a major lapse in etiquette and respect. Surrender is all about accepting and letting go, and asking "why" isn't typically a surrendering posture.

After a while, I got it. The Universe/Cosmos/Spiritual realm isn't really interested in giving out explanations or directives, lest we on this side of the veil continue with the perception of separation and subservience. The ability to question and be curious is a tool for the living. It sets up a whole slew of inquiry and wonder, and it's naturally present with innocence. The person who is genuinely making connections and contemplating both life and death at the end of their life is still expanding.

You can experience peace and still be engaged with curiosity. They aren't mutually exclusive. You can host a knowingness of perfection and still wonder at the mechanics of aesthetics. Self-awareness begins with a "why," as in "Why did I do that, say that, or feel that?" Spiritual development and maturity are created by such contemplations, and the more you respond with clear motivations and intentions, the less you'll question your decisions and environment.

I treated my life like a case study to help me understand what a life of isolation and fear, with major empathic sensitivities and feelings of disconnection from general society, would offer someone. I felt there was a gaping hole in the plotline of my life, as if the element that connected all the parts together with purpose was left out of my script. The more I leaned into my own healing and untangled myself from the denseness of the outer world, the more truths started to reveal themselves. The main one was that my sensitive nature is natural; just as nature is sensitive and resilient, so am I. My empathic sensitivities also revealed that I was connected to life by a unified field, so I had to reframe my thoughts and feelings of being alone and isolated. Moreover, this connection provided me with guidance and support in various forms. Ultimately, I accepted that this is the perfect life for bringing me a sense of belonging to myself, which my empathic senses facilitate.

Over the years, I've received guidance through meditation and automatic writing. One specific entry said,

> *"Your life may seem random, but by a design of intelligence to bring you to the exact and precise experience needed to propel you toward your own understanding of self and to be actualized. What does actualized mean? It means that you are no longer able to deny certain truths about your origin and your soul.*
>
> *"What is the dark night of the soul? It is just the opportunity to experience yourself without any tethering*

to concepts and constructs telling you who you are. It feels dark and bleak, yet it is filled with much light presence. It is the hand hold from your own soul reaching toward you from within."

Have you ever experienced *a dark night of the soul?* My own experience required that if I was to rise up and out of the darkness, I had to address my resistance to my own nature. It was a reckoning that required a transformation at a deep level of my heart to make room for self-love. That transformation was supported by a field of energy that interacted with me at first in my dreams and then in meditation. Then, I recognized it in the people I interacted with in my life. I surrendered to Mystery, an energetic field that presents as a benevolent intelligence. It's an intelligence that reveals itself through geometry, chaos, and paradox and even within our unique storylines. It's this presence that offers me a sense of oneness and guidance.

I took the liberty of naming this Part the Field of Mystery, but it has also been referred to as the Void, All-that-Is, God, Creator, Spirit, the Divine, and many other proper nouns. Please use what relates to your own sensibilities and knowingness.

I heard a joke decades ago that framed the Field of Mystery appropriately for me: Two scientists, proud and beaming, approach the Creator and proclaim, "We've made Man; we have figured it out!"

God says, "Oh, so pleased for you lads. Tell me, how did you do it?"

The eager scientists begin by saying, "We took a little dirt and then . . ."

Spirit cuts them off. "Well, now, how did you make the dirt?"

Most empowered empaths are seasoned in the ways of Mystery, as they center themselves in the space between the physical and nonphysical. This means that Mystery is always there to reveal more ways to feel and expand truth, as well as bring people who feel disconnected into the fold of humanity. More than likely, your own path of self-discovery has included mystical moments that revealed you're more than just a physical body and mind meant to toil or suffer.

I've written this guidebook while acquiescing as much as I can to the point of view of being in the body, leaving mystical elements to a minimum. I did this because I wanted the focus to be on the embodiment of our intuitive sensory selves. This is central to each of our lives as authentic empathic people.

I purposefully chose not to embellish empathic reception as a superpower or gift because I want to normalize intuition as part of our integrated human intelligence. Your gift is what you can offer humanity by way of healing your own limiting perception of who you know yourself to be. Your gift is your ability to stay present and grounded with an open heart and to love yourself unconditionally. Your gift is your willingness to respect another's life path even though it may not be what you would have chosen.

What part has your empathic nature played in your own personal development? My invitation to evolve your empathic sensitivities from just being a sponge into being a functional energy-aware empath is based on my own awareness and experience that our empathic traits are spiritual in nature. They serve to connect us to a consciousness of unity and oneness and to humbly sense balance.

Part V is an opportunity to share how I have interacted, witnessed, and observed the Field of Mystery throughout my life. The point of contact can be subtle or profound, and it has revealed itself in many varied ways. But I will feature three themes that demonstrate how this field has revealed itself to me: through the form of guides, through the cycles of life and death, and through developing spiritual maturity.

The Field of Mystery was present at the beginning of my story, holding space for me to unfold and find my voice, my balance, and my truth. This is what I want you to consider for yourself: How has this Field of Mystery supported you?

Chapter Nineteen

Field Guides

In his famous poem, "The Great Wagon," thirteenth-century Sufi poet Rumi mentions meeting the reader in a field beyond the ideas of right and wrong. The field he refers to is a state of consciousness that transcends duality. It's the universal field of everything and nothing—a creative field of potential and completion. It's the realm of the soul and its perfection.

I've always enjoyed the lines about the field in this poem because Rumi grounds the image in the physical world—a field, that grass, the posture of lying down—all of which can be sensed, imagined, and experienced in this world. The field is beyond mental activity and rumination—no words needed. We're self-actualized. Just lie down in *that* grass and be. But before we can reach this field of fullness, there are many other fields and landscapes to cross, terrains to explore, and truths and biases to uncover.

Self-discovery is indeed a journey, a labyrinth of emotions, and a gut-wrenching cliffhanger filled with anxiety and fears. It's a pastoral walk through a meadow contemplating and questioning life and death, a bog of dreariness and stagnation, a sunset beach with dimpled footprints, a solitary pilgrimage through a dark valley, a summit, a descent, a mysterious cavern, and so much more. It's a journey that in this instance lasts a lifetime in *this* one body.

In the natural world, no one thing exists singularly, and this is true for Rumi's field. *That grass* in Rumi's poem is everything at once—the grass *that* makes a nest, *that* is food, *that* is home, *that* holds the soil in place, *that* receives the sunshine, *that* drinks the rainfall, and *that* balances the nighttime dew upon its bent blades. It is *that*, which is everything and more. *This* one body and the growing understanding of *that* grass have been my field guides as I've traveled along my path.

Guidance emerges from the field and takes the shape and form of the familiar and the unfamiliar. It's all part of the Mystery: part sublime, part profound, and wholly unforgettable.

Kindness Emerging From the Field

When my father died, I found myself traveling alone internationally back to the US, raw with grief. I was suddenly aware of how fragile and sensitive I was, but also thankful that I knew the routine of international travel so that I could be somewhat on automatic pilot. It was a surreal feeling to be so vulnerable, yet at the mercy of public transportation during its busiest time—summer holidays.

I managed the flight without too many interactions. I forced myself to try to sleep, and as the plane landed in Denver, I committed my focus to putting one foot in front of the other, gathering my luggage, and finding my shuttle transport.

The hour-long ride from the airport to Boulder was spent replaying the last conversation I had with my dad forty-eight hours earlier, just hours before he succumbed to the infection that shut down his organs. I pictured him in the hospital bed. My memory scanned his voice for the tones of tenderness that were usually accompanied by a wink—his trademark way of letting me know everything would be okay. I'm not sure why I felt the need to replay that moment, but it comforted and gutted me at the same time.

The people in the shuttle were dropped off at various hotels and hubs along the way until it was just me and another passenger, who sat adjacent to me. With less than a mile to my drop-off, we started to talk. He was in town for a world-class climber's birthday party—it was Boulder, Colorado, after all. I gathered that he worked for a big mountaineering company based in Utah that must have employed the famous climber at some point. He asked what brought me to Boulder.

I hadn't spoken my new reality to anyone since I'd left my husband at the airport in Oslo the day before. I found the sentences forming, and without too much effort, I simply told him that I'd returned because my father had died suddenly. As he was extending his condolences to me, his phone rang, drawing him into a business call. At the same time, the shuttle turned into my driveway, and I began to collect my belongings. As I stepped out of the van, he told the person on the phone to wait a minute, and he set his phone down. He looked at me and held my gaze. "I'm very sorry for your loss," he said again with genuine compassion.

I was touched, but I did perhaps what many people do. I said something like "Thank you. My dad had just turned eighty-three and had some health issues."

Still holding his phone against his thigh and holding my gaze, he insisted, "Don't rationalize this. Too many people do that when someone dies. I really want you to know I am sorry for your loss."

I felt his deep witnessing of my pain. I had been in a bubble on the trip, just wanting some privacy since I'd received the news. Instead, I had been constantly surrounded by strangers and the hustle of travel. Yet here was a total stranger creating a space for me to express my truth and witness the depth of the loss I would have to absorb in the days, months, and years to come.

I have found that field guides like this appear when you need them. I've had my moments of helping others by being present and discerning when I needed to step forward or step back, and I've had the good fortune to encounter guides when I needed them, too. Experiencing and witnessing a field guide in action helps me trust humanity's reach. It isn't just a social construct; it's an agency with faculty and depth, and the world needs us all to be active members.

As an empath, whose life is somewhat attuned to witnessing others, the experience of being unexpectedly witnessed by someone else, a stranger even, filled me with so much gratitude and appreciation. But it also helped to correct an imbalance that was building within me—a subtle difference between resilience and resistance.

Having a strong center and knowing of your strengths and resilience need not keep you from receiving what you need to feel supported by the larger field. Kindness typically finds us when we're at a point of imbalance, fueling us to stay present and in our hearts.

Milk Teeth and Fading Pixie Dust

The remarkable gift of children is the opportunity to witness their innocence and wisdom—something that we as adults may not be able to recall after a lifetime of stresses. I honestly consider my four children to be among my greatest teachers. They are their own special kind of field guide.

Each one has helped me along my path, giving me more awareness about how each of us is born with unique sensitivities and dispositions and how our natural connections to this Field of Mystery have different expressions.

Our four children were like the Darling family children from Peter Pan when they were younger—seeing and experiencing things unseen in the so-called normal world. Then, as slowly and as quickly as the last light dims at the edge of the horizon, they stopped. In the story of Peter Pan, childlike wonder and the ability to see beyond the veil of reality come to an end when the children get their first adult teeth, the symbolic first sign of maturing that pulls the child fully into the physical world.

Our kids engaged their surroundings with the healthy imagination that enlivens childhood, but each one, at one time or another, entertained connections beyond this physical place. I witnessed these moments without too much inquiry from my side because I didn't want to place pressure on them to justify what was a natural part of their world's experience. But by the time they were seven or eight years old, they no longer spoke about these remarkable interactions or contemplations.

From about the age of two to six, my daughter Grace talked to a female presence whom she called by name—a rather odd name, at that. I sensed this presence myself but had no direct interaction with it. Grace could see the different colors of the chakras as well when she received energy clearings, even though she was never taught which color was associated with each chakra or in what sequence the energy was being directed.

My son Per brought forth channeled bits of wisdom that astonished my husband and me, making us truly wonder about his language disabilities. He would often be deep in thought, and I would ask where he was, joking a bit. But he would answer matter-of-factly that he was somewhere there were only geometric shapes.

At the age of seven, my son Finn was under the influence of a sedative before a medical procedure when he started an eerie soliloquy on the profound eloquence of nothingness—a time before the duality of light and dark.

The kids sometimes echoed my observation that a room's energy felt weird or stagnant. This often happens with my son Michael, who is a very sensitive empathic person. We will enter a room and almost simultaneously turn to each other, declaring that there's a funky energy present.

They are adults now and have their own journeys. Other than the recent experiences with Michael, they don't recall their experiences from childhood when I bring up those memories. It's as if the pixie dust from Neverland lost its magic as they aged. Their behaviors and interactions appeared mysterious, just as the stories about the elderly who are visited by deceased friends and relatives before they pass, or when we have unsettling messages delivered in our dreams.

Shake and Rattle: The Body's Wisdom

When I was in my early twenties, I participated in a week-long river course with Outward Bound on the Colorado River. Among the many necessary items that supported the staff and participants were field guides of the region, which pointed out plants, wildlife, topography, and river currents. Instructors were also well-versed with the region and gladly shared their own personal experience of the landscape, as well as how to uncover more than just what meets the eye.

Layer upon layer of multidisciplinary fields unfolded before us—geology, land management policy, forestry, indigenous history, plant life, ecosystems, erosion, climate contribution, wildlife, and practical health and wellness issues—mainly centered on how to stay warm and dry while limiting sun exposure. These outdoor immersion courses expand each person uniquely. Though it may be a shared group experience, it's also an intimate and private journey.

Each of us rotated positions on the raft to learn the importance of teamwork and develop specific skills, from captaining in the back to taking commands in the front. A few days into our trip, I was positioned at the bow and instructed to get out of the boat and anchor the rope. As a crew we needed to disembark and get an overview of the upcoming rapids, and this was the only spot left on the embankment for our boat to tie up. I rushed through some smaller willow bushes on the riverbank to secure the rope around a more substantial tree, only to stop dead in my tracks. I can still recall the narrowing of all of my senses. Gone was the sound of the rushing river behind me. Instead, I heard the distinctly hurried pulse of my heart pounding as I held my breath.

I was confused but actually remember questioning, "Why am I stopping? Why am I seemingly paralyzed and not moving forward?" My hearing was the first to come back on board and give me sensory input: a deafening rattling surrounded me. My vision cleared as I scanned the shadows before me. Six feet in front of me at the base of the tree that I was approaching to secure the rope, there was a large rattlesnake cocked and attentive, rattling its tail in warning.

Meanwhile, the five-person crew, paddling to keep the nose of the boat close to shore in a moving current, began to tire. I stood in complete stillness like a game of statue from my childhood with the end of the rope firmly gripped in front of my chest. I registered that our instructor Huck was urgently asking what was taking so long, his voice cutting above the sound of water and rattling.

I swallowed and considered whether the sound of my voice, which I would need to project loudly enough to travel behind me to reach Huck, would startle the snake. I felt I was having an out-of-body experience, one that made room for a completely calm inner dialogue. I wasn't panicked, but I was hyper-conscious that my actions would be the catalyst for whatever was to transpire. I somehow managed to respond that there was a snake. How my voice, with its calculated volume and frequency, reached Huck is still a mystery to me, but reach him it did. I was told not to move and that he was coming ashore.

Soon, I heard his voice behind me, stating, "Don't move. You also have snakes behind you." I had unknowingly rushed ashore into a loosely formed rattlesnake den. The crescendo of rattling surrounded me.

I had no idea what Huck witnessed behind me. I had blindly walked through that patch of ground focused on one thing—securing the rope. I stood frozen but thankful that the snake before me also remained in its own statuesque form, apart from the rattling of its tail. If it had started to move in any direction, I'm certain that I would have succumbed to hysteria and then shock. I barely registered or considered what the snakes behind me were doing.

Remarkably, my body listened to Huck, who spoke quietly behind me. He instructed me that at the count of three, I was to throw the rope as high and as far back as possible. We would then both run toward an opening on the shoreline to our right. There was no discussion, no idle chat. It was his voice and his instruction that I grabbed on to. I no longer heard the rattling, only Huck's voice. The count to three came impressively quickly and succinctly, and my body somchow shifted from a paralytic state to one of flight. The rope left my hand as I bolted to the right, clearing the willows with five sprinting strides. Huck also ran with a look of shock and bewilderment on his face.

My body and my mind struggled to come together. The burst of adrenaline that surged through me and seemingly propelled me out of danger danced around my chest as my knees buckled, and I found myself not sure if I was laughing or crying.

Admittedly, I still have a physical reaction whenever I see a live snake, venomous or not. My heart leaps, and I move away quickly. It's a reaction that comes involuntarily, and it can bring great laughs from my children, particularly when a puny garden snake slithers into view. But what they don't register is the absolute respect and gratitude I feel toward those rattlers on the shores of the Colorado River in Glen Canyon. They gave me a warning—a chance to get out of there without injury.

That experience also holds an element of mystery for me regarding how my body's innate wisdom took over even while my mind was trying to figure out what was going on. It didn't go into fight, flight, or freeze; it went into stillness. I was present in a way that I still can't fathom when faced with such potential danger.

No matter how many times I replay it in my mind, I'm in awe of the intelligence that saw what I did not, heard what I had not, and seemingly knew the exact spot that I needed to stop, stand still, and wait, as if locating the middle of an electromagnetic field. In that field, I encountered a part of me that was beyond the "I" of me. And the humble gratitude for Huck's calm voice guiding me out of harm's way will forever symbolize a trust and surrender that I'd rarely experienced before in my life.

We all have guides, teachers, and supporters who calmly, excitably, or even dramatically encourage us from the side that we can do it, whatever it is—a change of careers, healing from a health crisis, making new friends, or escaping from a rattlesnake den. Yet it's us, the ones in the seemingly impossible position, who must take action to facilitate the growth. It's us who have to host the courage, resolve, bruises, and exhilaration of our efforts. But at least if we acknowledge that we aren't alone but are supported and trust that support (without dictating the form of the support), it's easier to take action.

Questions for Reflection

Take some time with your journal to write down your impressions and feelings in response to these questions. Then, reflect on how your experience in your answers may have affected you emotionally or affected your development as an empath.

1. Write about moments of unexpected kindness by strangers or loved ones. What have these experiences shown you? What stands out to you about the gestures extended to you? How did they make you feel, and what was the effect they had on your energy? Do you see them as "field guides" of a sort?

2. Do you recall if you experienced any non-ordinary encounters as a child? Did your family ever share how you had special abilities or an overactive imagination? Reflect on any interesting memories that you perhaps didn't share with others out of fear of being labeled weird.

3. Have you ever had an experience that reminds you of mine with the rattlesnake and my reaction of stillness? Has your body's innate wisdom ever kicked in like that? If so, write about it and how my story affects your thoughts and feelings about it.

4. Write about some of the field guides you've had in your life who have encouraged you from the sidelines.

Chapter Twenty

Death—Forget Me Not

As a child, I spent a lot of my time alone, escaping into my thoughts and queries about the expansive starlit Colorado skies. I found comfort in being still, surrounded by nature. I also felt vulnerable and of little worth next to all of the beauty and pulsing life around me.

Without knowing it, I managed to find a form of meditation that allowed me to elevate myself out of the worries and confines of my life. Time and again, I sat on the banks just outside of the current of Life, watching, observing, and oddly enough, not thinking. I would "return" to my physical life, appreciating something more deeply than I had before, but I also felt the paradox of feeling more out of touch with the people around me. I had no one in my life reflecting to me that these deep contemplations on the essence of beauty, questions about existence, and the nature of consciousness were normal or worth pursuing.

I wonder if I visited that bank so often that I became a fixture of its own particular landscape of nothingness and everything-ness. I always felt protected and safe, but I also didn't feel the need to go beyond that spot and explore more deeply into the embankments—beyond the shores of where Life and Death touch, or the so-called veil.

Life is a current, a constant moving stream—sometimes fast, sometimes babbling—and it pulses with activity. Life is something you join by slipping into that stream, and it teaches us through experience. Death is the banks, the container of Life, but it's also part of the structure of the stream, helping knit together everything in existence.

Death came to me, not as an entity fully developed with a personality but with an essence of calm and knowingness, with a profound level of comprehension and patience. And with a profound intelligence. My awareness of Death was slow and very gradual. Time-lapse photography might still show my spirit sitting on that bank, tethered to my life here.

It was Death that helped open my understanding of the mechanics of the physical world to make it more accessible for me. I've never tried to capture this relationship in words before. It isn't so different than trying to describe the relationship between the sky and the air. There is air above me, but it's also in front of me. Do I call the space immediately before my face the "sky"? At what distance does air become sky? It's like that with Death and Life. Many wouldn't be able to sense that within their life is death. To many, it's a finite reality—black and white, Life and Death.

As an empath who wanted context and to understand my nature, I wondered a great deal about the dynamics of structures and systems—the need to look under the hood of the car, so to speak. But it's impossible for anyone to simultaneously drive a car and pop the hood to examine the engine while the vehicle is moving.

I came to appreciate the physical world of the living through holding the hand of Death. Not the death of myths and legends with a Grim Reaper, dark-cloaked and frightening. Rather, Death with a tender and compassionate essence of gifting understanding and peace. The energy I call Death is much more than just the antithesis of Life. I can call it "All that has potential in the physical world," but that's a mouthful. So I shorten it to "All that is."

Recently, I heard someone talk about the angel Metatron in very much the same way—as an energy that's a template of structures that Life is built upon. Each intuitive person, including an empath, perceives the expansive energies that come from the Field of Mystery/Oneness with our human consciousness. It's a tall order for our minds, but we give it a go by building an identity around the energy so that we may understand it in some fashion that makes sense. For me, as a child, whose source of comfort was the natural world and its representation of Life, the only way I knew how to understand this energy that met me was that it had to be Death. Rightly or wrongly labeled, it didn't bother to correct me.

As a subject, Death tends to be loaded with fear and anxiety in the human psyche. So many people fear the unknown, and Death is the biggest unknown for us on the mortal side of the veil. How can we spend an entire life finding a sense of place and cultivating a sense of belonging within ourselves—our life, our body, our relationships—to only hand it over once we take our last breath? Our life is reduced to a sand mandala swept away or fading with the elements.

When we experience the loss of a loved one, there is pain, sorrow, and grief. These are healthy responses when reflecting on the beauty and richness of relationships.

Death, however, doesn't kill anything in the physical world. A life ends, but the essence of love merely changes form. We just typically can't see the new structure with our physical eyes. It's truly faith that helps us accept that what was once before us and is not now is still present, just in a different form. Death isn't a verb in the realm of the living; it receives Life and transforms it and is in perfect harmony with oneness. Accepting change is inevitably part of mastering Life.

Just as my own children's mystical interactions faded, my visit to the bank faded as my focus shifted to managing my complicated home life. Only as an adult, triggered by what can be called a dark night of the soul, did I remember the familiarity of the bank and the tenderness it possessed. Many of my visits to the bank were for the benefit of mastering my own energy systems and seeking resources to help me understand what I was learning from reading books on energy anatomy, or to better understand a touted spiritual principle. I had matured and moved well beyond asking "why" to more nuanced questions about the nature of consciousness, as well as suffering and compassion.

I would find myself eager to go to bed and open my mind for an explanation, knowing that any impressions I received would only be a fraction of the depth and truth of the contemplation I held. I would often drift off to sleep but would awaken with impressions still fresh in my mind, wanting to be released in my journals.

I have encountered concepts and truths written by mystics throughout history from different faiths that align with the knowingness I have about the nature of consciousness and the Beloved. I've stumbled upon quotes from scientists and literary figures who have likewise sought understanding and awareness of the sublime qualities of the aesthetics of Life. Each time this occurs, I feel the lightness of being that comes from the recognition that I'm not alone in this sea of humanity, nor am I the only one who innocently sits on the banks to contemplate the balance between meaning and mystery.

Point of Departure

I was in my midtwenties when I started to sense the energetic presence of people who had died, otherwise known as disincarnate energy. This skillset developed as I expanded my sense of reality to include the threshold of "the veil." This is silent work, done simply and respectfully. I don't channel their narrative, I don't engage their life story, and I don't relay messages. I just relay the essence of their spirit as it transforms its form and identity. An empath is suited for this kind of service because we're grounded with our intuitive senses at a point of balancing in between the physical and the nonphysical—exactly at a place where a disincarnate energy can, on occasion, benefit from some assistance to move closer energetically to the veil. It's an intimate and honored role, though I didn't always view it that way.

I have discovered that this service of assisting departing energy goes in waves. I don't know the whys and wheres of it, and that's part of the Mystery. These days, I rarely intercept disincarnate energy needing help, which contrasts sharply with where I was fifteen years ago when I felt I would never get a moment of "normal" living without needing to help a presence at the edge of my energy fields.

Initially, I resisted and felt intimidated by this work. I felt put upon, which seemed to amplify the number of encounters I received. But it was these relentless periods of assisting the deceased that broke my immature stance of "why me?" I got over my fear of this work and realized that I had to find the truth for myself and not be misled by Hollywood storyboards. I matured and began to see the continuum between Life and Death, which only further assisted me in experiencing unity and oneness.

The more comfortable I became with the rhythm of Life cycles, including Death, the more my subconscious mind didn't need to attach fear and anxiety to my interactions. But helping a disincarnate transition when they've already died isn't the same as being present with someone who is still transitioning from Life to Death.

I'm ending this chapter with a deeply personal story from my life that incorporates all the critical components that I have come to know as the essence of Life: a receiver, a transmitter, and a message. But in this moment Life, Death, and Mystery are all present and interchanging seamlessly between giving and receiving messages.

Breaking Point

Texas rain, typically a torrential downpour, created an uncharacteristic blanket of mist on the afternoon I drove the unknown country roads of Montgomery in search of an address scribbled on a piece of paper. I had a feeling that I was driving through a low-lying cloud and needed help from ground control and radar to navigate the bending, tree-lined roads. With my headlights and windshield wipers on, my shoulders tensed, and my hands gripped the steering wheel of our minivan. I tried to calm my building nerves by reminding myself that I had agreed to this assignment.

The mist, the fog, the unfamiliar countryside, and the pressure to get back home before my kids returned from school all added to my stress and doubt. When I'd answered the phone just after lunch on that early spring day in 2002, I was already deep into doubting my real purpose in volunteering at a hospice.

I had lived in Texas for less than two years when a friend who was a bereavement counselor for a hospice in Conroe asked if I would be willing to volunteer. I said yes, but with some trepidation. I knew I wanted to be of service in some capacity, and Death, as strange as it sounds, suited me. I'm comfortable with the fact that everyone dies. I respect that hospice offers support to terminally ill people and their families. But I still felt a tug inside me—an uncomfortable feeling of being pushed out of my comfort zone. The intense feelings of sadness and the energy of a terminal illness can well up within the walls of a family's home.

I understood that I needed to humanize my experience of Death. Without giving it much thought, I had become comfortable with the task of helping disincarnate souls transition, like hailing a taxi for someone who is unable to wave or whistle. By the time these souls reached me, they were no longer attached to their body or their family. They were simply looking for the way forward, and I obliged by setting an intention for their passage. That was me—roadside assistance.

My first assignment as a volunteer was to help a woman with breast cancer in her late fifties as she organized her files of newspaper clippings and documents on various subjects that had consumed her attention during the last twenty years. She desperately wanted to pass them on to those who might be interested in taking up her causes after she passed. Her family, however, no longer had the energy to entertain her devotion to those boxes of paper. For years, they'd heard her espouse her concerns and anger about special education, pharmaceuticals, supplements, and the FDA's regulation and control.

Despite her late-stage condition, she was a strikingly pretty woman with simple and delicate features. She looked much younger than her years. Her hair was gray, and her skin was remarkably fine and smooth as porcelain. She had chosen not to have any invasive or aggressive treatment, so her tumor had eaten its way through her left breast, leaving an oozing and pungent open wound that required daily bandage changes. The smell was an affront to my senses that I needed to accept and adjust to as her body began its descent toward Death.

I went to her home once or twice a week for nearly three months, and she came to look upon me as her personal assistant. In addition to my visits, hospice nurses came by, house cleaners attended to the growing medical waste and kept the house tidy, and the clergy from her church came to offer blessings.

I began each visit by making us tea, and I sat beside her bed, which occupied the living room. A file, extracted from one of the boxes, sat in my lap, and I held up article after article for her consideration. There were many duplicates to be extracted, so I created a filing system to organize her different causes. This was tedious work, but it was my intention to give her a sense of being seen and heard. As she got weaker, it became less about the boxes and more about me sitting with her and holding her hand, which she liked. She commented once that she felt warmth from my hand. I smiled, and we talked about why she became so passionate about some of the issues in the boxes.

It was right before Christmas, and I was making dinner when I had a sudden knowingness that she was getting ready to pass. I sensed a movement of energy traveling up her spine, halfway out of her body. A few hours later, I received a call that she had passed. She had a beautiful memorial service that her husband created much on his own, and his eulogy of his strong-willed, passionate wife was an eloquent testament to his love and her life.

I would often sit with an ailing unconscious person, keeping their spouse company while clearing the room energetically or invoking mercy and grace to be ever-present with the family. I learned to multitask in those few hours a week spent outside of my family life as a mother and a wife. Those hours were filled with pockets of intense denseness and lightness. Few knew or understood that my presence involved a level of energy work that prepared a space for a soul's transition. I felt like a doula for the dying. I'm not sure if I felt underappreciated or exhausted from oscillating back and forth from my domestic life to that of being a witness and guide for those on the brink of dying. But something was missing for me.

The hospice experience provided me with the opportunity to experience the breaking point between the physical and the etheric—the two separating like a yoke from the white. I suppose I needed to understand this pivotal moment, and that came from being a witness to a person's life while still living, surrounded by family, photos, furniture, and personalized expressions of their time spent here in physical form. Yet I felt a burden.

The hospice provided service to a large area, often requiring me to drive hours outside the city. I felt alone a lot of the time. I often found myself knocking on the doors of various homes, not always feeling as if I was totally wanted there. After all, dying in your home is a choice, and people usually make that choice because it affords intimacy and privacy for the family.

As I drove in the fog, feeling lost on many levels, I felt useless and found myself taking inventory of what this volunteer position looked like on the surface: time away from my family; driving my car many miles; using gas; inserting myself into strangers' lives who may or may not want me there; witnessing pain, suffering, and grief; and having to interact with noxious energy that fed off the person like a parasite. What did it matter, really, if I volunteered or not?

After driving for nearly forty-five minutes, the fog began to lift, and I arrived at a modular-home community. I had been told to expect a woman in her thirties with four children. She had been diagnosed with cancer of the liver.

The family had requested someone assist them in making video diary entries that she hoped to leave behind for her young children. I wasn't a videographer, but as a volunteer, you recognize that a lot of the time, what's needed is just someone to step up and help in whatever capacity. And it didn't take much for me to put myself in her shoes and know that I, too, faced with death, would want to leave something for my four children—a chance for them to hear from me about my wishes and hopes for each one of them.

At the door, I was greeted by a middle-aged woman and told to come inside. I was impressed that the modular home looked so big from the inside. There was a scattering of people spread throughout the kitchen and the living room, a buffet of food arranged on folding tables, and small children playing beside a TV in the corner of the room. I followed her toward a door adjacent to a small washroom on the right side of the house. The woman explained that they had made a mistake in calling me. Her daughter had seriously declined, and there was no way they wanted to document how she looked now for the kids to remember her.

She paused, and I was unsure if I should just return to my car and drive home. But she opened the door and indicated that I should enter, immediately closing the door behind me. I entered a small dimly lit room. The twin-sized bed held a gravely ill young woman whose staggered breath rattled and paused. She was terribly thin, and her face was nearly a skeleton with a casing of skin. Her husband was beside her, holding her hand and so present with her that it was both heartbreaking and heart-expanding to see his willingness to absorb the whole scene into his being. He wasn't looking away; he was holding his heart open and his eyes wide.

I introduced myself in a whisper, and he offered his chair for me to sit beside his dying wife. I was moved by his acceptance of me, a stranger and just a volunteer, in the incredibly intimate scene. I declined his offer and suggested that I would like to just stand at the foot of her bed. He returned to his chair, and we both focused on the jaundiced body barely breathing in the bed. I was quiet and still, and I began to sense the energy in the room. I sensed the sheer magnitude of her spirit—the beauty, the boldness, and how it no longer was contained in her physical body.

I spoke through my third eye, or my mind's eye, to her spirit, her essence, her soul. I told her how absolutely beautiful she was, how brave and bold, and how her family and children were equally beautiful extensions of her life. I told her how she was safe and how she was free from pain and suffering. I said these and other prayers in my mind, so in awe of everything I was experiencing in that room. Suddenly, she opened her eyes and revealed yellow-brown pupils with dark rings under each eye that dug shadows into her features. Alarmed by her sudden emergence from her resting state, her husband reached forward to her. She raised her arm and pointed a finger toward the end of the bed where I was standing.

Her husband introduced me to calm her, but she spoke directly to me—the first words she had spoken in hours. "I hear you!" she proclaimed, and a smile stretched across her cracked lips. "I hear you," she repeated more quietly and then closed her eyes and returned to her death-rattle breathing. Her husband looked to me for an explanation. I told him that I had been speaking to her soul and preparing the space for her to receive peace in her transition. I said this, knowing it might offend or confuse him. But instead, he said they were open-minded, and it was wonderful to know her beauty shone beyond her diseased and decaying body. He embraced me with so much gratitude that I was humbled and also grateful.

I went to the car, aware that this beautiful soul had delivered to me a much-needed message at a point of great intimacy for her and her family so that I would know that my witnessing others is also witnessed. I wasn't alone. And yes, I was not only seen—I was heard.

Questions for Reflection

Take some time with your journal to write down your impressions and feelings in response to these questions. Then, reflect on how your experience in your answers may have affected you emotionally or affected your development as an empath.

1. What do you contemplate about your life and about Life in general? Have you been the recipient of wisdom and knowingness that stands out as extraordinary?

2. Does the idea of death scare you or cause you anxiety? What encounters have you personally had with death and dying?

3. As an empath, have you sensed the presence of disincarnate energies around you? If so, describe how you came to understand that this sensation correlated with disincarnate energy. Describe what you typically do when you have such encounters.

4. My hospice experience was intimate and deeply personal. What did it reveal to you that you may not have considered about dying and Mystery? Or if you have your own experience, journal about a moment when you felt a contact point between the realms.

5. Five Wishes, a living will that some hospitals require to be filled out before surgeries, prompts the applicant to express how they would like to be remembered in the event of death. How would you like to be remembered? Do you need to modify anything in your life to align to your testimony?

Chapter Twenty-One

Spiritual Maturity

In Dante's *Inferno*, written in the Middle Ages, the reader encounters a level of hell for soothsayers—fortune tellers and psychics whose punishment for selling visions of the future is having their heads attached backward so they must look only at their past. People who use their intuition—whether historical oracles guiding a court, such as the Greek Oracle of Delphi or today's psychic hotline—must consider the services they provide and to what end they are helping or harming others. This is true for empaths. Remember, just because you may feel something emitting information from someone else's energy doesn't mean that you're meant to confront them with the information without discerning your own motivation and intention.

When Helping Is Hurting

A friend of mine who enjoyed yoga and wanted to deepen her journey decided to attend a yoga mindfulness workshop in the Midwest. The instructor announced to her that out of everyone there, she had the most work to do in developing herself. My friend shut down. She was handed a negative assessment, and she took it in and doubted herself.

Another friend told me her then boyfriend attended a weekend spiritual retreat, wanting to heal what was standing in the way of his ability to commit and be available in a relationship. Someone attending the retreat felt the need to share an image she "received" for him. This image was a heart with barbed wire and bristles around it—not really a Hallmark-worthy picture to empower a person. Like my friend at the yoga workshop, he felt miserable, not knowing how to open and clear such an obstructive image. Would he ever be able to give and receive love?

These are two examples of why someone working with their intuitive channels should be supported by a mentor or group who can help them develop their discernment process and build a neutral channel to receive impressions. There's a strong correlation between doing your inner work, clearing limiting programming, and getting clearer intuitive receptivity. Strengthening your receptive channels needs to be balanced by integrating and applying the wisdom into the physical realm of your life and relationships—just as someone who weight trains has to stretch their muscles to promote flexibility. It's designed as a feedback loop. Life is not theoretical, and sometimes, it can take years of practicing to make real an experience that can be felt—like forgiveness.

Embody the Teaching

There's a well-known story about Gandhi, the late political and peace activist, that illustrates the essence of spiritual maturity. A woman who was concerned about the number of sweets her son ate traveled a great distance to Gandhi's ashram to ask for his help. She approached Gandhi and told him to please tell her son to stop eating sweets, as they weren't good for his health. Gandhi told her to come back in two weeks. She traveled the distance again two weeks later with her son.

Gandhi told the boy to stop eating sweets, as they weren't good for his health. The woman, a bit dismayed, asked him why he didn't tell them the first time they came. Gandhi told her that he had to give up sweets himself before he could advise the boy to do the same.

Can you practice what you preach? Can you walk the talk? Can you embody the teaching? Can you embrace your nature without diminishing another? These are all important truths to be assessed by any well-meaning person on a spiritual path.

"Spiritual bypassing" is a term that has been used to describe people who are, more or less, imitating and espousing spiritual tenets of surrender, forgiveness, and self-love without attending to the inner work—the hollowing of oneself to be hallow. Of course, I'm not passing judgment on anyone's path, as I know how tempting it is to set down your family suitcase of generational programming, say "no, thanks," and then go read a book from a great master or attend a retreat full of temporary serenity. I sat mine down for decades before I realized that if I opened it up, I would also find empathy, compassion, forgiveness, and self-love.

The Spiritual Subtle Body—Made for Grace

I was a young mother living in a foreign land when I began to question and contemplate how to heal the obvious holes in my sense of being. I was contending with the tumor in my neck region, as well as facing the consequences of not dealing with my own baggage that I was still carrying from my childhood, which impacted my perception of safety, even as an adult. I was experiencing a perfect storm from all directions. My mental, emotional, and physical body joined together to give me the message that I had one more subtle body that offered me comfort and grace—my spiritual body.

I felt my spiritual body mostly in nature—about nature—and it was opening up for me in a manner that required I place myself within this field as well. The entrenched pattern of separating myself from all that I revered and loved was nonetheless a version of duality and separation consciousness. I was unable to move forward until I honored myself and extended to myself the same respect and love I naturally and unwaveringly extended to nature, the cosmos, and my closest family and friends.

I felt deeply with my heart, but more or less directed it outwardly. I was desperate, but still, I couldn't find the audacity and boldness to pray for myself. Remarkably, though, I could imagine all the other people in the world (men, women, and children) perhaps feeling as I did—alone, lost, and needing a deeper connection to something kinder and gentler. So I prayed for all of those people, whoever they might be, and threw myself into the mix. Even in my misery, I no longer wanted to be alone, yet I didn't want the company of misery. I wanted hope, movement, and betterment.

The more I engaged in a universal prayer practice designed by my own creative imagination, the more I was able to individualize and vocalize what I wanted to call forth into my own life. In my summation, I entered my path to spirituality through the back door of humanity. I snuck in on the pain and suffering of all those like me. My prayers were lifted for mothers, young and old, exhausted and filled with doubt about how to parent and nurture young children without repeating generational patterns of neglect or abuse. For wives who felt invisible in the eyes of their husbands and family as they tried endlessly to be good enough and to be the perfect nurturing vessels. Prayers lifted to the idea of a soul and that this life was more than a futile passage of time. Prayers for my body, that it ceased its undefined fatigue and aches. I prayed that the mystery that cloaked my understanding of my life's purpose be lifted to let me have a glimpse behind the curtain.

Soon after I started my nightly prayer practice, I had the dream that held such specific guidance and led me to the first energy practitioner who helped facilitate my body's response to heal the tumor without medical intervention. Would the dream and guidance have come if I hadn't started my prayer practice that finally included myself? I do believe there's a connection.

Spiritual maturity requires that you put yourself in the equation of your own life, because displaced authority equals a diminished voice. You don't need to shout, but you do need to be able to hear your own narrative. Spiritual maturity accepts that your healing is the most important healing for your attention. You are your primary relationship; how is that relationship?

A Necessary Purge

Becoming aware and accepting your empathic nature doesn't instantly provide you with the maturity you need for balance and centeredness, but they're certainly prerequisites that will assist you. In Chapter 9, I described feeling overwhelmed at a parents' conference to discuss and support each other when a student in my son's class died. In that moment, I felt I was held hostage by my empathic reception that had to process the pain of the other adults, as well as my own. But there was another level of awareness that this moment served me, which I've waited until this chapter to discuss.

Initially, I did the pendulum swing of first feeling defensive about my emotional display of grief and sadness. Then, I comforted myself by projecting inadequacies of the other adults who were stone cold and rigid, leaving me with the burden of processing this deep, raw emotion. I experienced tears for three days that flowed from a seemingly bottomless well. Pure exhaustion washed over me like a cleansing, and I wrung out layers of grief from depths and landscapes I didn't know I held within me. The pendulum at last came to rest in the middle, and on the third night of what I came to call the big purge, I dreamed I was transported somewhere otherworldly with white sand dunes and fields of columbine flowers. I was laid by a sea the color of deep purple that ebbed and lapped with celestial sounds, and I was told to rest. I was shown mercy and an awareness that the Field of Mystery had given me a chance to purge the tears of a lifetime out of my system.

The version I share in Chapter 9 was from the part of me that was still learning about my sensitivities and still using my mental body to define my sensitivities and experiences. What I experienced after this purge was humbling and expansive from a mature spiritual body. I prayed with such devotion to the young boy, whose tragic loss of life pricked open a floodgate of my own repressed tears. It's true that I helped transmute the displaced emotions that were present in the room from the other adults to the point that several reached for tissues to wipe away their own tears. But it was my own well of tears that provided me the physical release I needed for my own healing. We cannot cry someone else's tears.

A week after the memorial, I was driving on the road where the accident happened at a crosswalk. I was the only one on that section of the road, and without explanation, the pedestrian crosswalk light turned red. I pressed on the brake and came to a stop, though no one was physically there. But for me, it was a chance to honor the healing that was extended to me very generously by Mystery and a young boy who helped me open my heart. It was a moment of contact between two souls and the field witnessing each other.

Mystery is always there to reveal more ways to feel, expand truth, and bring people who are feeling disconnected into the fold of humanity. The capacity to care never ages. Everyone is helping everyone grow into loving themselves.

Often, it's after someone has healed from an illness or from a destructive behavior that they find themselves helping others in the same situation. Our life experiences, particularly when mastered, give us a sense of authority in sharing our stories, including our challenges and successes. As tested and self-realized individuals, we recognize the landscape and can offer to be an unassuming guide and companion for someone on a similar path or trajectory. We offer a hand, some advice, some kindness, some caution, and some contact.

The Path of Healing

There is some poignancy that the word "pathogen" contains the word "path." A pathogen is a microorganism that can cause disease, and it has its own *path* into and within the body. Anyone who has ever sought out a spiritual path has simultaneously sought to heal an imbalance or sense of loss and separation. Something being out of balance is a message, not an identity. This is important for anyone on a healing journey—to not overly identify with what's perceived as being wrong with you.

Have your sensitivities ever made you feel as if something is wrong or broken within you? If you've carried such feelings, I truly hope this book has been a guide to reclaim your truth. For that matter, what is your truth? Can you articulate it and hold it in your center? What's missing for you to feel whole?

A family member once asked me if I ever got cancer or another life-threatening disease, would I feel as if I'd failed at what I thought to be true about a holistic lifestyle and the energy work I offer to others? It's a legitimate question, but no, I wouldn't feel I had failed or that I would be discredited as an energy-aware empath. We have lessons brought to us in many forms. Illness is just one variation of a catalyst to look within and see what needs to be heard, healed, or accepted. I would hate to think that anyone who discovers they have a severe illness, contracts a virus, has an accident or injury, or experiences severe trauma would feel they'd failed at something as fundamental as living.

Spiritual Maturity and Service

If I've learned something along my path as an empath, it's that I'm not alone. Sustainability is a necessity in maintaining a pace—do what is yours, and you will find that you'll always have what you need when you need it. Humility affords you the posture to ask, "Is this mine?" If it is, lean in and support, assist, witness, and be an instrument of service. If it isn't, observe and extend acknowledgment of the situation. Then, disconnect your energy. This is the practice of maintaining energetic boundaries.

When I was new to the path of service, I wanted to understand everything. I was so full in my head with theory, determination, and impatience. Nowadays, I'm content to accept Mystery. I'm willing to be an instrument without understanding all of the ins and outs. I have become comfortable dancing with myself. I'm still letting the dance reveal itself to me—its rhythm and beat, a pulse that I hear on occasion echoed in my own heartbeat.

Questions for Reflection

Take some time with your journal to write down your impressions and feelings in response to these questions. Then, reflect on how your experience in your answers may have affected you emotionally or affected your development as an empath.

1. Have you received an intuitive message from someone when you didn't ask for it? If so, how did it make you feel? Was it a positive experience, or did it feel invasive? Journal about the scenario and what you learned in hindsight.

2. Have you experienced spiritual bypassing? Is it easier to give advice but not follow it? What aspect of yourself do you sense you're avoiding or simply willing to put up with? What would help you begin that inner work? Look at the resource page at the back of the book to see if there's a modality that would support you.

3. I have a friend who is going through cancer treatment. She has described it on occasion as "a healing journey into joy." If you've had a serious illness or traumatic event in your life, describe any insights or wisdom that was revealed to you through the experience.

4. What life experiences have provided you with growth and the opportunity to be a guide for someone else in a similar situation? Has grief seasoned you to be a counselor, or has recovery from addictions brought you empathy and compassion for those still struggling? Explore where your empathy can connect with others.

5. What is your soulful truth? Can you share that with someone close? I invite you to share with me what you know is your essence. Contact information is provided in the back of the book.

Chapter Twenty-Two

The Aging Empath

The sweeping arc of life is a steady current. Our infant self enters the stream, floating at various speeds, experiencing many wonders and obstacles over time until our body, our lifeboat, has run its course. It's a rare individual who's conscious of their journey from birth. Most of us awaken in stages to what our life offers and how we can consciously experience it as a creative endeavor. A path, however, is created out of our intentions.

Every one of us has or will face difficult moments in life, where we wonder how we'll get to the other side of an intimidating obstacle. The best advice is one step at a time. For many, a serious illness propels them on a journey of self-awareness: how their lifestyle is impacting their health—smoking, eating, drinking, drugs, excesses in any areas; the health of their relationships; what their inner dialogue sounds like; and an existential contemplation of existence and mortality.

My personal journey has been centered in authenticity, focused on how to strip off the layers of fear and doubt, embrace my true empathic nature, and expand upon my senses to balance the seen and unseen. It's a journey to arrive at Rumi's field of grass with no need to seek, long, or try. Even now, I'm certain the journey has just begun, and I'm intrigued and full of wonder. The spiritual services I provide are to help others who struggle to feel connected to their center and reclaim authority over their own energy. I'm not a career empath, meaning it isn't a title I use to exclusively identify myself. My empathic nature is part of sensory perception and my spiritual sensibilities.

The Aging Empath

As I age, my hormones are changing, shifting gears from the reproductive years to the wise and sage years—or at least that's the hope. My empathic receptivity has changed as well. I suspect the neurotransmitters and the molecular biology that sustain my life and measure its vitality are also changing and impacting my sensitivity and how it's communicated. I tend to receive fewer individual impressions, unless purposely working a space or working with a person. I now tend to get a teaching steeped in what presents as a pattern in humanity that also has some bearing on my own life.

Most recently, I picked up an energy impression from someone who had committed suicide. I didn't recognize at first what was happening to me. My vision changed, and I began to see in black and white. This is what usually happens if a disincarnate energy enters my energy fields before I register its presence. My appetite can change as well—somewhat like accounts given by organ recipients who suddenly have similar likes and dislikes as their donors.

When that happened, I was distracted and not attending to my own advice about being aware of my boundaries. I was settling into a new country, and I wasn't meditating regularly or getting bodywork. Yet this somewhat intrusive exchange of hosting another's pain and suffering was a very personal teaching for me. I accept that Mystery brings forth experiences needed to deepen my own understanding of suffering and surrendering.

I have family members who have depression and suicidal thoughts. It's a difficult illness to be present with and support in an unconditional way. According to the World Health Organization, more than 264 million people of all ages suffer from depression globally, it's a leading cause of disability worldwide, and it's a major contributor to the overall global burden of disease.

When I had this energy exchange, I was instantly struck by a localized dense pain in my upper chest region—a dull, nearly imploding point of despair that made it difficult to breathe or to even want to breathe. To shift this feeling from my body, I had to work on my own energy systems by going back to the fundamentals of centering myself as I breathed up and down my central channel. I had to ground into the Earth, recall my sense of what I know is true, build up my presence, and flow energy through my heart. What I gained through this active clearing for myself was great compassion for people who feel disconnected from their core, their heart, the essence of their life, and the challenge they face to articulate their experience to others.

Your Essence: Passion and Purpose

I began this guidebook with the quote from an ancient poet Pindar, "Know who you are and be such," and I also opened the Field of Definition with a quote attributed to Socrates. Poets and philosophers are drawn to examine the meaning and essence of Life. They're magnetized by the depth of mystery that surrounds us, unknown yet known. I, too, fall under its rather divine spell to wonder at what suspends and animates our life at the same time.

Essence is defined as "the intrinsic nature or indispensable quality of something, especially something abstract, which determines its character." Undeniably, our empathic sensitivity is part of our essence, which sets us up to experience life with depth. But it's our passions, cultivating a sense of purpose, that transmit our essence as a soul creating a life.

The awareness that your life is an interactive field with limitless choices opens up opportunities to explore and discover your own passion and purpose. Passion is one of those energies that's naturally raw and untamed. It actually takes cultivating. It has a pendulumlike spectrum: On one end it can be overwhelming and all consuming, madness even. On the other end, it's the fuel that fires incredible action and pursuits. Social justice and activism are two of the many expressions advanced by individuals who have tapped into passion to help them contribute to the whole in a purposeful way.

We all have passions that we resonate with: the environment, education, civil rights, artistic expression, athletic prowess, food, sustainability, and so on. How we channel or sprinkle our passion into our lives gives us a sense of purpose. We *feel* passionate, and we *sense* purpose. Ultimately, these two elements influence how we feel about ourselves and our connection to our external world. They are our ambassadors, forging relationships and opportunities on our path to authentically express and reveal ourselves.

My innate passion has always centered around the sublime beauty of words, language, and artistic expression. Then, quite unexpectedly, my life presented me with a different expression of this passion. As a mother with two children challenged by expressive language disabilities, I found myself engaged in pursuing social justice in the area of special education and upholding a federal act entitled

Free Appropriate Public Education, or FAPE, which was appealed to the US Supreme Court. I was also motivated to adopt a child with a severe cleft impairment so that she could receive care and love. These pursuits, which propelled our family into costly and difficult environments in high courts and international ministries, defined for me what motivators love and passion can be. These efforts took many years, many dollars, and large amounts of mental and emotional focus—but this is the profound power of love in action.

My life experiences deepened my passion by demonstrating that language initiates an individual into being a creator and sovereign of their own energy. Life's circumstances place opportunities before us to demonstrate our love, our awareness of inequality, and what's out of balance, not just for an individual but for the whole. Ultimately, I experienced the bravery, boldness, and courage demanded by passion. It can be nuclear and no doubt transformative.

What are you passionate about? How does your empathic nature add to your expression or experience of your passion? Does your passion lend a sense of purpose and meaning to your life?

Small Things Like That

The details of the small things in our lives bring depth to the mystery of existence—for what is truly small? When I sit still, mark my breath, and am made aware of the inner world it traverses to give me life? Or when I watch twin lambs rush to their mother's teats simultaneously for comfort, as any newborn does when startled? As I blow on a stubborn and resistant ember to light the fire in the cold belly of a wood stove, I wonder if these small endeavors, witnessed with mindfulness, are filled with more life than all the wishing and dreaming of my fantasies.

Each of us is created from the biological mechanism of sperm and egg uniting and given, more or less, nine months to develop. We are then named, like any worthy vessel. We're called into being. We journey through our life, possibly even renaming ourselves, forming our identity around precious syllables that identify us. Our family and friends tease, shorten, and playfully alter our names as an offering of intimacy and affection. Or our name may be cursed in anger and with slurs and slander to shake us to our core so that we may examine what drama is flowing through our life.

When our sons Per and Finn were confirmed at the Norwegian Seamen's church in Pasadena, Texas, part of the sermon of the port ministry was to call out each Norwegian vessel that would be making port that week. Each vessel and crewmember were a long way from home but welcomed by her compatriots on a foreign shore. I was unexpectedly moved by this gesture that's so symbolic of every single soul's journey—the recognition that as we sail on our way and visit different ports to refuel and restock for the next leg, our friends and family call out our name, witnessing our arrival and blessing our journey.

Part of my life's exploration is coming to feel at home in my own name—a name that has been somewhat of an enigma. Signe was a name my parents found in a book and thought it unique and different. They weren't aware of any Scandinavian heritage; there were no gods to honor. Nonetheless, my siblings and I all received Nordic names. Ironically, my name finds its root in my husband's language. Small things like that make you take notice. Who would ever imagine that a name my parents found in a book and adopted with ignorant mispronunciation would guide me to this country like a homing pigeon—to this family with a mother-in-law and sister-in-law who both have the same name as me?

Throughout my childhood, my name was something I stumbled over, uncertain how to wear it, let alone own it. My mother-in-law, Signe, is the one who informed me not long after I joined their family that our common name has two meanings. The older Viking version means to invoke victory, and the more modern one is a blessing.

My empathic nature was something I also struggled with and had to grow into. I finally arrived at a place of acceptance and can call it a blessing, too.

Both my name and my empathic nature have grafted and fused into the marrow of my life to the point that they have their own unique presence and power. They were the small details from the beginning of my story, waiting for my focus to step forward and be embodied.

This has been a guidebook to assist you in honoring and understanding better your empathic sensitivities, but it's also written to tell you who I AM, as your guide. I am *that* girl who looked for meaning and purpose and turned outward toward nature. I am *this* woman who turned inward to find a sense of belonging and authenticity. I am both *this* and *that*, which is why my story of discovery isn't linear but is nonetheless unified. The process of unification came through personal acceptance and self-love, through respect and wonder of nature. I have placed my Self in the space between *all that is* and *all that can be*.

If you find yourself reflected in my exploration and contemplations, it's because we are part of the One Field. I hope the questions that have been provided throughout the book help you discover your "I AM" and how to honor and embrace your own unique voice and sensitive intuitive nature.

What is the space in between us? Everything and nothing.

The space between

The space between me and you
Is no farther than that quality in me
that you represent.
The space between me and you is absent
when I find that you and I are one;
And in that, my freedom I have won.

—Signe Myers Hovem

Bibliography

"33: Convention of 29 May 1993 on Protection of Children and Co-operation in Respect of Intercountry Adoption." Hague Conference on Private International Law, May 29, 1993. https://www.hcch.net/en/instruments/conventions/full-text/?cid=69.

Alexander, Jessica. "Why Danish Students Are Happier and More Empathetic." *The Atlantic,* August 9, 2016. https://www.theatlantic.com/education/archive/2016/08/the-us-empathy-gap/494975/.

Aron, Elaine. "The Highly Sensitive Person." The Highly Sensitive Person. https://hsperson.com.

Beck, Martha. "The Sponge People." *Oprah Magazine,* June 2006. https://oprah.com/spirit/martha-beck-the-sponge-people.

Bergland, Christopher. "The Cerebellum Deeply Influences Our Thoughts and Emotions." *Psychology Today,* March 17, 2015. https://www.psychologytoday.com/ca/blog/the-athletes-way/201503/the-cerebellum-deeply-influences-our-thoughts-and-emotions.

Bergland, Christopher. "How Do Your Genes Influence Levels of Emotional Sensitivity?" *Psychology Today,* May 9, 2015. https://www.psychologytoday.com/ca/blog/the-athletes-way/201505/how-do-your-genes-influence-levels-emotional-sensitivity.

Campos, Marcelo, MD. "Heart Rate Variability: A New Way to Track Well-being." Harvard Health Publishing, October 22, 2019. https://www.health.harvard.edu/blog/heart-rate-variability-new-way-track-well-2017112212789.

Cherry, Kendra. "What Is Negative Bias?" Very Well Mind, April 29, 2020. https://verywellmind.com/negative-bias-4589618.

Coleridge, Samuel Taylor. "Answer to a Child's Question."

Daily, Mary. "Neuroscientist Marco Lacoboni On How Mirror Neurons Teach Us To Be Human." *UCLA Newsroom,* October 19, 2016. https://www.uclahealth.org/neuroscientist-marco-iacoboni-on-how-mirror-neurons-teach-us-to-be-human.

Fallows, James. "The Boiled-Frog Myth: Stop the Lying Now!" *The Atlantic,* September 16, 2006. https://theatlantic.com/technology/archive/2006/09/the-boiled-frog-myth-stop-the-lying-now/7446/.

"Family Constellation." https://www.hellinger.com/familienstellen/.

"Home – InSitu." InSitu Foundation. https://dogsdetectcancer.org.

"How Much of the Ocean Have We Explored?" National Oceanic and Atmospheric Administration, February 26, 2021. https://oceanservice.noaa.gov/facts/exploration.html.

Jain, Shaili. "Cortisol, the Intergenerational Transmission of Stress and PTSD: An Interview with Dr. Rachel Yehuda." Coyne of the Realm, July 18, 2016. https://www.coyneoftherealm.com/2016/07/18/cortisol-the-intergenerational-transmission-of-stress-and-ptsd-an-interview-with-dr-rachel-yehuda/.

Johnson, J. Paul. "Dalai Lama Leads a Prayer for Orlando, Urges Compassion in USIP Visit." *United States Institute of Peace,* June 13, 2016. https://www.usip.org/press/2016/06

/dalai-lama-leads-prayer-orlando-urges-compassion-usip-visit.

Keller, Hellen. "Before the Soul Dawn." *The World I Live In*. New York: Century Company, 1908.

Klein Indep. Sch. Dist. V. Hovem, 690 F.3d 390 (5th Cir. 2012). https://www.supremecourt.gov/Search.aspx?FileName=/docketfiles/12-875.htm.

Lacuone, Robyn. "Heyoka: The Most Powerful Type of Empath." *The Minds Journal*. https://themindsjournal.com/heyoka-powerful-type-empath/.

MacKinnon, Matthew. "The Neuroscience of Mindfulness." *Psychology Today,* October 11, 2009. https://www.psychologytoday.com/us/blog/your-brain-work/200910/the-neuroscience-mindfulness.

Marsh, Jason. "Do Mirror Neurons Give Us Empathy?" *Greater Good Magazine,* March 29, 2012.https://greatergood.berkeley.edu/article/item/do_mirror_neurons_give_empathy.

"Martin Cooper (1926-)." *Time Magazine*. http://content.time.com/time/specials/2007/article/0,28804,1677329_1677708_1677825,00.html.

Morrison, Toni. "Toni Morrison – Nobel Lecture." Nobel Media AB 2021. Delivered December 7, 1993. https://www.nobelprize.org/prizes/literature/1993/morrison/lecture/.

Mosaic, Gaia Vince. "There's a Single Nerve That Connects All of Your Vital Organs—And It Might Just Be the Future of Medicine." *Business Insider,* June 1, 2015. https://www.businessinsider.com/vagus-nerve-stimulation-2015-6.

Moss, Laura. "Trail Trees Are a Living Native American Legacy." Treehugger, June 17, 2019. https://www.treehugger.com/trail-trees-living-native-american-legacy-4862242.

Nannup, Greg. Indigenous Tours WA. http://www.indigenouswa.com.

Nepo, Mark. *The Book of Awakening*. Newburyport: Red Wheel, 2020.

Osbon, Diane K. "Reflections on the Art of Living: A Joseph Campbell Companion." New York: HarperCollins, 1991.

Padgett, Jason, and Maureen Ann Seaberg. *Struck by Genius: How a Brain Injury Made Me a Mathematical Marvel*. Boston: Houghton Mifflin Harcourt, 2014.

Perez, Jason, and Brian Dunbar. "Why Space Radiation Matters." NASA, October 8, 2019. https://nasa.gov/analogs/nsrl/why-space-radiation-matters.

Perry, Susan. "Mirror Neurons." *Brainfacts.org*, November 16, 2008. http://www.brainfacts.org/Archives/2008/Mirror-Neurons.

Pigliucci, Massimo. *Answers for Aristotle: How Science and Philosophy Can Lead Us to a More Meaningful Life*. New York: Basic Books, 2012.

Quigley, Elizabeth. "Parkinson's Smell Test Explained by Science." *BBC Scotland News,* March 20, 2019. http://bbc.com/news/uk-scotland-47627179.

Resnick, Brian. "The Silent 'Sixth' Sense." *Vox,* December 26, 2019. https://www.vox.com/the-highlight/2019/11/22/20920762/proprioception-sixth-sense.

Roemmelt, Ronda. "The History of Marker Trees." Deeproot, October 5, 2015. https://www.deeproot.com/blog/blog-entries/the-history-of-marker-trees.

Saftler, Kiri. Peacekeeper Circles. https://www.peacecircles.com.

Sheldrake, Rupert. "Morphic Resonance." Rupert Sheldrake, 2018. https://www.sheldrake.org/research/morphic-resonance.

Thackeray, William Makepeace. *Vanity Fair: A Novel Without a Hero*. Auckland: The Floating Press, 2008.

Thoreau, David Henry. *Walden; or, Life in the Woods*. Boston: Ticknor and Fields, 1854.

"The Three Brains: Why Your Head, Heart and Gut Sometimes Conflict." Australian Spinal Research Foundation, July 26, 2016. https://spinalresearch.com.au/three-brains-head-heart-gut-sometimes-conflict/.

Watts, Alan. "The Tao of Philosophy 5: Myth of Myself." *The Library*, 1965. https://www.organism.earth/library/document/tao-of-philosophy-5.

Whitfield, Stephen E, and Gene Roddenberry. *The Making of Star Trek*. New York: Ballantine Books, 1973.

Whitman, Walt. *Leaves of Grass*. Project Gutenberg, August 24, 2008. https://gutenberg.org/files/1322/1322-h/1322-h.htm.

Wild, Allison. "8 Times 'Star Trek' Accurately Predicted Future Technology." *The Portalist,* December 20, 2018. https://theportalist.com/star-trek-tech-predictions.

Yehuda, Rachel. "How Trauma and Resilience Cross Generations." On Being Project, July 30, 2015. https://onbeing.org/programs/rachel-yehuda-how-trauma-and-resilience-cross-generations/.

"Your 8 Senses." Star Institute. https://sensoryhealth.org/basic/your-8-senses.

Resources

This is not a "how to" book. This has been written as a guide, an illustration of what my life looked like at different stages of my own empathic awareness. The following are resources that I've tapped into to assist me with feeling comfortable in my body, mind, and spirit. Undoubtedly, there are many other modalities out in the world. The fact that I have not included them in the list below does not discredit them. Trust your own intuition about what works best for you. A trained facilitator can assist you in healing pain and perceptions that may limit your ability to know and share your true nature.

Supplemental Meditations

I am offering three meditations to support you in connecting with your energetic self-care. Access available for download at: https://www.smhovem.com/book-meditations

Meditation One: Subtle Body Clearing
Meditation Two: Projection Clearing
Meditation Three: Relaxation Ebb and Flow

Body awareness and therapeutic measures:

Cranial sacral therapy:

Upledger Institute International
11211 Prosperity Farms Road, Suite D325
Palm Beach Gardens, FL 33410-3487
info@upledger.com

Visceral and neural manipulation:

The Barral Institute
11211 Prosperity Farms Road, Suite D324
Palm Beach Gardens, FL 33410
info@barralinstitute.com

Rolfing® and fascia work:

5055 Chaparral Court, Suite 103
Boulder, CO 80301
www.rolf.org

Integrative energy systems and instructional coursework:

Barbra Brennan School of Healing

500 NE Spanish River Boulevard, Suite 208
Boca Raton, FL 33431-4559
www.barbarabrennan.com
bbsh.office@barbarabrennan.com

Melaney Ryan Institute of Applied Consciousness

www.mriac.com.au
admin@mriac.com.au

Eden Method Energy Medicine

www.innersource.net
https://edenenergymedicine.com
https://edenmethod.com

Dr. Sue Morter, Morter Institute
10439 Commerce Drive, Suite 140
Carmel, Indiana 46032
https://drsuemorter.com

Acknowledgments

This book has lived in me in various stages for the past fifteen years. To say I grappled with the writing process is a bit of an understatement. I was often isolated in my writing as I uprooted and replanted myself in new homes and new countries. Yet I was incredibly fortunate to have many forms of support throughout every stage—especially from family and friends, who witnessed me lean in and unearth aspects of myself to share with other sensitive persons.

To Rose Hart, an ageless, extraordinary, sensitive human who has been there from the beginning—you grounded me with wisdom and gave me a space to contemplate, regardless of the physical distance that separated us on the globe. I am beyond grateful for all that you held for me during this time—particularly the faith you had in me to find the words to express an empath's nature.

To Mike, Vegard, and other spirits whose visits prompted me to open up my senses and let in more than the physical realm—I thank you for your patience and your willingness to get my attention. It was not in vain. And to Thomas, who replaced doubt with trust.

To the many editors who have steered and supported me throughout each phase of this journey, I am humbled by your skill and grateful for your guidance: Max Regan, Lisa Birman, Debra Evans, Kristine Carlson, and Melanie Votaw. Each of you helped me to focus and bring clarity and more depth to an already deep and abstract subject. Thank you.

To Publisher Brooke Warner of She Writes Press—I am deeply grateful for the opportunity to put this book in the hands of readers who will benefit from understanding more fully their empathic nature. Thank you for providing me a path forward to share what I know with the public. Additional gratitude to Julie Metz's art department for the beautiful cover, Tabitha Lahr for her equally great interior pages, Shannon Green for keeping me on track with good humor, and to my fellow SWP authors who shared their own journeys and resources.

To my early test readers who were presented a voluminous draft of this book—thank you for your time and your feedback. Each one of you helped me narrow the scope and fine-tune the purpose of the book: Jason Scott, Sapna Sadhir, Angela Phatouros, Jo Parfitt, Marieke Bruin, Sue Ventris, Jill Brooks, and Jennifer Lakshmi Dove.

To my writing community scattered here and there—thank you for answering author questions throughout the years and for sharing your creative genius with me. I am very fortunate to have the company of such wit, humor and intelligence offered to me by Melanie Dufty, Lee Lenyk, Sindee Ernst, Dorothy Van Soest, and Melanie Miller.

To mentors, guides, and friends, in no particular order, but still named in love and with gratitude for all of your support: Rosa Glen-Riley, Polly Tsai, Sonya Downes, Diana Byrnes, Melaney Ryan, The Mahat community, Melissa Italiano, Anne Hansen, Lys Shonnard, Gail Hackett, Cathy Brett, Nicole Pavlica, Janet Light, Pam Stockton, Lynne Løge, Nicki Baldi, Ida Høtzel, Tammy

Walters, Lynn Abraham, Heidi Wagner, Cathy Chittum, Nancy Vadstein, and Beth and Lars Hübert.

And most importantly, I honor my family in all the various forms they have taken in my life: my mom, Joanne; my parents, Rex and Sharon; and my in-laws, Jens and Signe. To my children—Per, Finn, Michael, and Grace—you all continue to be my teachers and guides. And to Knut, my husband, who has waited patiently for me to step out, be bold, and state this is who I AM—thank you for giving me the space and the opportunity to express myself. Cheers to all the joy!

About the Author

Signe Myers Hovem has created homes on five continents over twenty years, raised four uniquely sensitive children, pursued a special education lawsuit appealed to the US Supreme Court, and volunteered in a hospice in Texas and an orphanage in Azerbaijan. She has worked as a spiritual counselor in Houston Texas and taught workshops and trainings in the art of being an empath and the power of language in many countries around the world. For more information and contact details visit www.smhovem.com.

Author photo © Heidi Wagner Photography

SELECTED TITLES FROM SHE WRITES PRESS

She Writes Press is an independent publishing company founded to serve women writers everywhere. Visit us at www.shewritespress.com.

Think Better. Live Better. 5 Steps to Create the Life You Deserve by Francine Huss. $16.95, 978-1-938314-66-7. With the help of this guide, readers will learn to cultivate more creative thoughts, realign their mindset, and gain a new perspective on life.

The Art of Play: Igniting Your Imagination to Unlock Insight, Healing, and Joy by Joan Stanford. $19.95, 978-1-63152-030-3. Lifelong "non-artist" Joan Stanford shares the creative process that led her to insight and healing, and shares ways for others to do the same.

The Complete Enneagram: 27 Paths to Greater Self-Knowledge by Beatrice Chestnut, PhD. $24.95, 978-1-938314-54-4. A comprehensive handbook on using the Enneagram to do the self-work required to reach a higher stage of personal development.

This Way Up: Seven Tools for Unleashing Your Creative Self and Transforming Your Life by Patti Clark. $16.95, 978-1-63152-028-0. A story of healing for women who yearn to lead a fuller life, accompanied by a workbook designed to help readers work through personal challenges, discover new inspiration, and harness their creative power.

She Is Me: How Women Will Save the World by Lori Sokol, PhD. $16.95, 978-1-63152-715-9. Through interviews with women including Gloria Steinem, Billie Jean King, and Nobel Peace Prize recipient Leymah Gbowee, Sokol demonstrates how many of the traits thought to be typical of women—traits long considered to be soft and weak in our patriarchal culture—are actually proving more effective in transforming lives, securing our planet, and saving the world.